the amazing Page

650 *New Scrapbook Page Ideas, Tips and Techniques*

~ 12 years together ~ love of my life ~

LAUGH

~ We've been married for 12 years and you still make me laugh! ~

MEMORY MAKERS BOOKS

Denver, Colorado

Managing Editor MaryJo Regier

Art Director Nick Nyffeler

Editor Amy Glander

Photographer Ken Trujillo

Art Acquisitions Editor Janetta Abucejo Wieneke

Craft Editor Jodi Amidei

Graphic Designers Jordan Kinney, Robin Rozum

Production Coordinator Matthew Wagner

Administrative Assistant Karen Cain

Editorial Support Emily Curry Hitchingham

Contributing Writer Trisha McCarty-Luedke

Contributing Photographers Camillo DiLizia, Jennifer Reeves

Copy Editor Dena Twinem

Contributing Memory Makers Masters Jessie Baldwin, Amber Baley, Jennifer Bourgeault, Jenn Brookover, Christine Brown, Sheila Doherty, Kathy Fesmire, Kelly Goree, Jodi Heinen, Jeniece Higgins, Nic Howard, Julie Johnson, Kelli Noto, Suzy Plantamura, Valerie Salmon, Torrey Scott, Trudy Sigurdson, Jessica Sprague, Shannon Taylor, Danielle Thompson, Denise Tucker, Lisa VanderVeen, Samantha Walker, Susan Weinroth, Angelia Wigginton

Memory Makers® The Amazing Page

Published by Memory Makers Books, an imprint of F+W Publications, Inc.
12365 Huron Street, Suite 500, Denver, CO 80234
Phone (800) 254-9124

First edition. Printed in China.
10 09 08 07 06 5 4 3 2 1

Library of Congress Cataloging-in-Publication Data

The Amazing Page : 650 new scrapbook page ideas, tips and techniques.
     p. cm.
   ISBN-13: 978-1-892127-91-4
   ISBN-10: 1-892127-91-1
     1. Photograph albums. 2. Photographs--Conservation and restoration. 3. Scrapbooks.
   I. Memory Makers Books.

   TR501.A465 2006
   745.593--dc22

                                                    2006046215

Distributed to trade and art markets by

F+W Publications, Inc.

4700 East Galbraith Road, Cincinnati, OH 45236

Phone (800) 289-0963

Distributed in Canada by

Fraser Direct

100 Armstrong Avenue

Georgetown, ON, Canada L7G 5S4

Tel: (905) 877-4411

Distributed in the U.K. and Europe by David & Charles

Brunel House, Newton Abbot, Devon, TQ12 4PU, England

Tel: (+44) 1626 323200,
Fax: (+44) 1626 323319

E-mail: mail@davidandcharles.co.uk

Distributed in Australia by Capricorn Link

P.O. Box 704, S. Windsor NSW, 2756 Australia

Tel: (02) 4577-3555

Memory Makers Books is the home of Memory Makers, the scrapbook magazine dedicated to educating and inspiring scrapbookers. To subscribe, or for more information, call (800) 366-6465. Visit us on the Internet at www.memorymakersmagazine.com

We dedicate this book to our contributors and reading audience who continually seek the joy and fulfillment of this creative hobby.

contents

playing in the

enjoying the

sipping cold

eating yum

the Fabric of Our Lives 8-49

Celebrate the people and things that add richness and fulfillment to your life. Family members (10-11), sons and daughters (12-19), siblings (20-25), cousins (26-27), the special men in your life (28-33), heritage and generations past (34-37), friends (38-43) and even the four walls you call home (44-49) are all worthy of documentation.

you are my Sunshine 50-101

Just like the popular song touts, our sources of warmth and affection comes from the ones we bring into our home as babes, and our lives would be gray and dreary without them. Babies (52-57), toddlers (58-65), kids (66-83), teens (84-91) and pets (92-101) make our lives complete with their sunny smiles and cheerful dispositions. Frame the moments of love and laughter in pages all about them.

let the Good times Roll 102-137

Merry times call for merry pages chronicling our gaiety and good times with those we love. Traditions (104-107), good times (108-115), fun with water (116-119), fun with snow (120-121), at play (122-131), and spending quality time with that special someone (132-137) can be forever immortalized in scrapbook pages freezing each moment in time.

seize the Day 138-177

Time passes by way too quickly, so cherish all the moments of spontaneity and adventure with adrenaline-infused layouts that jump right out of your albums. Travel (140-145), adventure (146-151), sports (152-160), the discovery of nature (161-162)), the four seasons (163-171) and the bliss of the long-awaited wedding day (172-177) will never fade from memory, but will be remembered more easily when framed in scrapbooks that say "Carpe Diem" like nothing else.

up close and personal 178-219

The inner fibers of our character and those we love should be recorded for both living and future generations to understand our are true essence. All-about-me pages (180-189), hopes and dreams (190-195), faith and spirituality (196-204), favorites (205-215) and hobbies (216-219) are all insights into our soul. Share a piece of yourself with those you love and they'll forever thank you for it.

Ginger

3 DAYS later

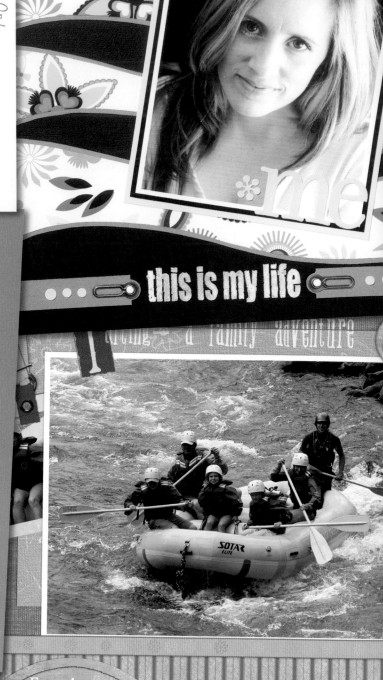

*me

this is my life

racing a family adventure

Hendrickson

what is it like
to be
1 of 6?

Janet, Barbara, Patricia
Jean, Dick, and Jane

The things this gang of 6 does often surprise me. My mom and her sisters and brother (tho I think Dick is a bit of a reluctant participant) just feel so free to get wild together. I remember antics, alliances, disruptions, and reunions between them since I was a child (Grandma sometimes leading the way back then). As a girl with 2 brothers, this behavior is foreign, exotic, even. Oh, to dance the night away together, to play wild pranks on your sister at 60, to go away for a weekend of shopping, crafting, dominoes, over-the-top matching outfits and lunches out. It is a joy and a wonder to watch how their shared history gives them such comfort and freedom when they are together. photo 6/03, journaling 11/03.

FAMILY ADVENTURE
ON THE CLEAR CREEK
RIVER IN COLORADO. WE WERE
THE LAST RAFT OUT FOR THE DAY
OUR TOUR GUIDE LET US HAVE
PLENTY OF TIME TO PLAY. WE SPUN
CIRCLES, AND THE KIDS ALL JUMPED OUT TO
SWIM AT ONE POINT.   JULY 2005

Most kids like to **swing**.
Tyler is no exception. He
absolutely loves to **swing**.
Even before he was sitting up
alone, **swinging** made him
smile. Now when we get to the
park he runs straight over to
the **swing**, points to them &
says "Gah!" He giggles in
delight as I push him.

little man

JE T'AIME TOI !

Lorsque j'ai rencontré la jolie
petite Morgan, ce fut un réel
coup de foudre réciproque entre
elle et moi alors quand elle m'a
lancé candidement un *"je t'aime
toi "* j'en ai été très touchée!
Morgan a 4 ans et elle est la
fillette de Sandie, une amie de
Design Team.

Je t'aime   TOI

What makes a scrapbook page *amazing*? Is it the perfect combination of funky patterns or bold colors that unify every element on the page? Maybe it's the stellar photos that shine on an artistic background. Perhaps texture, dimension or handmade embellishments provide the perfect finishing touch. Maybe it's the sizzle and sparkle from glitter, paint jewels or embossing powder. Whatever the ingredients, after seeing multitudes of scrapbook pages over the years, we've discovered that the recipe for "amazing" results when an artist uncovers his or her own definition of scrapbook beauty and creatively expresses it on the page.

The Amazing Page offers an abundance of remarkable scrapbook pages sure to make your eyes pop. The book is divided into five chapters organized by the most popular topics seen in scrapbooks. Topics include the family unit, the special place we call home, generations who have walked before us, precious babies, lovable kids, exuberant teens, our special sweethearts, good times spent with friends and family, far off places worthy of travel, dynamic sports, the beauty of nature, hopes and dreams, faith and spirituality, favorites and the true essence of ourselves captured in all-about-me layouts.

Whether you're a beginner or an advanced scrapbooker, you will find a large selection of never-before-seen pages— covering a wide variety of themes and styles—that will spark your imagination to create your own "amazing" pages. In addition, helpful tips and tricks from contributors are sprinkled throughout to offer additional inspiration and pointers, as well as a CD-ROM of 75 printable page layout sketches that will take all the guesswork out of designing great pages fast. You'll find an additional sampling of stunning pages on the CD-ROM as well.

Turn the pages of this colossal gallery of astounding artwork from our reading audience, and you'll surely be inspired to capture your precious memories and everyday moments in your scrapbook pages. See examples and techniques that will help you create your own portrayal of "amazing," a portrayal that only you can depict in the illustrative biography you are creating.

Amy

Amy Glander

Associate Editor, Memory Makers Books

...because she is
...ere to protect you
...you the way.

...cause he looks up
...thinks that you
...on and the stars.

...use she lets you
...her friends and
...overs.

...use he calls you
...eally means it.

...cause she will
...there for you,
...what.

...use he is
...innocent, and
...long every time.

YOUR BROTHER

V&N

Yep. We're Sisters. There's no denying it. Kimmie and I both love so many of the same things. Straight hair, high heels or rainbow flip flops (depending on our mood!), Banana Republic, veggie sushi, the perfect shade of brown lipstick, expensive jeans, Coach bags, imported Italian pasta, tanning, white bedrooms, Coco Mademoiselle perfume, and so much more that I'm forgetting... We even wear the same size - I just wished we lived closer!! Love ya tons! XoXoX Susan (photo 11.04)

K S sisters

the Fabric of Our Lives

Pure **Girl** cousins

silly
music
sweet
nail polish
talkative
...crets
...girlfriends
shoes
squealing
...p gloss
beads
attitude
frilly
whispers
...onytails
style
...ewelry
sassy
snuggly
...elicate
shopping
...litter
blue jeans
...ancing

The special bonds we have with the loved ones in our lives deserve celebration. The family unit, sons and daughters, the special men in our lives, our best friends and even the homes we build all add to the richness of our lives. The following pages provide examples of scrapbook pages that reflect the love we share with the people we choose to share a piece of ourselves with. Use them as inspiration when creating your own pages that chronicle these special relationships.

iLOVE u

vinhicks

hang out in coffee sh
sleep han
love homemade baked go
read before bed
play boardga
talk... a lot!
well, most of
love being toge

YOU, MY SON
Y LOVE FOR

LIKE WAVES IN THE OCEAN AFAR

BILL & JOSIAH

f
ends

at different times
d be gradual or instantaneous.
t doesn't happen at all. It is the
ger feel like a child around your parents.
ally feel like an adult. Making your own
own way in the world.

my dad. I feel like our relationship has
ere I no longer have to explain myself.
hat I may be doing something wrong. It is
ces in the decisions that I have made and
I have established. He is supportive and
mental. He respects me and adores my
s proud of the life that I have made and
s my father and also my friend.

Father AND

friend

This family portrait that donned Ursula's Christmas card may seem perfect. The truth is, when one of her sons fussed and fidgeted in the shot, she pasted his smiling face photo over his frown with image-editing software. Ursula says it sums up the family's year perfectly as "overall good with a few flaws that can only be seen when you look closely." She further customized the photo with a handwritten title and doodles.

Ursula Page, Thomasville, Georgia
Photo: Jennifer Newton,
Altamonte Springs, Florida

Supplies: Patterned papers (Imagination Project); white pen

This is it – the official family picture for our 2004 Christmas cards. I have to laugh because when I sent this picture out with the cards, I got so many compliments on it. Many people wrote to tell me how much they loved this picture and every time I read that I snickered to myself. You see, this picture is what you could "doctored." In November, Chris and I took the kids to Disneyworld for the first time. While we were there, we met an online friend, Jennifer Newton, and she agreed to take some pictures of our family. After snapping a few shots of us individually, we huddled together to get a group shot. I desperately wanted a family picture for our Christmas cards and I didn't want a cheesy department store photo of the four of us. Jennifer managed to snap eight pictures before Preston officially lost it and refused to sit still anymore. When I got home, I studied every one of the wonderful pictures that she took. I was thrilled with the results, but when I got to the family photos, there was not one good one. Chris and I were smiling in every picture, but if one kid was smiling in a picture than the other one was not. I was so disappointed because I knew this meant I had to rethink the family photo I hoped to send out. Then, I got a brilliant idea. I decided to take the best picture of three of us and use that as my base photo. I then found the best picture of Sterling and I used Adobe Photoshop Elements to cut out Sterling's smiling head and paste it onto the base photo. Of course, it was a little tricky because in the base photo Sterling's head was tilted, but somehow I made it work. If you look closely, you can tell that this photo was "doctored" because the angle of Sterling's head is a bit odd and my chin looks a little too perfect. I think this pictures sums up the year 2004 perfectly – overall good with a few flaws that can only be seen when you look closely at the year overall.

it's beginning to look a lot like

A play on words from a popular Christmas song forms this title that encapsulates an extended family's world trip together. With first, second and third cousins all posed together in Europe, Hera's large distant family, though far from their homes, feel at home together as captured in this red matted photo. Hidden tag journaling tucked behind the family photo tells about their world travels.

Hera Frei, Kusnacht, Zurich, Switzerland

Supplies: Patterned paper, patterned vellum (Plaid); rhinestone brads (SEI); snowflake and heart eyelets (source unknown); chipboard monogram letters (Basic Grey); grosgrain ribbon; chalk ink; cardstock

1st, 2nd and 3rd cousins in Europe...a long long way from home... we all decided to take the plunge and travel the world, for better or for worse. Paul married to Caroline, from England and with their girls, Olivia and Jessica live in the South of France; Tania recently arrived to work in London; Richelle is in Switzerland for a year working as an au pair; Patrick, Tane, Mika and I live in Switzerland. We all met in Zurich for the weekend and drove to this castle in Austria for their famous Wiener Schnitzel! Though New Zealand is what we all have in common! Sometimes I wonder what I'm doing so far from home, sometimes I wish that what I left in New Zealand could also be here, sometimes I love that my home can be in two places...but I'll never forget the words of my Dad when I left almost 10 years ago...Home will always be here! Go see the world and know we'll be here waiting for you. So I guess for us all there'll be a place in our hearts that nowhere in the world can replace, HOME!

October, 2005

winnicks:

hang out in coffee shops

sleep hard

love homemade baked goodies

read before bedtime

play boardgames

talk... a lot!
Well, most of them

love being together

This simple page captures Sara's family's togetherness. An enlarged photo shows the family hand in hand accented by jumbo punched photo corners and thin, patterned-paper strips. Coordinating patterned-paper hearts accent Sara's handwritten list, detailing her family's favorites during this precious stage of their life.

Sara Winnick, Issaquah, Washington
Photo: Desiree Swanson, Issaquah, Washington

Supplies: Patterned paper (Chatterbox, Fontwerks); ghost hearts (Heidi Swapp); photo corner punch (EK Success); letter stickers (American Crafts); stamping ink; staples; black pen; cardstock

"**I wanted to capture my family 'right now,' focusing on the things we have in common. I expect we'll cherish pages like these that give us glimpses into our life 'back then.'**"

A family love story is played up with "love" patterned paper accentuated with machine-stitching. Jeniece changed her family photo to sepia to coordinate with the red and pink color scheme. A chipboard frame highlights the Higgins family and carries the page's title. Jeniece's handwritten journaling on pink paper resembles a traditional love letter.

Jeniece Higgins, Lake Forest, Illinois

Supplies: Patterned papers (Karen Foster Design, KI Memories); notebook paper; chipboard letters (Heidi Swapp); metal heart (Making Memories); chipboard frame (Rusty Pickle); flowers (Prima); acrylic paint; beads; transparency; thread

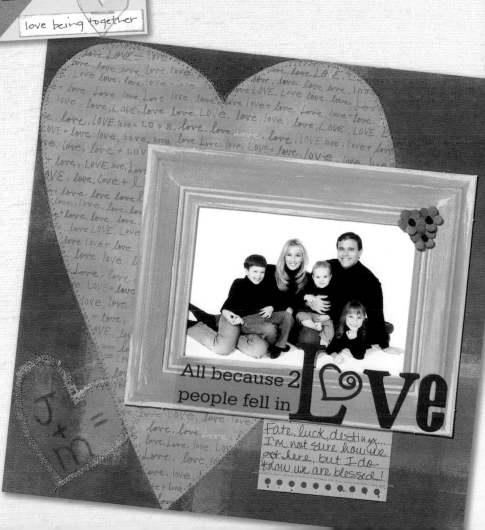

All because 2 people fell in Love

Fate, luck, destiny... I'm not sure how we got here, but I do know we are blessed!

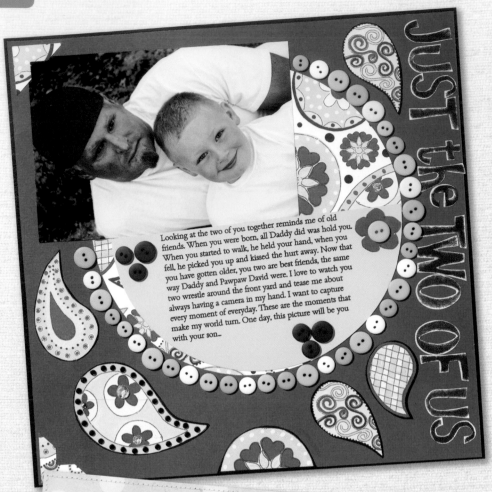

Julie's husband and son are inseparable. She preserves their sweet bond with printed journaling on a circular journaling block that doubles as a photo mat surrounded by buttons. Paisleys handcut from patterned papers and adhered randomly to punchy red cardstock add a sense of fun. The mix of circle, paisley and square shapes makes this a playful page reflective of this father-son relationship.

Julie Johnson, Seabrook, Texas

Supplies: Patterned paper (Junkitz); letter stickers (Bo-Bunny Press); buttons (SEI); gems; photo corner punch (EK Success); cardstock

Being the youngest child with an age gap between him and his siblings allowed Nic's husband to spend quality time with his father. She created this page in tribute to his memory and the special relationship they shared. A large photo shows Nic's husband thinking about his late father and smaller photos show him and his pop in earlier times. Handdrawn doodles and rub-on scrolls accent the page.

Nic Howard, Pukekohe,
South Auckland, New Zealand
Photo: Lesley Cooper,
Auckland, New Zealand

Supplies: Patterned papers (Basic Grey, Scenic Route Paper Co.); chipboard letters (Heidi Swapp); rub-ons (Basic Grey); stamping ink; white pen; cardstock

Despite their 2-year-old son's fussiness during a photo shoot, Danielle and her husband still managed to capture these precious snapshots. To highlight the focal photo, Danielle silhouetted stars from patterned paper to slightly overlay the photo. Handcut stars from bold patterned papers pop with dimensional adhesive. Hand-stitched floss and stars add a touch of contrasting color and texture.

Danielle Thompson, Tucker, Georgia

Supplies: Patterned papers (American Crafts, Cherry Arte, Provo Craft); floss (DMC); number stickers (Making Memories); stamping ink; pen

Ask two boys to stand still for a serious photo and what do you get—a series of silly shots. From rabbit ears to a wrestling hold, Beth captured her boys at their silly best and placed the painted-edge photos against a playful geometric background. For a twist, Beth placed her printed journaling block sideways on the page. See sketch on CD-ROM.

Beth Sears, Quispamsis, New Brunswick, Canada

Supplies: Patterned papers, die cuts (Basic Grey); letter stickers (Provo Craft); stamping ink; cardstock

What's the perfect way to spend a cold winter's day? Playing video games in front of the fire with Dad, as shown in Nic's photos. To keep the players as the stars of the page, Nic used neutral colors. Layers of stitched papers, twill tape and ribbon add rugged texture. Decorative square brads brushed with paint act as bullet points for journaling details of the day. See sketch on CD-ROM.

Nic Howard, Pukekohe, South Auckland, New Zealand

Supplies: Patterned papers, decorative brads (American Traditional Designs); chipboard letters (Making Memories); clear gloss medium (Plaid); solvent ink (Tsukineko); letters (Paper Bliss); ribbon; cardstock

Written through the eyes of a child, Samantha printed her journaling directly onto her photos with image-editing software, and feathered the photos' edges for a distressed look. Grass paper anchored over concrete patterned paper with metal screw brads brings a nature-meets-urban feel to the page, complementing the photos' subjects.

Samantha Walker, Lehi, Utah

Supplies: Patterned paper (Far and Away Scrapbooks); grass paper (FLAX Art & Design); sticker sentiments (Pebbles In My Pocket); screw brads (Karen Foster Design); washers (Making Memories); label holder (Jo-Ann Stores); cardstock

A mother's love is everlasting, as is evident in this playful layout. A poem expressing the joy of a daughter is printed on journaling strips and placed strategically on the left border. Dominique matted two photos and her title enclosed in a cirlce and a rectangle to balance the right side.

Dominique Quintal, Longueuil, Quebec, Canada
Photos: Martine Giguère, Longueuil, Quebec, Canada

Supplies: Patterned paper (Polar Bear Press); alphabet stickers (source unknown); metal plate (Karen Foster Design); flower (Prima); rub-ons (K & Company); stamping ink; cardstock

A heartbreaking struggle with infertility ends with a mother's love for a much-prayed-for daughter. Heather says she created this page for her daughter to know that "she was one prayed for and wanted little girl." A photo of mom and daughter is softly complemented with pinks and greens. A flower handcut from patterned papers and stitched to the background expresses Heather's feelings on motherhood—joy.

Heather Preckel, Swannanoa, North Carolina

Supplies: Patterned papers (Chatterbox); buttons (Junkitz); embroidery floss (Making Memories); ribbon (May Arts, Michaels); acrylic letters (Heidi Swapp); stamp (Hero Arts); epoxy stickers (Creative Imaginations); black pen; cardstock

"I wanted this layout to reflect the relationship I have with my one and only little girl. The journaling is very personal and something I wanted to get down so years from now my daughter will be able to read this and know how blessed we feel to have her in our lives."

This photo of Heather's daughter jumping up into her dad's arms for a smooch proves one thing—she's a daddy's girl. The endearing photo is set against a playful mix of energetic geometric shapes. A jumbo monogram "d" for "daddy" gets a girly touch with an outline of beads. Woven labels and printed sentiments are juxtaposed for added fun and secured with staples.

Heather Preckel, Swannanoa, North Carolina

Supplies: Patterned papers, jumbo monogram (A2Z Essentials); beads (Blue Moon Beads); woven labels (Me & My Big Ideas); ribbon (Michaels); pen; cardstock

A patchwork of patterned paper joined with decorative machine stitches makes for a homespun background. Lisa rounded the edges of the focal photo of her and her daughter for a softened effect. Photo turns secure the file folder collaged with a flower, stitched label sentiments and a letter tag dangling from a ribbon. The folder opens to reveal Mom's heartfelt journaling and a transfer tape photo of the two.

Lisa Tutman-Oglesby, Mundelein, Illinois

Supplies: Patterned papers (Imagination Project, Sandylion); metal letter (Collage Keepsakes); flower brads, chipboard letters, photo turns, acrylic paint, clear definition stickers (Making Memories); ribbon (Jo-Ann Stores, Sandylion); file folder; rub-on sentiments (Sandylion); mini paper flowers (Prima); daisy charm; cardstock

BILL & 'JOSIAH

LIKE WAVES IN THE OCEAN AFAR

SO IS MY LOVE FOR YOU, MY SON

2005

A quilt of stitched, wavy-cut papers and layered squares creates a cozy backdrop for this precious photo. Sharon captured this shot of her husband kissing their youngest son while vacationing in the family's old hometown near the ocean. Her stamped journaling borders the page and hints at the now faraway ocean waves. Dad's and son's names are stamped onto the photo accented with a clear heart adhered with brads.

**Sharon Laakkonen,
Superior, Wisconsin**

Supplies: Patterned papers (Mara Mi); clear heart (Heidi Swapp); mini brads (Queen & Co.); letter stamps (PSX Design); stamping ink; cardstock

All in the Family

Stumped for ideas for your family album? Consider these topics that will bring your family photos to life on your pages.

- The common personality traits you share with family members.
- The role each family member plays.
- The daily routine or quirky habits.
- Traditions or annual family gatherings.
- Unique phrases or nicknames known only to family insiders.
- Special talents or abilities unique to each family member.
- Passions or favorites that you share with family members.
- Physical traits passed down from one generation to another.
- The reasons why you love each member of your family.

Precious moments between a great-grand-mother and great-grandson will be cherished for years to come with Sheredian's page. She documents her grandson sitting on his great-grandma's lap with a spunky backdrop with heritage touches. A tag inked with walnut ink describes their precious relationship while aged die-cut sayings add further sentiment.

Sheredian Vickers, The Woodlands, Texas

Supplies: Patterned papers (Arctic Frog); hinge sticker, die-cut letters, die-cut sentiments (Crafty Secrets); flowers, brads, flower button (Making Memories); heart charms (All My Memories); rub-on sentiment (Melissa Frances); tag (Paper Reflections); cork (LazerLetterz); ribbon (American Crafts); walnut ink; stamping ink

Maegan's daughter is lucky to have a dad who loves spending time with her. Maegan showcases their relationship with a green color scheme and quotes that play up the lucky-girl theme. Photos of Dad and the apple of his eye pop against a green mat and a painted chipboard frame. Acrylic letter tiles on ribbon-topped tags begin Dad's precious journaling written in his own words.

Maegan Hall, Virginia Beach, Virginia

Supplies: Patterned papers (7 Gypsies, Doodlebug Design, KI Memories); ribbon, letters (Doodlebug Design); button, metal plaque, flowers, letters (Making Memories); chipboard; photo corners (Pioneer); acrylic paint; foam core; cardstock

An enlarged photo of a grandmother with her granddaughters shines against this whimsical patterned paper. To add dimension to the circle patterns, Heide layered the design with smaller punches in contrasting colors adhered with brads. Punched flowers centered with brads add a feminine touch. A multicolored title printed on the mat frames the photo.

Heide Lasher, Englewood, Colorado

Supplies: Patterned paper (American Crafts); flower punch; hole punch; brads; cardstock

Jessica knows what the good stuff is all about. The focal black-and-white photo perfectly encapsulates the precious moments between mother and daughter. Geometric shapes and straight lines add rhythm and unity to her uncluttered layout.

Jessica Sprague, Cary, North Carolina
Photo: Jared Sprague, Cary, North Carolina

Supplies: Patterned paper (American Crafts); cardstock

"This page was so easy to put together because the paper had diagonal stripes. I simply cut a straight strip off the edge and turned it until the stripes were perpendicular—no measuring!"

Despite their ages, these six siblings sure know how to play hard together. Debbie celebrates the camaraderie between her mom and her brothers and sisters with the group's photo accented by ribbon borders. Her printed journaling matted on three up-side-down tags secured with brads details the gang's fun antics. A tag title block is aged with brown ink for a heritage effect.

Deborah Hodge, Durham, New Hampshire

Supplies: Patterned paper (Anna Griffin); label holder (Jo-Ann Stores); decorative brads (American Traditional Designs); flower (Making Memories); ribbon charm (Maya Road); ribbon (Wrights, Offray, Michaels); photo corners (3L); copper leafing pen (Krylon); floss (DMC); chipboard numbers (Heidi Swapp); clip art (Dover Publications); button; tags; metal photo corner; stamping inks; cardstock

Jane's daughters share a close relationship, so close they even decided to attend the same university 2,000 miles from home. To express the special bond these two have, Jane used a quote in place of her journaling. Repeated flower elements add an air of grace and femininity.

Jane Davies, Westbank, British Columbia, Canada

Supplies: Patterned paper, ribbon, fibers (Gin-X); die-cut monogram (Basic Grey); rub-ons (Chatterbox, Heidi Swapp); flowers (Prima); brads (Doodlebug Design); acrylic paint; decoupage medium; chalk ink

friends to the end

SISTERS SISTERS

you

love

best buds

r & b

Never let an angry sister comb your hair. -Patricia McCann

TOMBOY ❁

Of all the rights of women, the greatest is to be a mother. -Lin Yutang

girly girl

Lord help the mister that comes between me and my sister. -Irving Berlin

A friend is like a good bra, close to your heart, hard to find and supportive. ~Anonymous

In the spirit of sisterly love, Rebecca sets a sassy tone with punchy patterns and colors as well as humorous sentiments on this page. The black-and-white photo of the smiling sisters pops against brightly colored retro patterns. A pink paint-stamped vertical title on a playful circle pattern adds movement to the page while zigzag stitches add texture.

Rebecca Cantu, Brownwood, Texas

Supplies: Patterned papers, tags, acrylic charm (KI Memories); rub-ons (Doodlebug Design, Making Memories); foam letter stamps (Making Memories); alphabet brads (Queen & Co.); stickers (Me & My Big Ideas); acrylic paint; cardstock

100%

Pumpkin Patch - Goebberts in WI Oct 05

Being your mom.... I'm truly the spoiled one! Thanks for making these the best years of my life! Love,

Katie 10, Mikey 7 & Anna

per me

me

ove me

ease me   love me

me

spoil me

sp●iled

When you read Felicia's title and glance at this photo, you may think she's referring to her kids as being spoiled. The truth is, she feels so blessed and spoiled herself to be their mom that she celebrates it with this heartfelt layout. Bright cardstock squares layered over floral patterned paper create a punchy mat to this sweet photo. Clear stickers spell out her title.

Felicia Krelwitz, Plainfield, Illinois

Supplies: Patterned paper, die-cut flower (Urban Lily); letter stickers, flower sticker (Mustard Moon); cardstock

Maria pays tribute to the love between her children with an endearing close-up of the hugging siblings and a list of reasons the two should love one another. Aged wood patterned paper in yellows and reds conveys the warmth of the loving photo. Maria printed "love him" and "love her" reasons in red on cream paper and highlighted the journaling strips with brad-centered flowers. See sketch on CD-ROM.

Maria Gallardo-Williams, Cary, North Carolina

Supplies: Patterned papers (Daisy D's); wooden word (Li'l Davis Designs); flowers (Prima); brads; ribbon (Offray); fabric (Legacy Paper Arts); photo corners (Club Scrap); letter stamps (Post Modern Design); stamping ink; cardstock

The focal photo shows an exchange of brotherly-sisterly love, but Julie explains the cute story behind the backward-hat-wearing dude and dudette in her vertical block of journaling. A close-up shows the great relationship of Julie's kids while smaller shots tout separately their sweet faces. Polka-dot paper strips add a bit of playfulness in gender-neutral colors. See sketch on CD-ROM.

Julie Laakso, Howell, Michigan

Supplies: Patterned paper (Second Avenue); letter stickers (Imagination Project); date stamp (Autumn Leaves); rub-on letters (Making Memories); label holder; brads; cardstock

"I adore this photo of my son, Cole, whispering into his sister's ear how much he loves her. For a fun twist, I overlapped the large monogram letters."

Julie captured this precious photo of brother-sister love and knew it was a scrapbook gem. Mom's letter to the sweet siblings is handwritten on a tag tucked behind the focal photo. Large monogram letters make a bold title while straight and zigzag stitched borders add homespun appeal.

Julie Geiger, Gold Canyon, Arizona

Supplies: Patterned paper, monogram letters, die-cut tag, cardstock stickers (3 Bugs In a Rug); brad; thread; pen; cardstock

Susan compares the similarities between her and her sister on blue cardstock that doubles as a photo mat. Contrasting patterned papers meet under the mat but directly between the long-distance sisters to draw focus to them. A mailbox letter for each sister's initial slightly overlays the photo.

Susan Weinroth, Centerville, Minnesota

Supplies: Patterned papers (American Crafts, FiberMark); photo turns (7 Gypsies); letter stickers (Basic Grey) ; mailbox letters (Making Memories); rub-on letters (Scrapworks); brads; cardstock

Sisters always make the best of friends. Karen wanted to convey the special bond between these two girls and felt the quote perfectly summed up their relationship (and added a bit of humor, too). She printed the black-and-white focal photo on a fabric sticker for visual interest and added pretty girly flowers against a fun and funky color palette.

Karen Cobb, Victoria, British Columbia, Canada

Supplies: Patterned paper, die-cut tags, phrase labels, rub-ons (Scrapworks); fabric sticker (Paper House); die cuts (QuicKutz); ribbon (American Craft); flowers (Prima); acrylic word, metal frame (Li'l Davis Designs); circle punch (EK Success); chalk ink; brads

A hectic day ends with a precious moment and a prayer to slow time. After tending to fights between her son and daughter all day, Courtney couldn't wait for bedtime. But when she captured this precious moment in the photos, she wished bedtime wasn't so soon. Her circular stamped title accented by a crescent of buttons proves her double-mindedness. Psychedelic patterns symbolize the chaos while blue shows the peace Mom finally enjoyed.

Courtney Walsh, Winnebago, Illinois

Supplies: Patterned papers (EK Success); ribbon (Making Memories, May Arts, Michaels); buttons (Junkitz); thread; staples; cardstock

There is no FRIEND LIKE A sister

August 2004

The bond of sisterhood proves unique and strong for these two sisters. Metal and distressed touches dress the unconventionally feminine page with tres-chic flair. Heather tore, inked, sanded and curled paper to create the distressed yet soft feel. A paper strip secured with a series of brads accents the focal photo of the sisters. The small frame accented with a heart clip opens to Heather's sister-tribute.

Heather Uppencamp, Provo, Utah

Supplies: Patterned paper, zipper pulls, typewriter key stickers, brads (All My Memories); heart clip, metal frame, label holder, ribbon (Making Memories); fasteners (Creative Impressions, Karen Foster Design); stamps (Hero Arts, Making Memories, PSX Design); acrylic paint (Delta); sandpaper; solvent ink (Tsukineko); stamping ink; cardstock

How to describe my sister... Tiffany is simply my dearest friend. She has been a source of unconditional love and a great example to me for as long as I can remember. Her strength and sense of humor have lifted me more times than I can count.
Her example of love and patience as a mother inspires me, and helps me with my own children.

The funny thing is, she is my little sister. I feel like she should be the oldest, she seems to have wisdom beyond her (and my) years. She is far more calm and grounded than I am, and has been my rock.
I am glad we can openly tell each other, "I love you". Neither of us takes our relationship for granted, and we both treasure the other. There is no one like my sister!
-journaled Aug, 2004-

These siblings may claim they hate each other, but Trudy knows her kids are all talk—deep down their love for each other reaches to the stars. Whether hangin' out or just chilling with the dog, these two can't get enough of each other. The black-and-white photos complement the harlequin and polka-dot design.

Trudy Sigurdson, Victoria, British Columbia, Canada

Supplies: Patterned papers, die-cut letters (A2Z Essentials); chipboard letters (Pressed Petals); die-cut photo turns (QuickKutz); textured cardstock, brads (Bazzill); letter stamps (PSX Design); date stamp (Making Memories); chipboard brackets (Basic Grey); chalk ink

aysha & alex at butchart gardens

August 2005

CHILLIN'...

OK, so you both constantly say that you

HATE

each other.........yeah right, as if!

The saying goes, "You can pick your friends, but you can't pick your family," but for these close cousins, family and friends are one and the same. Renee matted the photos of her children goofing around with their cousins on a tapestry patterned backdrop with stitching for a warm homespun feel. Acrylic hearts tied with polka-dot ribbons add texture and fun while die-cut sentiments add endearing expression.

Renee Hagler, Birmingham, Alabama

Supplies: Patterned paper, frame, die-cut sentiments (My Mind's Eye); vellum (The Paper Company); ribbon (May Arts); acrylic hearts (Heidi Grace Designs); letter dies (Sizzix)

As her son and his cousin played until the setting sun, Vicki captured these playful photos shining with golden light. The photo montage is set on a color-blocked background of patterned paper squares. A frayed fabric strip adds rugged texture while paper-strip journaling preserves the sweet boyish friendship.

Vicki Boutin, Burlington, Ontario, Canada

Supplies: Patterned papers (Imagination Project, Chatterbox); rub-ons (Scenic Route Paper Co.); chipboard (Heidi Swapp); metal letters (Making Memories); fabric strips (Imagination Project); brads (Making Memories); cardstock

Close cousins huddled together for this precious photo. A citrusy mix of warm patterned papers complements Suzy's photo matted in avocado green. Printed journaling strips name each cousin while a handcut patterned paper flower highlights Suzy's stamped title. Orange rickrack on a striped patterned paper strip adds further spunk and movement to the page.

Suzy West, Fremont, California

Supplies: Patterned papers (Chatterbox); rickrack (May Arts); letter stamps (Li'l Davis Designs); cardstock

Shades of neon capture the vibrant energy of these young cousins. Lisa printed words describing the girls' interests onto a transparency over a lime green background attached with bright ribbons. Paint brushed onto the back of the transparency highlights key words and lends to the look of nail polish. Pink tags adhered with brad-centered flowers label each girl in the photo, listing her name and age. See sketch on CD-ROM.

Lisa Schmitt, Easton, Connecticut

Supplies: Fabric paper, transparencies (Artistic Impressions, K & Company); letter stickers (Creative Imaginations); ribbon (May Arts); acrylic paint, flowers (Making Memories); mini brads (Provo Craft); die-cut tags (AccuCut); pen; cardstock

"To add a bit of spice to this girly layout, I brushed acrylic paint to the back of some of the words on the preprinted transparency. It really made the color pop off the lime green background."

Susan stitched a love quilt with strips of kraft and love patterned papers to form a homespun backdrop to her hubby's photo. She lists each quality she loves about him on paper strips accented with zigzag stitches. Handcut hearts are outlined with straight stitches for a bit of whimsy.

Susan Weinroth, Centerville, Minnesota

Supplies: Patterned papers (FiberMark, KI Memories, Li'l Davis Designs), rub-on (Making Memories); ribbon (May Arts); cardstock

what i **love** **About YOU**

Your smile.
Your kisses.
Your eyes.
Your attitude.
Your energy.
Your being.
Your Love for Me.

no ReGrETs

After two failed marriages, I no longer believed in love or marriage and I didn't want to ever try it again!!! BUT, I wanted more children, so I had no choice but to give it one more try. Tom had no idea what he was getting into when he started dating me. I had developed a "Rate-A-Mate" test to weigh and score each trait that was important to me in a future spouse. I was going to use my head this time and finally make a good decision. I put him through a lot during the two years we dated, constantly testing him and questioning our relationship. It took lots of courage, but I said yes when he asked me to marry him. I was so scared and almost backed out many times. I did NOT want to fail again. I knew Tom had impeccable character and would be a good father and provider. I could not have married a man with more loyalty and commitment to his family. Now that we have been married for seven years and have two little girls together, I have NO REGRETS! Not only did he give me more children, he also taught me to believe in love and marriage again – an added bonus! *Valentine's Day, 2006*

TOM ON OUR HONEYMOON 1998

7

After two failed marriages, three's a charm for Suzy as she's learned to trust her now husband of seven years. She showcased her appreciation for him with this focal photo taken on their honeymoon. A filmstrip of photos set at an angle and bordered with rickrack adds movement and insight to the couple's happiness.

Suzy Plantamura,
Laguna Niguel, California

Supplies: Patterned papers (KI Memories); plastic letters (Heidi Swapp); brads (Junkitz, SEI); rickrack; vellum; white pen; cardstock

Sometimes tongue-in-cheek and sometimes strictly serious, Angelia lists her heartfelt reasons she's glad she married her husband 17 years ago. She printed her list on a paper strip accented by chipboard symbols. The enlarged photo of the guy she'd marry all over again is highlighted with a row of circles and punched hearts.

Angelia Wigginton, Belmont, Mississippi

Supplies: Patterned paper (Chatterbox); chipboard numbers, chipboard brackets, silhouette circle, photo corners (Heidi Swapp); heart punch (EK Success); tiny flowers (Savvy Stamps); mini brads; cardstock

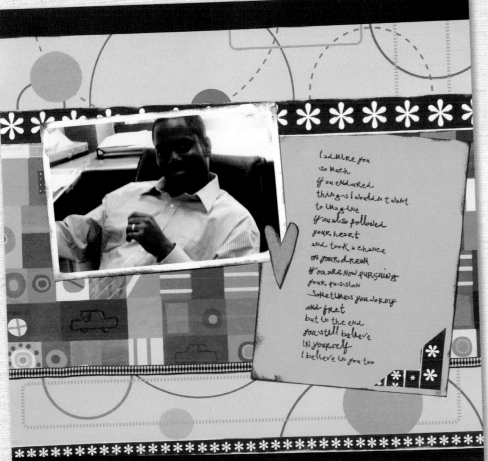

Muriel admires her husband for his passion for life and his job. He's shown here smiling as he sits at his desk, and to convey his happy attitude toward his work, Muriel used spunky patterned papers in masculine colors. She purposely combined an eclectic mix of papers and a ribbon border to reflect her husband's busyness.

Muriel Roseman Croom, Chula Vista, California

Supplies: Patterned papers (Imagination Project, KI Memories, Provo Craft); ribbon (Making Memories); stamping ink; cardstock

Wanda pays tribute to this special man in her life by placing him front and center with a large black-and-white focal photo. The image immediately captures the eye, while the icicle letters placed vertically down the page add movement and complement the retro feel.

Wanda Santiago-Cintron, Deerfield, Wisconsin

Supplies: Patterned paper (Die Cuts with a View); icicle letters (KI Memories); black pen

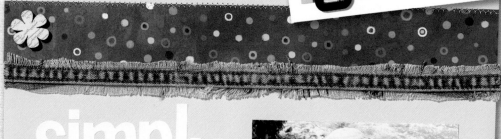

simply sam

Clothed in his standard dress of denim, Jodi's husband is the star of this page. To enhance his shorts and blue-lens sunglasses, Jodi adjusted the hue saturation of the photo. A frayed seam from an old pair of blue jeans borders the top of the page. Jodi's journaling about what is simply Sam is printed on the background along with a digital design element.

Jodi Heinen, Sartell, Minnesota

Supplies: Patterned papers (KI Memories, Scrapworks); letter stickers (American Crafts); denim; wooden accents (Li'l Davis Designs); digital graphic (Rhonna Farrer); cardstock

Sam is predictable, but that is one of the things that I love about him I know that on any given day he will be wearing a white t-shirt, jeans or jean shorts, tennis shoes and a baseball hat.

I swear that the older he gets the younger he looks.

JUL 2005

fishing in maine

June

2005

A few words from Dad about his fishing adventure in Maine with Tim this past summer:

"While I have had many opportunities to go fishing with my eldest son, I enjoyed this particular trip most of all. This was a rare time in which it was just he and I. I faithfully got out of bed very early every morning and ventured out onto various lakes and ponds near our camp in Maine. It was rainy and chilly most mornings, but the warmth and enjoyment of being out on the water with Tim made it all worthwhile"

rain

memories

Just a note: Dad caught his first small mouth bass on that trip. ☺

The proud smile of Dee's darling dad is the true catch on this page. Dee journals in her dad's words on a sanded journaling block about the treasured fishing trip he took with his son. A wavy line of stitches, circles and cardstock add vertical movement while Dee's tiny touches, such as a side note on a torn notebook paper and sentiment tags, add a homespun feel.

Dee Gallimore-Perry, Griswold, Connecticut
Photo: Tim Gallimore, Sprague, Connecticut

Supplies: Patterned paper, die cuts, stickers, ribbon (KI Memories); tag, notebook paper, safety pin (Making Memories); brad (Junkitz); rub-on word (Li'l Davis Designs); photo corners (Heidi Swapp, My Mind's Eye); leather folio closure (EK success); ribbon (Offray); sandpaper; staple; thread; cardstock

> **"I used my dad's own words as my journaling for this layout. It worked great to share the story from his own personal perspective."**

FATHER...

family ties family ties family ties

family ties family ties family ties

A father is, by definition, someone who gives you life. But a dad is so much more. Fathers are fathers because they care, because they love, because they're there. Unfortunately, I lost my own father when I was just 17, nearly 13 years ago. A father is not someone you can ever replace. My dad is still right here with me, in me. Fortunately, also 13 years ago, a father figure came into my life. As I was losing a father, I was gaining a father-in-law. At first, our relationship was rocky: we didn't always agree on what was best for his son, the man I love. But time did its thing, it brought us closer. I look up to him like I would my father. He has not taken my father's place, but like a father, he cares for me, he loves me and he's always there. He's an amazing person, an extraordinary father and father-in-law, and an outstanding grandfather to my kids. He is simply...

...IN-LAW

IRREPLACEABLE

Caroline tributes her late father while paying homage to her father-in law with heartfelt journaling bordered by mesh. Clusters of paper flowers stitched with embroidery thread are decidedly masculine in neutral colors. Patterned paper strips in varying widths create a mat with a spice of color to her father-in-law's photo. How she feels about him as well as her dad are summed up with chipboard letters—irreplaceable.

Caroline Huot, Laval, Quebec, Canada

Supplies: Patterned papers (Basic Grey); mesh (Magic Mesh); letter stickers (Die Cuts With a View); flowers (Prima); ribbon (All My Memories); chipboard letters (Heidi Swapp); cardstock

This man owes his compassionate nature to his growing up with seven sisters, according to one of them, Becky. This is just one of her brother's admired traits as Becky explains in her heartfelt journaling. His photo shines against a rustic backdrop of masculine papers. Jumbo photo turns and screw brads add beefy texture. A definition die cut split between a metal-rimmed tag with a heart makes a loving sentiment.

Becky Heisler, Waupaca, Wisconsin
Photo: Jolynn Winkels,
Wisconsin Rapids, Wisconsin

Supplies: Patterned papers (A2Z Essentials, Basic Grey); die-cut sentiment (My Mind's Eye); metal-rimmed tags, screw brads (Making Memories); acrylic paint; stamping ink; cardstock

brother

charming /"ci____mi[ng]/ adj.
1. extremely plea____ ____ delightful, or facinating
2. captivating

When I think of my brother Tim, the first thing that always comes to mind is what a great friend he is. He is always ready to lend a helping hand. I admire him so much for his drive to be better person and succeed in his life and business. I love to watch him. With his family, he is a wonderful, participating husband and father. Of course, he does have other qualities we have to mention like being a pack rat and the fact that growing up he always had longer prettier hair than any one of us 7 girls always bought on some laughter. Tim is a kind and compassionate person, but then I would not expect any less growing up with 7 sisters!

Greta has reached the milestone of feeling on level ground with her father as an adult. Her father, who is also her friend, is pictured here with Greta's two children. Staggered patterned paper strips form the photo mat, and the page is accented with punchy polka-dot flowers and buttons. See sketch on CD-ROM.

Greta Hammond, Goshen, Indiana

Supplies: Patterned papers (Chatterbox, Daisy D's, Scenic Route Paper Co); chipboard photo corners (Scenic Route Paper Co.); buttons (Chatterbox, Foofala); chipboard sentiment (Bazzill); typewriter letter stickers (EK Success); cardstock

Father AND friend

It probably happens at different times for everyone. It could be gradual or instantaneous. Or maybe, for some, it doesn't happen at all. It is the time when you no longer feel like a child around your parents. The time when you finally feel like an adult. Making your own decisions. Making your own way in the world.

This is how I feel with my dad. I feel like our relationship has progressed to place where I no longer have to explain myself. Where I no longer fear that I may be doing something wrong. It is at a place where he rejoices in the decisions that I have made and the home that Wade and I have established. He is supportive and encouraging but not judgmental. He respects me and adores my husband and children. He is proud of the life that I have made and wants to be apart of it. He is my father and also my friend.

Uncle Ford's character and heart have touched Erin in a big way. She pays tribute to him with this page of rich masculine colors. The focal photo shows Erin giving him a squeeze, and smaller snapshots show the inspiring man in everyday moments. She details all about him that inspires her on a sage journaling block highlighted by velvet ties strung by photo hangers. Leather photo corners give a finishing touch.

Erin Campbell-Pope, Petal, Mississippi
Photos: Charlotte Campbell,
Carriere, Mississippi

Supplies: Patterned papers (Autumn Leaves, My Mind's Eye, SEI); chipboard letters, leather photo corners, brads (Making Memories); photo hangers (Jo-Ann Stores); velvet ribbon (Michaels); heart charm; acrylic paint; stamping ink; sandpaper; cardstock

In the 11th grade, Deborah's dad was drafted into the Army to serve his country. She tributes the now well-worn soldier for his sacrifices back then that changed both him and the world. A close-up shot shows Dad sporting his patriotism with a flag scarf. Ribbon ties and star buttons add a touch of American spirit while a die-cut sentiment and dog tags salute this freedom-fighting hero.

Deborah Barton, Rockingham, North Carolina
Photo: Leslie Barton, Rockingham,
North Carolina

Supplies: Patterned papers (Karen Foster Design); star buttons (Doodlebug Design); chipboard letters, label holder, brads (Making Memories); acrylic paint; ribbons (May Arts); dog tags (Li'l Davis Designs); ball chain (Wal-Mart); label maker (Dymo); stamping ink; cardstock

This is a photograph of my father, Jack Gallimore around 1943 or 1944 while living in Saxonville, MA. He was around 5-years old. I asked him to write a little bit about the memories this picture brings back...this is what he wrote:

"As best that I can remember, it had to be around 1943 or 1944. WWII was still going on and we lived on the block. The block was a long multi-family building that was made primarily for the mill workers. We lived at 24 Centennial Place. I think there were 28 or 30 families that lived there."

"I remember exactly as the fish was caught; my dad and I were out in the boat somewhere up the Sudbury River not far from the old icehouse, near the 'cove'. I had a pole, Dad had a pole, and I remember seeing this flash of silver through the water...my pole bent over and the line started out. About that time, Dad grabbed the pole and worked the fish into the boat. It was a 24" Pickerel; not bad for a 5-year old. In later years, my dad bested me by getting a 27" from the same river. I never turned out to be the fisherman my dad was. He could catch fish in the desert. I guess Tim takes after him that way."

"The boat is another story. Dad built it in the basement of 24 Centennial Place (this is the same place where we owned the 2 pigs, Skunk and Coca Cola.) He was having a very difficult time closing up the boards to make the bow, using clamps or whatever. My mom apparently heard him and went down to help. She took the bow boards between her knees, squeezed them together and Dad made the connections."

"I was standing on a box in the boat in this photograph. We had an outboard motor that my dad had 'made'. I will tell THAT story sometime, too."

LITTLE BOY...BIG FISH

The greatest oak was once a little nut who held its ground. ~unknown

Dee got more than a fish tale when she asked her father to write about his childhood photo with this big catch. Set against a backdrop of youthful patterned papers, the heritage photo stands as the focal point, but the lively storytelling lures you into the page. Dee's dad brings to life memories of fishing in his father's handmade boat, hinting at a difficult yet perhaps simpler time.

Dee Gallimore-Perry,
Griswold, Connecticut

Supplies: Patterned papers, die-cut stickers, rub-ons (KI Memories); circle cutter; thread; cardstock

"I have had this photo of my grand-mother for over 15 years. It was always special to me, however I did not know many details. So I used my journaling to express my wish to know more about the story behind this photo."

Though Kim has more questions than answers about her grandmother's life during World War II, she is happy to have found a shoe box full of forgotten photos including this one. With her grandmother's signature at the bottom, the photo preserves her handwriting as well as a glimpse of her youth. Smudges of brown ink lend an aged look while bright pastels add a lively touch to this heritage page. See sketch on CD-ROM.

Kim DuPree, Tyler, Texas

Supplies: Patterned papers, canvas stickers (Foofala); border sticker (Creative Imaginations); foam letter stamps, acrylic paint (Making Memories); letter stickers (EK Success); ribbon (May Arts); rub-on stitches; decorative rub-ons (7 Gypsies); buttons; eyelets; cardstock

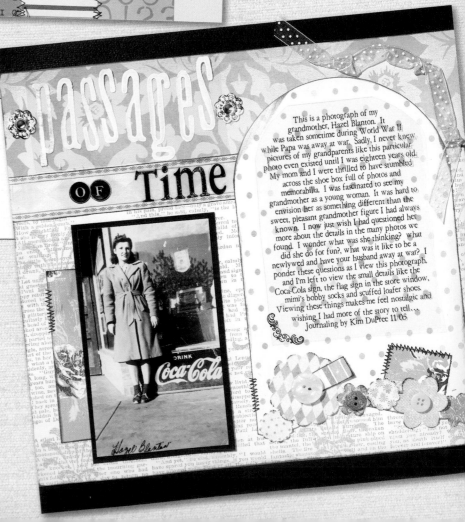

passages OF Time

This is a photograph of my grandmother, Hazel Blanton. It was taken sometime during World War II while Papa was away at war. Sadly, I never knew pictures of my grandparents like this particular photo even existed until I was eighteen years old. My mom and I were thrilled to have stumbled across the shoe box full of photos and memorabilia. I was fascinated to see my grandmother as a young woman. It was hard to envision her as something different than the sweet, pleasant grandmother figure I had always known. I now just wish I had questioned her more about the details in the many photos we found. I wonder what was she thinking?, what did she do for fun?, what was it like to be a newlywed and have your husband away at war? I ponder these questions as I view this photograph, and I'm left to view the small details like the Coca-Cola sign, the flag sign in the store window, mimi's bobby socks and scuffed loafer shoes. Viewing these things makes me feel nostalgic and wishing I had more of the story to tell...
Journaling by Kim DuPree 11-05

DRINK Coca-Cola

Hazel Blanton

Funky accents and patterns are a blast from the past, celebrating Danielle's parents' wedding day on this spread. Stripes, daisies and argyles in muted pastels are layered and machine-stitched in black to tie in the black-and-white photos. The bride's initial is punched from the focal photo and called out with 1960-reminiscent daisies. Rub-on sentiments on mirrors make groovy wedding decor along with the garter on Danielle's title.

Danielle Thompson, Tucker, Georgia

Supplies: Patterned paper (Anna Griffin, Chatterbox, K & Company, KI Memories); rub-ons (Chatterbox, Making Memories); wooden daisies (Li'l Davis Designs); large gems; beads (The Beadery); tag (Pebbles); key charm (Embellish It); ribbon (May Arts, Michaels); paper clip; die-cut flower (Colorbök); garter (7 Gypsies); chalks (Craf-T); staples; cardstock

Two women's lives during two different eras find common ground in circumstance and life challenges. Carolyn begins the comparison of herself and her mother during the same stages in life with a woven backdrop of modern patterned papers and a heritage photo of the two. She journaled their comparisons on a flower-topped tag tucked into a pocket.

Carolyn Cleveland, Maysville, Georgia

Supplies: Patterned paper (Imagination Project); rub-ons (Imagination Project, My Mind's Eye); stickers (KI Memories, Scrapworks); chipboard, flower (Making Memories); ribbon (May Arts); brad; stamping ink; cardstock

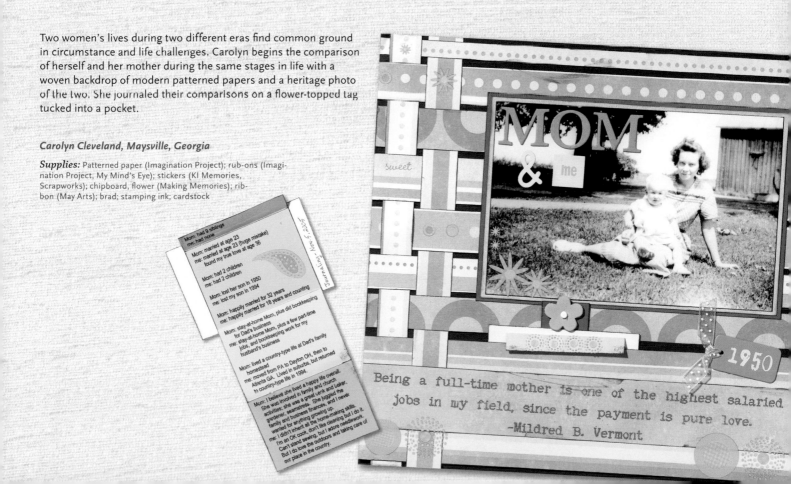

Sunny backyard memories came rushing back to Pam when she found this childhood portrait. A stitched slightly worn tapestry backdrop complements the black-and-white heritage photo. Pam stitched a photo mat to the tapestry, which doubles as a journaling block for fond memories printed on a transparency. A border made with stitched nostalgic-textile patterns accented with knotted ribbons adds a homespun touch.

Pam Sivage, Georgetown, Texas

Supplies: Patterned papers, cardstock sentiments (My Mind's Eye); flower; twill tape; ribbon; brad; cardstock

sunny

outdoors

warm

fun

This photo brings back summer memories of our backyard. I played for hours in the sprinkler, running on the lush green grass that was always weed free. I played in the sandbox my Dad made, building tunnels and castles. The trees always offered an adventure of seeing how high I could climb and picking fresh apricots and peaches when I needed a snack. 1947

Jennifer:

You were nearly a year old when you were given your first See's Candy sucker. The look of wonder that filled your face enchanted everyone in the room. It was pure magic! Your huge blue eyes widened as you tasted the buttery caramel that melted in your mouth.

Before too many moments passed, nearly half of the caramel had dribbled onto your bare tummy. How lucky for us to have had a camera in the room at that once in a lifetime moment. At such a young age, you had little verbal language to describe your feelings.

but this picture truly says 1000 words, and I think all of them would have been "yummy!" I love to remember those little "baby firsts" now after so many years, and can't wait to share "grandbaby firsts" when that day comes.
Love,
Mom   July 21, 2004

A heritage photo of Pam's daughter eating her first See's Candy sucker is remembered in sweet detail on this page. Bright red papers paired with vintage patterned papers create a spunky setting for the black-and-white photo. Actual suckers tied with ribbons and candy wrappers made into tags are custom accents. The hinged title opens to Pam's nostalgic journaling.

Pamela James, Ventura, California

Supplies: Patterned papers (Club Scrap); candy wrappers; candy suckers; ribbon; 3-D flower stickers (EK Success); safety pin; clear gloss medium (Judikins); decorative scissors; tags; brads; cardstock

When Carolyn saw these French Country patterned papers with a newspaper theme, she knew it was the perfect backdrop to complement this 1947 photo of her husband's mother. The photo, published in a newspaper, shows his mother holding the winning bird in the poultry industry's search for a meatier chicken. Matted on distressed patterned paper and cardstock secured with sticker hinges, the photo opens to the entire story told by Carolyn's husband.

Carolyn Cleveland, Maysville, Georgia

Supplies: Patterned papers (Daisy D's); stickers (Autumn Leaves, Daisy D's); rub-ons (My Mind's Eye); chalk; stamping ink; cardstock

The poultry industry looks for a better commercial bird.

In 1946 the Great Atlantic and Pacific Tea Company (now A&P) launched the 'Chicken of Tomorrow' contest to find a strain of chicken that could produce a broad-breasted bird at low feed cost. At the time, the most common broiler chicken was an expensive, scrawny bird with mostly dark meat and red and/or gray feathers, more apt to be seen on a rich man's plate than a poor man's.

One of the entrants to the Iowa 'Chicken of Tomorrow' contest was Myrick's Morris Hatchery in Morris, Illinois. Owner Burdell Myrick and his Office Manager Arline Cleveland had done some research among U.S. breeders and had found Arbor Acres Farms in Connecticut, where Henry Saglio had bred a heavy-breed of White Plymouth Rock. Hatching eggs had been obtained and the chicks raised with properly-balanced nutrition rather than the usual "grain scraps" fed to most chickens at that time.

For the 1947 contest, the birds were ready to be shown off. The meaty, white-feathered bird made a big impression on poultry processors. During processing, dark feathers would often leave a bit of a stain on the flesh, so a white-feathered bird was greatly desirable.

The picture shows Arline Cleveland holding "Ferdinand", a rather elegant rooster, which had been one of the top entrants.

(The actual background of the picture was a large map of North and South America with tacked-down ribbons showing the many places that the Hatchery shipped baby chicks. Part of it had been hand-painted to a gray background for publication purposes.)

(On the back of the photo it says:
Mrs. Arline Cleveland (correct)
Morris, Ia+, & Ferdinand,-
son of Iowa "Chicken of Tomorrow"

The back has rubber-stamped:
Photo by Herman Seid
Cleveland Press
Jul 23 1947
Return....)

A heritage photo from a poignant moment in Gislaine's life—confirming her faith—is framed with aged scripted papers with a torn and rolled scroll-like edge. Her layered die-cut title and tags are accented with ribbon and spiritual charms. A stamped initial block secured with brads memorializes the date of this special event.

Gislaine Vincent, Dorval, Quebec, Canada

Supplies: Patterned papers (Creative Imaginations, DDDesigns); rub-ons (Making Memories); word sticker, concho (7 Gypsies); charms (Dollar Love); photo turns (Junkitz); ribbon (May Arts); die-cut letters (Crafty Secrets); silk flowers; lace; date stamp; stamping ink; brads; cardstock

The adage "The getting there is half the fun" proved true for Maegan and a group of women as they set out for a shopping trip. They got stuck in traffic, but nothing slowed these ladies down as they talked and got better acquainted. Eventually, true colors showed, inspiring Maegan's painted chipboard title. Handcut daisies with bright buttons add spunk while rub-on letters on tags dangling from clips spell each woman's name.

Maegan Hall, Virginia Beach, Virginia
Photos: David Hall, Virginia Beach, Virginia

Supplies: Patterned papers, stickers, rub-on letters, buttons, stickers (Doodlebug Design); chipboard letters (Making Memories, Heidi Swapp); corner rounder (Creative Memories); acrylic paint; cardstock

A filmstrip of goofy black-and-white photos printed on textured cardstock and colored with bright chalks tributes a funny friend. Maegan matted the focal photo with custom word paper she created by looking up the word "admire" in a thesaurus and then printing the words in bright colors. A chipboard monogram carries the title rub-on "admire" accented with punchy ribbons and spunky buttons to represent this special friend's personality. See sketch on CD-ROM.

Maegan Hall, Virginia Beach, Virginia

Supplies: Patterned papers, buttons, rub-ons (Doodlebug Design); chipboard monogram (Heidi Swapp); ribbon; cardstock

> **"I made my own custom paper by looking up all the words that have the same meaning as 'admire' in the thesaurus and then printing them on paper placed behind the photo."**

A combination of stripes, daisies and polka-dot patterns is as spunky as the group of friends in the focal photo. Julie plays up her youthful theme with her playful title created from a template and chipboard letters that she then inked and painted to match the page. Flowers cut from patterned papers shine with clear gloss medium and embellish the pocket-like accent that carries her transparency-printed journaling.

Julie Eickmeier, Fort Myers, Florida
Photo: Petra Muetzel,
Garfield Heights, Ohio

Supplies: Patterned papers (Déjà Views); ribbon; lettering template; chipboard letters (Making Memories); Wet Look adhesive (Little Black Dress Designs); buckle; eyelets; stamping ink; cardstock

Tracy tributes a friendship that runs deep with this happy photo close-up and heartfelt journaling. The black-and-white photo of the best friends is placed on a sea of serene green papers that have been brushed with cream paint for a dreamy effect. Machine-stitching adds a homespun touch while a cluster of flowers adds feminine flair. See sketch on CD-ROM.

Tracy Weinzapfel Burgos, Ramona, California

Supplies: Patterned papers (Fiberscraps); letter stamp (PSX Design); date stamp, acrylic paint (Making Memories); flowers (Michaels); brads; stamping ink

With a shared passion to become professional scrapbookers, Michelle tributes a special friend as she rises to a scrapbook challenge to creatively use ribbon. The friendship story unfolds with close-ups and hidden journaling beneath the hinged focal photo. Rickrack adds movement as borders, expression as tag toppers and frames the tags as well. The dreams of these less-than-six-month scrapbookers look promising as both have joined manufacturer design teams.

Michelle Van Etten, Pensacola, Florida
Photo: Diana McGraw, Pensacola, Florida

Supplies: Patterned papers (Basic Grey); hinges, rub-ons, tags (Making Memories); stencil letters (Wal-Mart); ribbons (Offray, Shoebox Trims, Wal-Mart); ribbon charm; flowers (www.mermaidtears.net); clear gloss medium (Plaid); staples; cardstock

When Sheredian gets together with the ladies in her family, they are sure to be a powerhouse of fun, talent and beauty—in other words, true divas. The bold patterns and bright colors of Sheredian's backdrop complements the spirit of the ladies in the photo. Their diva qualities are printed on paper strips highlighted with neon brads. Silk flowers and monogram letters add bold diva touches.

Sheredian Vickers, The Woodlands, Texas

Supplies: Patterned papers, monogram letters (Basic Grey); brads, label holder (Making Memories); buttons (Die Cuts With a View, Jesse James); silk flowers (Michaels); stamping ink

FRIENDSHIP EVERLASTING

When I think of the word everlasting, many things come to mind. I think of all the things and people that claim to be everlasting but few rarely are. During my childhood, I remember the first time I got an Everlasting Gobstopper. Wow! Could it really last forever? Well, you know what happens to those Gobstoppers ... they stop Gobbing much faster than they ought!

Thankfully, I've come to find out that along with our heavenly father there are a rare few things in this life that also last. Michelle and I have been friends since junior high and from that moment forward, we have maintained a true friendship. This rare type of friendship can stand the test of time, distance, changed jobs, children, husbands and life. We have shared all of life's emotions and have encouraged one another to find the value in each day that God brings. I am thankful to call Michelle my everlasting friend.

He who walks with the wise grows wise, while the companion of fools suffers harm.
Proverbs 13:20

Pink paint, torn papers and machine-stitching lend a trés chic touch to this feminine friendship page. Sonia used strokes of paint to distress and frame the photos of her and her best friend. Brushes of paint and a gem transform a washer into a fancy flower on the left side of the horizontal photo. A handmade tag tucked behind a photo holds the story of their everlasting friendship.

Sonia Pancratz, Lewisville, Texas
Photo: Steve Pancratz, Lewisville, Texas

Supplies: Patterned papers (Kit-Love-4); ribbon, plaque stickers, silk flowers, acrylic paint, eyelets, hinges, photo turns, brads (Making Memories); molding strips, metal plaques, buttons, flower charms, label holders, gems, jump rings (Li'l Davis Designs); fabric letters; beads; staples; vellum; cardstock

WALKS and TALKS

Palm Island, Florida April 2005

Growing up, I was never one of the girly-girls. I don't have any memories of sitting around with a group of my girlfriends painting nails and gossiping. But that sure doesn't mean that I don't need my share dose of time with "my girls." I have a great time each time I am able to get together with any one of them, weather it be an hour at our house or a few hours out to dinner. However, nothing reenergizes me more than our biannual weekends away together. They are such fun and relaxing times and leave me with a feeling of "friendship fullness" like nothing else can. I am totally grateful for those times spent together... Just walking... just talking...and just being together. I love my girls!

Strolling along the beach on one of her biannual weekend getaways with girlfriends, Linda got this spontaneous photo by holding her camera out at arm's length. She framed the shot with a cluster of flowers, some with pearl centers. The floral motif and crisp white backdrop epitomize summer. Journaling printed in coordinating ink directly on the background tells of Linda's blessed feminine friendships.

Linda Harrison, Sarasota, Florida

Supplies: Patterned paper, rub-ons (Fontwerks); chipboard letters (Heidi Swapp); pearls (Westrim); flowers (Prima); hole punches; cardstock

> "I wanted to use my own handwriting on the layout to keep it personal. I feel it helps reflect my great friendship with these three ladies."

A unique photo treatment emphasizes these friendly faces. Sam printed his focal black-and-white photo twice and cropped one as a photo strip secured with hinges. He used a square punch on the duplicate photo to crop in on each face. He inked the square's edges and carefully adhered them in place on the hinged photo strip. The hinges flip down to show two color photos. Handwritten journaling details each friend's attributes with a personal touch.

Samuel Cole, Woodbury, Minnesota

Supplies: Patterned paper (EK Success, Karen Foster Design, SEI); stickers (SEI); square punch (Creative Memories); letter stamps (Hero Arts); label holders; circle punch; stamping ink; brads; pen; cardstock

friends

Jill & Andrea

It isn't exactly the easiest to get together every weekend with a friend that lives about 1700 miles away. So when Jill came to visit me for 10 days in August of 2004, it was such a treat. We had enough time to scrapbook and enjoy the warm weather. I was able to visit her in Kentucky 4 months later when she got married to her best friend, T.J. Time will only tell when we can meet up again.

A long-distance friendship is reaffirmed during cherished weekend get-togethers for these two women. Andrea highlights the black-and-white photos of her and her precious friend with a feminine background of pastel polka-dot patterned paper. The playful pattern is echoed in a circle journaling block and a series of polka-dot ribbons. See sketch on CD-ROM.

Andrea Graves, Sandy, Utah

Supplies: Ribbons (May Arts); digital kit (www.digitaldesignessentials.com); staples; cardstock

Common bonds bridge the 10-year age gap between these two friends. Rachel printed the black-and-white photo of her and her "me too" friend directly onto cardstock for a soft effect. Rachel's doodles, handwritten journaling and rub-on stitches lend a warm homespun feel.

Rachel Carlson, Highlands Ranch, Colorado

Supplies: Rub-on stitches (Autumn Leaves); stamping ink; pen; cardstock

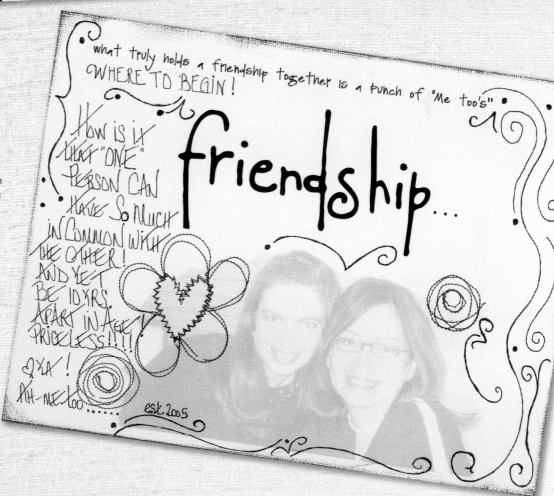

what truly holds a friendship together is a bunch of "Me too's"
WHERE TO BEGIN!
How is it that "ONE" PERSON CAN HAVE So Much IN COMMON WITH THE OTHER! AND YET BE 10 YRS. APART IN AGE! PRICELESS!!!!
JLA! RH-ME too

friendship...

est. 2005

A happy trip down memory lane always leads to Erin's special place—her childhood home. An enlarged focal photo of the road back home is secured with hinges and flips open to her sentimental journey printed on a transparency. A CD of a pictorial family history is set to music.

Erin Campbell-Pope, Petal, Mississippi
Photo: Campbell's Fine Portraits, Carriere, Mississippi

Supplies: Patterned paper (K & Company); fabric; ribbons (Offray); hinge stickers (Creek Bank Creations); gold paint pen (Krylon); letter sticker (Mrs. Grossman's); clock pieces (Magic Scraps); conchos, epoxy letter stickers (Li'l Davis Designs); fiber (EK Success); die-cut letters (AccuCut); key hole charm (Karen Foster Design); metal hinges, frame holders (Jest Charming); acrylic paint, rub-on letters (Making Memories); stamping ink; transparency; cardstock

With detail and sentiment, Maria revisits her childhood home in Venezuela bringing back comforting memories. The photo gives a glimpse of the wrought iron and brick she fondly remembers in her journaling. The architectural detail in the photo is given an old-world effect with a watercolor filter and is enhanced with rust embossed accents throughout the page.

Maria Gallardo-Williams, Cary, North Carolina

Supplies: Patterned paper (Provo Craft); ribbon (Legacy Paper Arts, Michaels); label holder (Legacy Paper Arts); charms (Magic Scraps, Provo Craft); embossing powder (Ranger); flowers (Prima); brads; stamping ink; photo corners; textured paper; cardstock

Danielle not only infuses her scrapbook pages with color and energy, but the rooms in her house as well. The spirit of Asian and Indian design comes alive on this computer-generated page about the favorite room in her house. She added a variety of fonts as well as faux stitching and brads to give the perfect finishing touch.

Danielle Thompson, Tucker, Georgia
Supplies: Shabby Princess digital kit (www.theshabbyshoppe.com); Rhonna Farrer digital kit (www.twopeasinabucket.com)

A wood stove warms Shannon's home as well as her family's hearts as they gather around it together. Shannon's page is all aglow warmed with burnt orange paper and a nostalgic patterned background. A twill tape sentiment is accented with strung gold beads and a stick pin dangling a heart charm. Sanded chipboard letters take on a worn look, adding meaning to the heirloom wood stove title.

Shannon Taylor, Bristol, Tennessee
Supplies: Patterned paper (Cactus Pink); chipboard letters (Li'l Davis Designs); heart charm (Anna Griffin); beads (Westrim); stick pin (EK Success); twill tape sentiment (K & Company); cardstock

After three years of hard work, I am finally feeling like our house is a home. When we first arrived our furnishings were from the early part of our marriage and were classically Midwest-contemporary. As I've grown older I've become more relaxed. I want a cozy house that my kids can enjoy with their friends and one I feel at home entertaining in. I want to wake to soothing colors and feel the warmth and love of our family in every room. I think we're finally getting there. We've painted and merchandised, recycled and discarded and we have stumbled upon our decorating style; French Country— and I love it. Not just the whole picture of it, but all the little parts that make it "home". And that's why all the pictures. Not of the room, but of all the little things that make up the rooms. I can finally step back, sigh and say, "I truly love our home."

Going
french

A photo montage commemorates all the little things that make Shay's house a home. She plays on her new decorating style with a paisley pattern in the same inspired theme— French country. Monogram chipboard letters covered in the same pattern paper begin the words in her title while whimsical French rub-on letters finish it.

Shay Brackney, Castle Rock, Colorado

Supplies: Patterned paper, chipboard monograms (Basic Grey); slide clip (Heidi Swapp); cardstock

"After moving from Phoenix to Colorado, our lives became more relaxed and our decorating style reflects that. Going from midwestern contemporary to French country was something worth scrapbooking!"

Photo snippets of Barb's favorite things give a glimpse into what she says makes her house a home. Chipboard coaster quotes accompany the photo montage. The photo and journaling mat is secured with machine-stitching to whimsically patterned papers for a homespun effect.

Barb Hogan, Cincinnati, Ohio

Supplies: Patterned papers (Cotton Art Tape); chipboard coaster quotes (Imagination Project); ribbon (Li'l Davis Designs); cardstock

It's the little things that make a house a home, and Lora documents with both words and visuals all that she loves about her abode. As the photos give a peek inside each of Lora's favorite rooms, journaling printed on vellum that overlays a photo of the outside of her house goes into detail about how each room uniquely provides comfort and joy. See sketch on CD-ROM.

Lora Covington, Superior, Colorado

Supplies: Patterned papers (7 Gypsies, Daisy D's, Paper Adventures); metal words (K & Company); stickers (Creative Imaginations); flower ponytail holders; ribbon; transparency; vellum; cardstock

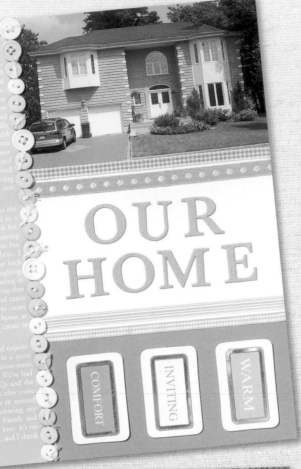

The photo may show the outward appearance of Nicole's house, but her journaling invites you inside to discover what makes it a home. She attributes the gift of creating a sense of home no matter the place to her parents as they moved often throughout her childhood. The story is set in a clean blocked design accented by ribbon and threaded buttons.

Nicole Cholet, Beaconsfield, Quebec, Canada

Supplies: Ribbon (KI Memories, Making Memories, May Arts); chipboard tags, metal-rimmed tags (Making Memories); chipboard letters; buttons; embroidery floss (Anchor); acrylic paint (Delta); cardstock

A long-awaited dream of a frilly nursery finally came to fruition for Kelly when her husband surprised her with this freshly painted room. To complement the nursery photos, Kelly used a soft yellow cardstock with muted patterned papers. Yellow hand-stitching and chipboard accents anchored with soft ribbons give a soft homespun feel. See sketch on CD-ROM.

Kelly Goree, Shelbyville, Kentucky

Supplies: Patterned papers, chipboard accents (Basic Grey); floss (DMC); ribbon (May Arts, Making Memories); green stamping ink; cardstock

Snapshots of an incredibly organized work space draw interest to the 8½ x 11" spread created in a horizontal format. A half sphere created with machine-stitching and epoxy circle charms house Gayle's journaling about her new scrapbook digs. The series of photo close-ups are eye candy against daisy and spiral patterned papers, and along with detailed journaling, they host the grand tour.

Gayle Hodgins, Philadelphia, Pennsylvania

Supplies: Patterned papers, epoxy charms, rub-on (MOD); letter stickers (American Crafts); date stamp; stamping ink; thread; cardstock

At first glance, this page may seem to boast a beautiful work space. But when the eye is curiously led to the tabs that read "pull," the journey to the heart of the story begins. The enlarged sepia photo of Teri's work space hints at a place that is ultimately a mind-set she calls the zone—her creative zone. The journaling details the self-empowerment and therapeutic benefits her creative time gives her.

Teri Davis, Lafayette, Louisiana

Supplies: Patterned papers (SEI); ribbons (American Crafts, Michaels, Offray); letter tabs (Scrapworks); die-cut letters (QuicKutz); stamping ink; cardstock

Don't get me wrong. I love being a wife and I love being a mother. My family gives me the greatest joys I could ever imagine, but it is the hardest job I've ever had. It's harder than working retail and even harder than teaching eighth graders. And I am extremely hard on myself. I am my biggest critic. Even though I *know* I am a good wife and a great mom, I don't always *feel* like I am despite my best efforts. It definitely isn't my comfort zone. But put me here, in my creative zone and I know I am safe, especially from my critical self. I love to organize and re-organize my scrap room. I can spend hours cleaning and straightening it, hours just pouring through my thousands (yes, literally over 8000) of sheets of papers. Yes, I know it's ridiculous, but when I am stressed it is the thing I love to do best. After a long day of cleaning and grocery shopping and playing and disciplining and raising a family, I know that I can retreat to my zone to unwind. I know that here I can leave all of the routines, the structure, the rules lying at the door. In here, I am free to do whatever I wish. If I don't like something I can throw it away and start over not feeling like I've made the most horrible decision in the world; not feeling like every decision will have some major impact on my family's future. And when I'm in my zone, I lose all track of time. Naptime is over much too quickly. Sometimes I even set the alarm to remind me it's time to pick the boys up from school and get one to speech therapy and then back home to romp around with them outside and then inside to fix dinner and do the laundry and the dishes until finally it's bedtime. It's here, in my creative zone, in my comfort zone, that I can just sit and relax. It is here that I can create and think and *be*. There is no greater joy in the world than what my family gives to me, but in my creative zone is where I am reminded of that daily and where I find myself remembering that I really *am* a great wife and a great mother and that this is who I am meant to be for now. And that is the sweetest joy and the most comforting realization of all. August 2005

er
IS

s is
y,
e guy
six
n just
ow
ne go
= just
much!!

My ♡verflows ♡

Bailey

PULL

...15 years old...goofy...sensitive...artistic...messy...awesome cook

my
girl

...enjoys badminton...dislike...   ...homework...reads a ton...stays up late...loves lattes...

coo

shelby and y
getting ready f
the game at th
Barnes. I love all th
cool outfits you
two come up with. The
scarves, sunglasses,
fun h

There was a time in my life where I began to grow concerned about your speaking ability. Your third birthday
was approaching quickly and you had not even uttered
your first word. At the beginning, I wasn't too concerned
because both of your brothers had a slow start to their
talking days. But as the days wore on, I began to grow a
little worried. Then one day, while at the beach house,
you watched your first Thomas the Tank Engine movie.
We played it over and over again during the whole trip,
and lovingly called it the "choo-choo movie". You would
bring us the video box to let us know you wanted to
watch it again. By the end of the trip, the four of us were
tired of Thomas, but you certainly were not, and continued to point to the movie screen in the car wanting to
watch more Thomas as we drove home.
Back at home, we had no Thomas movies, and you were

you are my Sunshine

When we look into the eyes of those who make our hearts sing with joy, we are reminded of the moments that make life worth living. It is these moments that are worth documenting in scrapbook pages that articulate the love in our hearts. Babies, toddlers, kids, teens and pets bring us those warm fuzzy feelings that match no other. Whether they are making us laugh or teaching us life's greatest lessons, the ones we hold most dear will always be front and center in our albums.

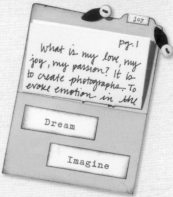

Evoking emotion through photography is Danielle's passion and is evident as she captured the unique expressions of these darling cousins. The contemporary photos take on a heritage look printed in sepia and accented with distressed embellishments. The focal photo of the threesome in the tub is played up with brads, machine-stitching and a mat raised with dimensional adhesive.

Danielle Pearson-Reier, Draper, Utah

Supplies: Patterned paper; embossed patterned paper (K & Company); brads, sticker sentiments (All My Memories); file folder (EK Success); flowers, photo turns (Making Memories); twill tape (7 Gypsies); buttons; lace; paint; thread; cardstock

When Amy tried to get a grin out of her daughter, all she got was this serious shot. She chose the dark color scheme to tie in the photo but added feminine touches to make this page all-girl. Threaded buttons bloom as feminine flowers with ribbon stems. A crocheted lace border is anchored with patterned paper-backed buttons, a buckled ribbon and a safety pin for more delicate touches.

Amy Farnsworth, Brighton, Colorado

Supplies: Patterned papers, chipboard tag (W R Memory Keepers); chipboard letters (Li'l Davis Designs, W R Memory Keepers); buttons (Buttons Galore); circle clips, safety pins, crocheted lace, floss (Making Memories); ribbon (May Arts); tape measure sticker (Provo Craft); buckle (Le Bouton); watch parts, walnut ink (7 Gypsies); flowers; transparency; metallic rub-ons (Craf-T); cardstock

Shannon credits her late father's love for photography to her baby albums filled with negatives and slides. Since she only has boys, Shannon finds it exciting to go through her albums and pull out some "girl" photos to scrapbook. Stitched layers of soft neutral papers complement the heritage photos. A neutral flower and ribbons tied on a paper strip add subtle femininity without distracting from the darling baby girl. See sketch on CD-ROM.

Shannon Taylor, Bristol, Tennessee

Supplies: Patterned papers, tag, ribbon, letter stamps, leather sentiment, flower (Rusty Pickle); typewriter letter stickers (K & Company); transparency; cardstock

"I decided to go with a softer look since these are baby pictures. I matched up the browns and tans in my skin tones and hair color. Yellow would have been too intense for this warm layout."

Gislaine's son won't nap in his bed, but he'll fall asleep anywhere else as seen on this footrest. Gislaine rounded the edges of the photo and mat and then stitched it to the background for a homespun feel. Her subtitle translated from French means "Little Dreamer" while her printed border on a ribbon says, "My boy has this soft and gentle dreamer's look; my boy is a real charmer."

Gislaine Vincent, Dorval, Quebec, Canada

Supplies: Patterned papers (Basic Grey, Creative Imaginations, DDDesigns); die-cut number (DDDesigns); wooden letters, silk flowers (Dollarama); metallic rub-ons; acrylic paint; ribbon (Offray); letter stickers (Basic Grey); metal photo corner, brad (Making Memories); skeleton leaves; cardstock

A baby boy's love for swinging is showcased in shades of blue to signify the swing gliding through the sky. Sheila changed these photos of her son to black-and-white to unify them with her blue color scheme. Folded paper strips stapled to one of the photos gives expression to Sheila's boy's face while swinging. She highlights variations of the word "swing" throughout her journaling with larger bold blue print. See sketch on CD-ROM.

Sheila Doherty, Coeur d' Alene, Idaho

Supplies: Patterned papers (Bo-Bunny Press, Karen Foster Design, KI Memories); chipboard sentiment (Li'l Davis Designs); stickers (Chatterbox); mini brads; washer (Making Memories); sentiment charm (Go West Studios); rub-on stitches (K & Company); ribbon (Offray); corner-rounder punch (Carl); paper clip; staples; cardstock

All the cute features of a friend's baby inspired Moon to create this layout. Moon matted the baby's photo vertically with a long stripe patterned paper offset by a green vertical border. The baby's endearing traits, including pudgy arms and a peculiar expression as well as his dad-inherited earlobes, are printed on the backdrop in coordinating green. Letter stickers spell out the title, summing up this baby—cute from head to toe.

Moon Ko, Versailles, Kentucky

Supplies: Patterned paper (KI Memories); letter stickers (Chatterbox); brads; cardstock

It was love at first sight when Maegan's daughter met Elmo. She documents her daughter's instant friendship with the stuffed Sesame Street creature in a series of photos. Playful polka-dot patterned paper strips and torn alphabet patterned paper create a youthful backdrop to the sweet photos. A collage of handcut hearts, tags and acrylic sentiments adds a loving touch.

Maegan Hall, Virginia Beach, Virginia

Supplies: Patterned papers, tags, die-cut letters, acrylic sentiments (KI Memories); photo corners (Heidi Swapp); handcut hearts; stickers (Doodlebug Designs); cardstock

Milestone moments of Sheila's 8-month-old son are listed directly on the background paper and bullet-pointed with brads. Sweet-face close-ups tout the page subject while a flattened bottle cap with ribbon medallion shows when the photos were taken. See sketch on CD-ROM.

Sheila Doherty, Coeur d'Alene, Idaho

Supplies: Patterned papers (Imagination Project); bottle cap (Li'l Davis Designs); mini brads; ribbon (American Crafts)

Nicole celebrates the joy her beautiful baby daughter brings to her life in this computer-generated layout. The precious baby photo is set against a sunny yellow background, adding the perfect touch of warmth and love.

Nicole Durtschi, Spokane Valley, Washington

Supplies: Image-editing software (Coral Draw 11); Carrie Stephens digital kit (www.fishscraps.com)

Baby Olivia has her cake and eats it too as evident in Colleen's black-and-white shots detailed with captions made from rub-on letters and paper strips secured with brads. The clean-face focal photo is complemented by a double mat on spunky but soft patterned papers. A tag tucked behind the focal-photo mat gives endearing details of the hand-in-cake then cake-on-face adventure. See sketch on CD-ROM.

Colleen Stearns,
Natrona Heights, Pennsylvania

Supplies: Patterned papers, rub-ons, photo turns, buttons, brads (Junkitz); ribbon (May Arts); thread; stamping ink; staples; cardstock

A creative title treatment adds to the uniqueness of Danielle's page. A mix of rub-on letters circles the photo mat, and then the title is continued with handwriting. A silk flower with silhouette-cut letters blooms as a custom page accent. The flower stands out against patterned paper strips with two page corners cut with decorative scissors.

Danielle Thompson, Tucker, Georgia

Supplies: Patterned papers (Foofala, MOD, Wordsworth); silk flower (Wal-Mart); rhinestone spiral clip (Target); rub-on letters (7 Gypsies, Foofala, Making Memories); quote stickers (Cloud 9 Design, Me & My Big Ideas); canvas flower (Foofala); flower punch (EK Success); circle cutter (Creative Memories); staples; stamping ink; brads; cardstock

"I decided to try a cool technique by cutting out the letters of my son's name 'Coop,' short for Cooper, on a silk flower with a craft knife. I then matted the flower over a piece of dark patterned paper to make the letters stand out."

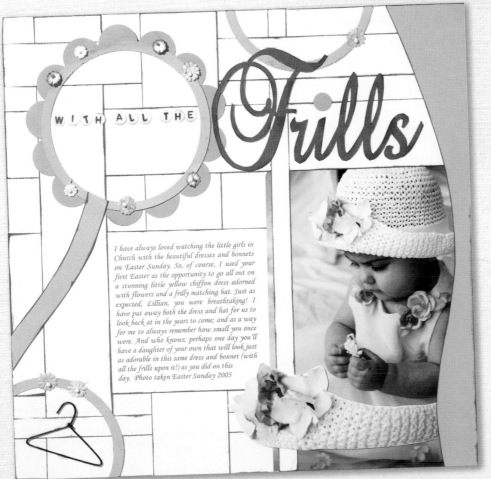

A simple basketlike backdrop made from inked and woven paper strips ensures Jennifer's daughter pictured in her Easter Sunday best is the page star. Jennifer enlarged and printed a duplicate photo from which she cut out the bonnet's brim to use as a custom accent. A handcut daisy encircles letter stickers that quietly begin the title. It is finished with a resounding extra-fancy handcut "frills," emphasizing the theme.

Jennifer Bourgeault, Macomb Township, Michigan

Supplies: Letter stickers (Doodlebug Design); flowers (Prima); hanger accent; stamping ink; cardstock

At the start of spring, you enjoyed your fist real trampoline experience. Sure, I put you on when you were a baby. But, you just sat there. At fifteen months, you ran and attempted jumping with complete confidence. You tripped, you fell, and through it all, a smile spread wide across your face. You pressed your face against the net enclosure and giggled at your sister, on the outside. I would venture to guess that by summer's end, you might be an old pro. In the meantime, enjoy learning. I'm certain that you will have **so much fun.**

Amber managed to get 10 photos on this page using large and small filmstrip-like mats. Black paper forms the large filmstrip holding three photos. A strategically placed red mat acts as a small film strip crossing the page with seven photos. Inspired by her son's sweater, Amber stitched striped patterned papers to accent the page and added bright jumbo brads for her title. See sketch on CD-ROM.

Amber Baley, Waupun, Wisconsin

Supplies: Patterned paper (American Crafts); label holders, brads, letter brads (Queen & Company); stamping ink; cardstock

A toddler playfully chasing after a gaggle of geese is chronicled in this adorable computer-generated layout. Kristie set her focal photo atop a series of mini photos depicting the tyke's grand adventure. Digital papers and embellishments alive with orange, blue and green accent the vivid photography.

Kristie David, Houston, Texas

Supplies: Image-editing software (Adobe Photoshop CS2); digital papers (www.theshabbyshop.com)

There was a time in my life where I began to grow concerned about your speaking ability. Your third birthday was approaching quickly and you had not even uttered your first word. At the beginning, I wasn't too concerned because both of your brothers had a slow start to their talking days. But as the days wore on, I began to grow a little worried. Then one day, while at the beach house, you watched your first Thomas the Tank Engine movie. We played it over and over again during the whole trip, and lovingly called it the "choo-choo movie". You would bring us the video box to let us know you wanted to watch it again. By the end of the trip, the four of us were tired of Thomas, but you certainly were not, and continued to point to the movie screen in the car wanting to watch more Thomas as we drove home.

Back at home, we had no Thomas movies, and you were very disappointed, and after a few days, the Thomas excitement was gone...or so I thought.

I really thought your first words would be "dada", or even better, "mama", but to our surprise, it wasn't. Instead, you muttered "choo choo woo-wee". It was music to my ears! You were finally talking! And I even knew what you said! You repeated it over and over again. For days on end, you would only say, "choo choo woo-wee", and for awhile, I thought you would never say anything else. Here I had prayed to God to teach you how to talk, and now I am begging him to make you quiet! I mean how many times in one day can you say, "choo choo woo-wee"? It started to drive me nuts!!!

Over time your love for Thomas and His Friends grew stronger. You have collected several Thomas trains and tracks and play with them everyday. Now your language has expanded to include a full array of train names and complete stories and descriptions of Thomas! And finally, you also say "mama". I love it!

CHOO CHOO love

A boy's infatuation with Thomas the Tank Engine inspired his first words, "choo choo woo-wee!" Holly documents the precious story with detailed journaling printed on a transparency. Her clean design allows her son in the photos to shine. A simple train die cut with eyelet wheels makes for a boyish accent, complementing the page theme. See sketch on CD-ROM.

Holly Corbett, Central, South Carolina

Supplies: Transparency; eyelets; train and letter die cuts (QuicKutz); cardstock

---

What is more delectable, melting ice cream or Linda's son's face in this photo? What details the photo doesn't give away, Linda's journaling fills in printed on a circle journaling block. The circular shape along with the rounded-corner rectangle and geometric patterned paper add a sense of fast fun, much like trying to eat ice cream before it melts.

Linda Harrison, Sarasota, Florida

Supplies: Patterned paper, letter stickers, decorative stickers (Arctic Frog); corner punch (Marvy); hole punch (Fiskars); pen; cardstock

Ice Cream

I knew ahead of time that getting ice cream in the drive-thru wasn't the smartest thing to do. Although we do only live about 5 minutes away from the nearest McDonald's, I still have to consider that you 'are' only two (messy) and that this 'is' Florida (hot). But who can resist the thought of a yummy cold vanilla ice cream cone on a hot Florida day. We did make it home, but the condition of the cone deteriorated at a rapid pace. Somehow you managed to get a few good tastes before it got a lot more ON you than IN you. Ahhhhh...the joys of ice cream to go.

{To Go

Robby • October 2005

Your tears always seem to make my heart melt. Every time you cry, I feel your emotion and your pain. Wishing that there was something I could do to make you feel better. Sometimes, you just have to let it all out. On this day, you were not a happy little baby. After leaving the doctors office for your flu shot, we walked across the parking lot to attend the Market Square Fall Festival. You weren't happy with the crowd of other toddlers and adults around. I tried everything I could to make you happy. We even had the chance to sit in a real fire truck. I wanted to get a picture of you. So, I let go of your hand and stepped away, you would stomp your feet on the ground, panting! No pictures were taken that day, like I wanted. Fortunately, someone else was there to capture the moment I missed. This photograph shows the deep emotion in your eyes, that I so love and adore looking into every day of my life!

tears

Tears flowing down her toddler's face make for this heart-wrenching yet heartwarming page. Cindy tore the edges of her son's photo for a worn look that matches his sad expression. Her stamped and embossed title in a grunge font runs like the tears down his sweet face. A stamped scroll design, decorative brads and shiny ribbon add rich textures. See sketch on CD-ROM.

Cindy Liebel, Fredericksburg, Virginia
Photo: Randi Gellis Photography,
Midlothian, Virginia

Supplies: Patterned paper (Daisy D's); transparency; ribbon (Michaels); rub-on letters (Chatterbox); letter stamps (Stampin' Up!); embossing powder; stamping inks; photo corners; cardstock

Like sprouts of new growth, fresh shades of green enhance fond memories of a child's development at age 2. Jessie listed her son's favorite pastimes during this precocious age on a citrus green cardstock that stands out against the dark green background and border. The green accents enhance her son's striped shirt and sparkling brown eyes in the photos. The enlarged focal photo placed with her son looking inward is a design-savvy move.

Jessie Baldwin, Las Vegas, Nevada

Supplies: Patterned paper (Rusty Pickle); textured paper (FiberMark); metal plaque (K & Company); ribbon (Offray); large brads; cardstock

> "I wanted to make the greens playful and fun. I especially wanted the journaling to stand out, so I printed it on the brightest color."

THE GOOD OLD DAYS

DECEMBER 2004
Turning Two...
LEARNING NEW WORDS EVERY DAY
POTTY TRAINING
CLIMBING ON THE COUNTERTOP
DRAWING CIRCLES ON THE FURNITURE
EATING STRING CHEESE CONSTANTLY
CUDDLING & NURSING AT NIGHT
HELPING CHECK THE MAIL
COPYING EVERYTHING VIOLET DOES
Loving every minute of you...

you are my Sunshine

The story behind her daughter's name is preserved for Nic's baby girl to someday relish. Nic created a pillowy pink backdrop to cushion her daughter's sweet close-up with layered patterned paper squares in shades of pink. The black-and-white photo is tied to the soft page with black-printed journaling telling the endearing details and a black patterned paper strip and mono-gram letter "a" for Abby.

Nic Howard, Pukekohe,
South Auckland, New Zealand

Supplies: Patterned papers (7 Gypsies, Déjà Views); letter brads (Queen & Co.); letter stickers (American Crafts); cardstock

You'd think after having 2 boys that we might have a girl name in mind for you, Abby. We had no idea. Daddy was determined to name you Emma, but after 3 out of the 20 girls at Jacob's kindy being called Emma, I wasn't so keen, as much as I loved the name. Daddy also loved Maya (pronounced My-uh) but I was afraid to give you a name that would forever be mispronounced. The options were Ella, Abby, Allie, Emily, Hannah, Holly, and I loved Kate. My favourite were Abby, Emily and Kate. We decided against Kate though, because with such a 'hard sounding' surname, it sounded wrong. 3 days after you were born the decision was down to Emily or Abby. We couldn't decide. In the end we left it to Jacob to decide. We gave him the choice, and he decided on Abby. Abigail Maya. 4 Feb 2004.

a abby

Your brilliant green eyes and perfectly highlighted hair.

Your engaging smile and pouty lips.

Your multiplying vocabulary and adorable pronunciations.

Your stubborn streaks and relentless need to imitate.

Your fascination with babies and love of the outdoors.

Your passion for music and overwhelming urge to dance.

Your ability to attract people to you and leave them with a smile on their face.

Your laugh. Your cry.
Your everything.

celebrate you

CAPTIVATING

All the quirks and endearments that make Greta's daughter truly captivating are captured in words and photos on this page. A close-up of her daughter's darling face light up against a girly backdrop of stitched floral patterned papers in shades of rose, greens and wines. Greta printed her journaling in a coordinating color and accented her journaling block and handcut title with paper flowers centered with brads. See sketch on CD-ROM.

Greta Hammond, Goshen, Indiana

Supplies: Patterned papers (Chatterbox); flowers, woven label, tag, safety pin (Making Memories); brads (Doodlebug Design, SEI); letter stickers, rub-ons (Chatterbox); handcut photo corners; cardstock

Scary or sweet? Looks can be deceiving as Nic's daughter sure looks sweet in this photo, but Mom's recollection of the toddler 2s says otherwise. Nic journaled her typical two-year-old moments on paper strips over a fiery backdrop with punchy patterns to match her little girl's spirit. The black background paper and letter sticker title tie the black-and-white photo to the page.

Nic Howard, Pukekohe, South Auckland, New Zealand

Supplies: Patterned papers (KI Memories); letter stickers (American Crafts); chipboard letters (Making Memories); paint; cardstock

GIVE ME THAT. NOW.

Tantrums and tears

our once baby girl

turns into a toddler

Pulling, grabbing, climbing

grumpy attitude to match

Finger pointed frowns set in stone.

It's like someone flicked a switch

our baby girl has gone and we are

approaching TWO

..That scary age...

"YOU are WORSE than A pet monkey!!"

One of the many hilarious things to come out of your mouth—and so self-descriptive!

Out of her daughter's mouth came the inspired title and Audrey's motivation for making this whimsical page. Bright colors and spunky patterns create a fun jungle-like stage for Audrey's daughter's funny-face photo. Audrey used a reverse-effect with her title, beginning each line with white letter stickers overlaying the photo then finishing them with black stickers on the background. Handwritten journaling contours a flower, and hand-drawn doodles delicately embellish the bold shapes.

Audrey Neal, Clinton, Kentucky

Supplies: Patterned paper (Provo Craft); stamp (Stampin' Up!); flowers (Prima); letter stickers (American Crafts, Doodlebug Design); stamping ink; brads; pen; cardstock

you are my Sunshine

OUR

back yard

It may not...

- Be on a cul-de-sac.
- Be very big.
  Contain a swing set.
- Be next to another child's.

But it does...

- Have nice green grass year round.
- Have a pond with ducks and turtles and a fountain.
- Have enough room for you to run your little body around.

And best of all...

- It's all your own!

7816 CREST HAMMOCK WAY

JAN 2005

It may not be the typical back yard, but Linda's boy loves romping around it just the same. To complement the playful page topic and the colors in the photo, Linda handcut a whimsically wavy border that moves the eye up the page and over to the corner title. Colorful punched dots provide bullet points to emphasize Linda's list journaling.

Linda Harrison, Sarasota, Florida

Supplies: Corner and hole punches (Marvy); label maker (Dymo); die-cut letters (Provo Craft); cardstock

Lightedhearted storytelling of a mother's near-nightmare ends with this precious memory of a fearless almost-2-year-old who just loves jumping on the bed. Jenn brilliantly begins the story with her curious title that lures you into the journaling that completes the tale. Strategically sewn floss borders the photos of her son and mimics the stitches she thinks he should've had instead of the glue and tape donned on his forehead. See sketch on CD-ROM.

Jenn Brookover, San Antonio, Texas

Supplies: Patterned papers (Karen Foster Design, Li'l Davis Designs, Paperloft); ribbon (Making Memories, Li'l Davis Designs); hinge (Foofala); rub-on letters, metal tag (Making Memories); bottle cap letters (Li'l Davis Designs); stamping inks; cardstock

Should've had stitches

But they glued it instead! I've never been so scared as when you busted your head open on our bed. I kept trying to keep you off, but in your "almost two" way…you insisted, laughing and running to get on it. No sooner did I take you away, than you escaped, hopped up and fell right on to the metal footboard. When you turned around, I knew it had split open and we both started screaming. As I drove frantically the block to the hospital, I kept shaking and crying…my poor baby! With the help of Grandma and the nurses, we kept you calm until the doctor came in to "glue" you back together. And when we arrived back home, what was the first thing you did in typical two year old fashion? You ran and tried to get back on the bed.

5769

Riley playing "the Dora Game" online—July 2005

Nick Jr.

Playhouse Disney

PBS Kids

Is two years old too young to be playing on the computer? Don't tell Riley! He's figured out how to log on, select his favorite websites, and play the games. I can't believe how fast he mastered the use of the mouse. Already taking after his daddy, Riley truly is a little whiz kid!

whiz kid

Is a 2-year-old using a computer a child prodigy or the wave of the future? Either way, it makes for a curious page theme. Layers of scribble and swirl patterned papers lend a playful touch, keeping the age of Jessie's "whiz kid" son playing a computer game in perspective. Brown half-circles soften the blocked design, and neutral colors give a boyish touch.

Jessie Baldwin, Las Vegas, Nevada

Supplies: Textured cardstock (Bazzill); patterned papers (Karen Foster Design, KI Memories), letter stickers (Li'l Davis Designs); brads; cardstock

Vicki's toddler daughter is on the go, wandering wherever her little feet will take her. Her vibrancy and energy is brought to the layout with bright neon paper strips stitched for texture. A stitched photo mat corrals three snapshots of the busy girl. Pink ribbon strung from loop brads to spiral clips adds playful visual interest to the title. See sketch on CD-ROM.

Vicki Boutin, Burlington, Ontario, Canada

Supplies: Patterned papers, stickers (Imagination Project); loop brads (Karen Foster Design); metal letters (Jo-Ann Stores); ribbon; buttons; cardstock

Nothing seems to make you as happy as the opportunity to walk! It must come from being cooped up in your stroller for so long, watching while the world around you was on the move. Now when ever the opportunity to walk presents itself you are on the go! We have come to refer to you as the Wanderer!

WANDERER

you are my Sunshine

Black-and-white photos against colorful retro patterned papers prove nostalgic of summer fun. Tarri documents her daughter's summer favorites by finishing preprinted sentences with a mix of die-cut stickers. Letter stickers on retro shapes and a phrase sticker mounted on a wooden plaque secured with brads complete the title.

Tarri Botwinski, Grand Rapids, Michigan

Supplies: Patterned paper, die cuts, wooden plaque, letter stickers, tacks (Chatterbox)

Jessica's girl is a bit camera shy, so this straight-on smiling shot is playfully celebrated for its rarity. A spunky mix of retro-colored flowers and polka dots coordinate with this smiling photo. Journaling strips are anchored under the photo and extend to the page's edge secured with tacks. A curved page corner, created by tracing a plate, highlights Jessica's ink- and paint-stamped title. See sketch on CD-ROM.

Jessica Sprague, Cary, North Carolina

Supplies: Patterned papers, tacks (Chatterbox); letter stamps (Making Memories, My Sentiments Exactly); acrylic paint; stamping ink; cardstock

"I printed my journaling and trimmed it into strips, anchoring one end under my photo and the other with a scrapbook tack. I strategically placed the strips in a fanlike arrangement to add movement and energy."

Inspired by her 6-year-old son's firecracker personality, Shannon showcased this black-and-white photo on an explosive mix of red, white and blue patterned papers. Plastic washers bound with tied ribbons border the page with energy and dimension. Red straight and zigzag stitches outline Shannon's heartfelt journaling with a burst of pizazz.

Shannon Taylor, Bristol, Tennessee

Supplies: Patterned papers (Rusty Pickle); washers, letter buttons, brad, rubber sentiment tab (Junkitz); ribbon (Offray); chipboard number (Heidi Swapp); heart charm; letter stickers (American Crafts); black pen

Capture the Silly Side

Kids tickle us pink with their silly stunts and sunny smiles. There are so many moments worth capturing as they explore their world and remind us how much fun it was to be a youngster in motion. Try capturing these amusing childhood moments:

- Silly facial expressions
- School moments
- Expressing love to pets or siblings
- At play with friends or classmates
- Accomplishments big or small
- Laughing and being silly
- Exploring their world

A luring slide, a willing participant and a camera-ready Mom make for this great focal photo. Ronnie stood with her camera resting on the bottom of the slide to catch the shot of her son. The smaller shots show the busy boy savoring the park. The photos are digitally layered over a clock image downloaded from the Internet. Ronnie created the other digital accents with image-editing software and her title with word art. See sketch on CD-ROM.

Ronnie McCray, St. James, Missouri

Supplies: Digital clock image by Cheryl Barber (www.cbdigitaldesigns.com); other digital elements (artist's own design); image-editing software (Adobe Photoshop Elements 2.0); word-processing software (Microsoft)

You can practically hear the laughter coming from Mary's daughter in this enlarged photo balanced by a bold chipboard title. Mom used a red hugs and kisses backdrop to her laughing girl that coordinates with the photo. Ribbons accented with threaded buttons are wrapped around the photo's edges. The words to Mary's journaling are spelled out with letter stickers, stamps and die cuts.

Mary Bautista Marty, Chula Vista, California

Supplies: Patterned paper (Carolee's Creations); letter stickers (K & Company); chipboard letters, die-cut letters, rub-on letters (Li'l Davis Designs); letter stamps (PSX Design); acrylic paint; stamping ink; label holders (Jo-Ann Stores); threaded buttons; ribbon (Making Memories); cardstock

Oh, the delights of summer spent with friends! Linda caught these candids of her son and his "older" girlfriend whose friendship shines as the star of this page. Citrus green, cool white and bright pink lend the essence of summer and the playfulness of youth. Linda's title begins with letter stickers and ends with handcut letters. She transformed wooden embellishments into custom accents with white paint and colored pens. See sketch on CD-ROM.

Linda Harrison, Sarasota, Florida

Supplies: Patterned paper (Christina Cole, Keeping Memories Alive); letter stickers (Doodlebug Design); wooden accents (EK Success, Over the Moon Press); acrylic paint (Plaid); silk flower; hole punch; pen; cardstock

Expressions this silly deserve an equally fun backdrop, which Suzy created with straight- and curve-cut paper strips adhered to cardstock. The photos matted on the left side of the page are balanced by handwritten journaling strips staggered on the right. Punchy pink chipboard letters and letter stickers form the title and complement the olive green cardstock.

Suzy West, Fremont, California

Supplies: Patterned papers; chipboard letters, letter stickers (Scenic Route Paper Co.); flower pin (Around the Block); ribbon (May Arts); cardstock

> **"The pictures of my daughter Sierra are so bright and pretty that I decided to complement them with really bright papers. The journaling cut into strips helps balance the page."**

Jill often finds her daughter caught up in sheer joy, dancing, singing and acting out favorite television characters. The expression of laughter on her face in these photos is strong evidence of her joy. The smaller photo flips up to reveal another close-up and Mom's celebration of her daughter's feisty yet sweet personality. Chunky and bright chipboard letters shout "unleashed" against spunky patterned papers that complement the smiling photo subject. See sketch on CD-ROM.

Jill Jackson-Mills, Roswell, Georgia

Supplies: Patterned papers (Anna Griffin, Basic Grey, KI Memories, My Mind's Eye); stickers (Bo-Bunny Press, Doodlebug Design); acrylic flowers (Heidi Swapp); chipboard letters (Bazzill, Li'l Davis Designs, Making Memories); rub-ons, die-cut letters (KI Memories); eyelets; cardstock

A tranquil setting in shades of green reflects the water and pensive mood of Julie's son in this photo. Julie hand-wrote on a tag of the wonders and thoughts running through her gazing son's head. Rub-on phrases on slightly sanded tags add boyish sentiment with a rugged touch.

Julie Johnson, Seabrook, Texas

Supplies: Patterned paper (Scenic Route Paper Co.); die-cut letters (Bo-Bunny Press); ribbon (Making Memories); rub-on sentiments (Creative Imaginations, My Mind's Eye); chipboard (Heidi Swapp); tags; stamping ink; cardstock

Angelina gives her daughter a lesson on true beauty. Mom journals with a letter, reiterating that beauty goes beyond skin deep. A large focal photo of her daughter sporting a faux tattoo is bordered by a grosgrain ribbon secured with a brad and bobby pin. A large die-cut circle with a printed-transparency center is anchored with a ribbon and mimics a magnifying glass focusing on the girl.

Angelina Schwarz, New Castle, Pennsylvania

Supplies: Patterned papers (Junkitz, Scrappy Cat); ribbon (Jo-Ann Stores); decorative brad, metal plaques (Making Memories); transparency (Great White); date stamp; bobby pin; flower; stamping ink; cardstock

Custom patterned paper adds a personal touch to this tribute page. For a page playing up the many facets of her son, Samantha printed bulleted descriptive words on cardstock in shades of blue. She used the printed cardstock to mat the focal photo and to create a custom monogram letter. See sketch on CD-ROM.

Samantha Walker, Lehi, Utah

Supplies: Brads (Making Memories); cardstock

Playful patterned papers layered with curvy strips and rickrack bring movement to Colleen's page about her boys' nonstop summer fun. The whimsical patterns slightly overlay the black-and-white photo, making it pop against the bright colors. Colleen handwrote her journaling on paper strips ending it with the word "happy" that also serves as her title.

Colleen Stearns, Natrona Heights, Pennsylvania

Supplies: Patterned papers (Chatterbox, Junkitz, Scenic Route Paper Co.); circle sentiment charm, brad (Junkitz); buttons; ribbon (May Arts); rickrack; stamping ink; staples; pen; cardstock

Whether there is music playing or not, Maddy's girl is grooving to the beat. Mom caught this series of great moves that preserve a typical summer's day with her daughter in their pool. Splashy bright circle patterned paper squares pump up the summer-fun volume with coordinating strips backing Maddy's clear punch label journaling. A few photos are cut and adhered sequentially to bring filmstrip-like movement to the dancing superstar.

Maddy Wright, Oviedo, Florida

Supplies: Patterned paper (Junkitz); rub-ons (Doodlebug Design, KI Memories); letter stickers (Li'l Davis Designs); flowers (Prima); photo corners (Heidi Swapp); label maker (Dymo); cardstock

A characteristic of the normal child is he doesn't act that way very often.
—Author unknown

enjoy life

SILLY

Nov '2

Gemiel may have an actor in her midst, as each time she gets out her camera, her son puts on a show—sometimes serious but mostly silly, as seen in this photo. A mix of striped, floral and polka-dot patterned papers adds playfulness to the page in neutral colors livened with punchy red, orange and green. A telling quote printed on vellum secured with a decorative brad goes perfectly with Gemiel's page theme.

Gemiel Matthews, Yorktown, Virginia

Supplies: Patterned papers (Scenic Route Paper Co.); ribbon, ribbon charms (Maya Road); chipboard letters (Pressed Petals); decorative brad (Making Memories); vellum quote (Flair Designs); chipboard sentiment (EK Success); stamping ink; pen; cardstock

"My son is at the age now that whenever he sees me pull out my camera, he has to perform. Sometimes he's serious, sometimes he poses like a model, but most often he's just his silly, adorable self."

the SIMPLE TRUTH

...or 'the world according to Sophia'...

open

This sassy grin is not without a story, which is what came first to inspire this page. Courtney's surprising conversation with her daughter unveiled a bit of Sophia's vanity, hence the subtitle "The World According to Sophia." It is on the outside of folded double-sided cardstock secured behind a paper slit. Unfolded, the conversation is revealed. The story is set in a sassy combination of orange and green accents.

Courtney Walsh, Winnebago, Illinois

Supplies: Patterned papers, ribbon, rub-ons, tacks, chipboard letters, photo corners (Chatterbox); letter stickers (Doodlebug Design); buttons (Junkitz); floss (DMC); cardstock

I am in my bathroom and I'm getting ready for bed when I hear Sophia behind me.

"Mom?" she says, "You really need to exercise."

"Oh yeah?" I ask, "Why is that?"

"Because if you exercised, then these wouldn't be so fat," she tells me, a grubby little finger pointing to my thighs.

And then she walks out.

As I am tucking her in a few moments later I calmly tell her, "Sophia, you shouldn't say things like that. It's not nice."

"Oh, why isn't it?" She so innocently wants to know.

"Well, because, God made all kinds of different people. Some are big. Some are little. Everyone is different."

"Oh, yeah, and not everyone can have these," she says matter-of-factly, throwing her leg into the air.

I think our next talk will be on vanity.

2005

you are my Sunshine

life is short... PLAY DIRTY

It doesn't matter how long you've been outside... you will always end up completely covered in dirt, grime and gunk. And you wouldn't have it any other way! I say live it up. you're only a kid for so long. July '05

Getting this dirty while playing is hard work but it sure is lots of fun, as shown in these photos. Jessie conveys the spirit of fun with dirt in bright shades of mustard and light brown. Paint splotches, ink smudges and a paint-stamped title add a messy look as playful as Jessie's dirty-faced boy. See sketch on CD-ROM.

Jessie Baldwin, Las Vegas, Nevada

Supplies: Patterned papers (KI Memories); stamps (Li'l Davis Designs); acrylic paint (Plaid); chalks; chalk stamping inks; pen; cardstock

Despite pleas to stop, Colleen can't resist taking a shot of her niece. Her irresistible face is matted on a shabby chic collage of patterned papers with handwritten journaling strips overlaying the photo. A whimsically layered flower made of mesh and patterned papers and accented with a button, stick pin and hanging tag corners the photo. A tag behind the photo mat reveals Colleen's heartfelt thoughts of her prized niece.

Colleen Stearns, Natrona Heights, Pennsylvania

Supplies: Patterned papers (Scenic Route Paper Co.); rub-on letter, stick pin (Making Memories); mesh (Magic Mesh); button (Junkitz); tag (Scrapping With Style); ribbon; walnut ink; stamping ink; pen; cardstock

"Aunt Ween, would you PLEASE stop taking my picture?" said my sweet Alyssa

honest,
caring,
handsome,
athletic,
Smart,
independent,
comical,
sweet,
thoughtful,
you're my son.

MARCH 2003

THINGS I LOVE ABOUT YOU 10 THINGS I LOVE ABOUT YOU 10 THINGS I LOVE ABOUT

Carla tributes her son with his charming photo and list of admired traits. Printed words and rub-on letters spell out the 10 things she loves about him. A masculine color mix of paper strips makes a simple photo mat. Her punch label title doubles as a page border.

Carla Jacobsen, Lebanon, Tennessee

Supplies: Label maker (Dymo); rub-on letters (Scrapworks); rub-on date (Autumn Leaves); staples; cardstock

A mom stops time, if for just a moment, to savor her little girl with this layout. Angelia created a watch-like accent with a circular-cut transparency as the watch face over patterned paper. Flowers punched from patterned paper and then stitched serve as whimsical clock parts. See sketch on CD-ROM.

Angelia Wigginton, Belmont, Mississippi

Supplies: Patterned papers, decorative brad, letter stickers, phrase stickers, transparency (K & Company); flower punch, circle punch (EK Success); mini brads

STOP TIME

Have you ever wanted to stop time, to just hold a moment in your heart a a little bit longer? I have. I do want you to grow up and be happy, and have children of your own, but I can't help wanting you to stay little for a bit longer. There is time enough later for all the questions about life and love. Time enough later for the teenage angst, and the college years. Today you are my little girl and I'm freezing this moment in my heart.

When Jessie first looked into her daughter's "baby browns," all her wishes for a blue-eyed baby melted away. Her brown-eyed girl takes center stage with the use of minimal accents and a simple design. The enlarged photo pops against the reddish-brown backdrop. And if that look doesn't grab you, perhaps the quirky glimpse in the small photo will. Matted on folded cardstock, the photo flips up to reveal heartfelt journaling.

Jessie Baldwin, Las Vega, Nevada

Supplies: Patterned papers (7 Gypsies, Rusty Pickle); woven tag (Me & My Big Ideas); letter stamps (Ma Vinci's Reliquary); stamping ink; ribbon; cardstock

Shannon's son laughed hysterically when his mom manipulated photos of other people with image-editing software. But when Shannon turned his portrait into an alien child, he wasn't laughing, and Mom couldn't resist scrapbooking it. The enlarged photo is draped with ribbons anchored to laminate chips that carry Shannon's rub-on title. A coaster sentiment dangling from a ball chain punched through the triple-layer background flips up to reveal Shannon's journaling.

Shannon Taylor, Bristol, Tennessee

Supplies: Woven paper (source unknown); letter buttons (Junkitz); coaster sentiment, chipboard numbers (Li'l Davis Designs); letter rub-ons (Making Memories); ribbon (Offray); brads; laminate chips; pen; cardstock

BALLET (bă-lā') n. A classical dance form characterized by grace and precision of movement and by elaborate formal gestures, steps, and poses.

Playful ballerinas kick back for a treat after their star performance. To let the photos of her ballerina daughter and friend steal the limelight, Courtney created a background with subtle dimension from layered and woven paper strips in the same shade of tutu pink. An organza ribbon is a whisper of elegance while with the mixed media title is as perfectly quirky as these two blue-lipped giggling ballerinas. See sketch on CD-ROM.

Courtney Walsh, Winnebago, Illinois

Supplies: Patterned papers (Rusty Pickle); rub-on letters (source unknown); label holder, sticker definition, metal letters and number (Making Memories); label maker (Dymo); ribbon (Michaels); brad; pen; cardstock

Handmade accents and mini gems enhance this photo of Suzy's daughter with girly delight. Suzy drew scroll, heart and dot borders on the background and the curved cut and layered cardstock design. A handcut and pen-accented butterfly flutters with dimensional wings. Suzy's pen handiwork and hand-sewn knot-centered flowers add delicate touches to this girly page.

Suzy Plantamura, Laguna Niguel, California

Supplies: Floss (DMC); mini gems (Li'l Davis Designs); flowers (Prima); pink gel pen; white paint pen; cardstock

Chloe's bright blue eyes were the inspiration for this graceful lavender page by Suzy. The close-up photo is the main focal point of the page while girly flowers and a script font add additional femininity and charm.

Suzy Plantamura, Laguna Niguel, California

Supplies: Patterned paper (KI Memories, Mara Mi); ribbon, acrylic paint (Making Memories); flower mask, transparency flowers (Heidi Swapp); black marker; white pen

> "I love this photo of my daughter, so I wanted to emphasize it by making it large and keeping it the focal point on the page. I chose my title based on her eyes."

you Mesmerize me with your Eyes

My beautiful Girl... you melt my heart with those big blue eyes...I love you! Mama 01/06

simply adorable

Jenn changed this photo of her son and his schoolmate to black-and-white to unify the otherwise clashing colors. She placed the photo on a playful purple background inspired by the colors in the woven label sentiment. Touches of patterns and texture are added to the monochromatic color scheme with fabric-tied metal buttons and a chipboard and metal letter title. See sketch on CD-ROM.

Jenn Brookover, San Antonio, Texas

Supplies: Fabric accents (Maisy Mo's); metal buttons (Karen Foster Design); chipboard and clay letters (Li'l Davis Designs); woven label sentiment (Making Memories); stamping ink; cardstock

For the first few weeks of pre-school school, Jake would come home chatting about "jeenwooeese". I had no idea what he was talking about! If I asked him, he'd just get mad and say it louder "you know, mom, jeenwooeese". Finally, at the first class party, I figured out what he was saying: it was Jean-Louise!

Jake & jean Louise

A mother's bittersweet thoughts on her boy reaching a milestone—kindergarten—warms as well as tugs at the heart. Though emotion stirred within her while creating this page, Nic used quiet neutral colors to create a serene mood to complement her sleepy son in the photo. Nic crumpled paper then smoothed and lightly painted it to lend rugged texture to the photo mat and silhouetted monogram square.

Nic Howard, Pukekohe,
South Auckland, New Zealand

Supplies: Patterned papers, decorative brads (American Traditional Designs); chipboard letter (Heidi Swapp); letter stickers (American Crafts); ribbon; stamping inks

Marie mimicked her son's soccer ball with a circular journaling block that doubles as a photo mat. A printed die-cut title underscores the photo. Punched circles and handcut squares from geometric patterned papers add movement and playfulness to the page.

Marie Cox, Springfield, Massachusetts

Supplies: Patterned papers, die-cut sentiment (KI Memories); circle punch; cardstock

This simple page is as refreshing as the page topic itself, taking a summer dip. Michele enlarged the black-and-white photo of her daughters engaging in their favorite summer activity to take up half of the 8½ x 11" page. Cardstock strips and a block of tile-patterned vellum create a nautical backdrop for Michele's handcut title and printed journaling. Lightly chalked punched sun shapes add subtle embellishment. See sketch on CD-ROM.

Michele Woods, Reynoldsburg, Ohio

Supplies: Patterned vellum (Chatterbox); sun punch (Marvy); chalk (Craf-T); cardstock

Her daughter's curious question asked with her own insightful answer validates Amy's reason for scrapbooking and inspired this page. A black-and-white close-up gives a look into Amy's daughter's wise young eyes. A rust photo mat and ribbons tied to jumbo leather photo corners add touches of texture and color. The precious conversation with Mom's not-so-little girl is documented on a series of printed tags.

Amy Sullivan, Wilmington, Delaware

Supplies: Patterned papers (7 Gypsies, Foofala); chipboard alphabet (Heidi Swapp); ribbons (Li'l Davis Designs, Strano Designs, Heidi Swapp); leather photo corners (Making Memories); rub-on letters (Chatterbox, Making Memories); metal index tab, sentiment sticker, reinforcement stickers (7 Gypsies); tags (Avery); pen; stamping ink; cardstock

fill my WORLD WITH color

I am so blessed with all the color you have brought to my life. Before you I honestly thought life was a black & white world you live and pass by. Now with you in my life I see the world so differently. Now I know what life is all about! It was almost as if when you were born the world became a new place. I wanted to do anything and everything just so...

You fill my world with color,
as your mother I now see.
On the day you were born,
they came alive for me.
I see the yellow of your hair,
that the sun has kissed.
I see the blue of your eyes,
I'm glad I've never missed.
I see the pink of your cheeks,
from the warmth of the sun.
I see the green upon your knees,
from a little backyard fun.
I see purple bruises on your legs,
from the tumbles that you take.
I see all the colors of the rainbow,
in the pictures that you make.
You fill my world with color,
my sweet pea, Gracie Leigh.
For without you in my life,
those colors would not be!

Color, used both literally and figuratively, passionately describes a mother's love for her daughter. In an original poem printed on a transparency, Jessica rhymes a letter of love to her daughter whose tiny handprint is stamped with paint. Further colorful sentiment is found on ribbon-topped pullout tags tucked behind the focal photo. Crayons coordinated to the poem topic accent the page as well as carry part of the title. See sketch on CD-ROM.

Jessica Delforge, West Allis, Wisconsin

Supplies: Patterned paper (Chatterbox); chipboard letters, washer, rub-ons, brad, acrylic paint (Making Memories); ribbon (Chatterbox, Offray); crayons (Crayola); letter stamps; flower; stamping ink; staples; cardstock

Jeremy
Paul
West

sweet.senstiive.
gentle.kind
100% BOY

brave
rowdy
explore
adventure
charming

no limits

tough guy

not.

These pictures of you are priceless. I look at them and they make me so happy. Looking at you is like looking at your daddy. You both are so much alike and yet different at the same time. Having you as my son has been such a joy for me. I am so lucky to have you as my son. I love you so much!

This "tough guy" layout shows the softer side of Suzy's son Jeremy. His charming smile lights up this page expressing Suzy's gratitude for having him in her life. She printed her journaling on strips and mixed them with word labels and other embellishments for a collage look.

Suzy West, Fremont, California

Supplies: Patterned paper, letter stickers (Scenic Route Paper Co.); metal frames (Jo-Ann Stores); chipboard stars (Li'l Davis Designs); brads (Making Memories); cardstock

Turning 5 is monumental in itself, but for Sheila's daughter, it was also the day she got her ears pierced as promised by Daddy a year before. Close-up shots show her ear before and after the piercing along with a focal photo of her brave smiling face. A ribbon with chunky letter charms vertically borders the page and leads to a gem-centered flower that mimics the big girl's new earrings. See sketch on CD-ROM.

Sheila Doherty, Coeur d' Alene, Idaho

Supplies: Patterned papers (Autumn Leaves, Crafter's Workshop, Scenic Route Paper Co.); epoxy word sticker (Autumn Leaves); letter charms (Doodlebug Design); ribbon (Michaels); flower (Prima); chalk; cardstock

"My daughter had never seen a gecko before. We were in Florida on vacation and her eyes just lit up when she saw it. When I saw her expression, I just had to grab the camera to get a picture."

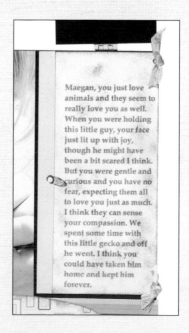

It was love right from the get-go for Darlene's daughter and this gecko. When the animal lover discovered the lizard on a Florida trip, she studied the peculiar creature as she held it in her hand. Darlene tells the endearing story behind her hinged title block. A black-and-white close-up in a clear pocket gives a good look at the gecko friend with a sticker sentiment describing her daughter's wild encounter—curious.

Darlene Sours, Erie, Colorado

Supplies: Patterned papers, buttons (KI Memories); photo turns, clips (7 Gypsies); clear pocket (source unknown); date stamp, hinges (Making Memories); ribbon (May Arts); brads; stamping inks; cardstock

Her daughter's milestone of losing a first tooth makes Mom realize that changes are coming. To savor her daughter's smile at age 7, Michele captured this photo before adult teeth set in, changing her into a young lady. A pink patterned paper strip adds a girly touch, bordering the snapshot vertically with a photo turn for emphasis. A printed and handcut title underscores the photo accompanied by Mom's bittersweet thoughts.

Michele Woods, Reynoldsburg, Ohio

Supplies: Patterned paper, photo turn (Basic Grey); mini brad; cardstock

The Before Smile

Last week you lost your first tooth. I feel like you're teetering on the edge of a major transformation. Your adult teeth coming in will forever change the look of your face as you start to grow into your pre-adolescent looks. I recently read an article about how important it is to take lots of photographs before this happens to remember what your smile looked like before. While I look forward to your new grown-up looks – your "after" if you will – I find myself with mixed feelings of happiness and regret. My little girl is growing up. –Chloe, Age 7

Piet Mondrian is one of my favorite artists. He started as a landscape painter who eventually turned to Cubism. At the end of his life he chose to only paint with color in what he said was it's purest form; red, yellow, blue, black and white. His graphic black lines and primary colored squares are so vibrant and striking, just like your gorgeous blue eyes. Every time I look at your sweet, innocent eyes, I am reminded of Mondrian's desire to keep his paintings pure, just like you.

COLOR

Inspired by Piet Mondrian, her favorite artist, Kathy created this graphic background with primary and white color blocks broken up by thin black lines. She chose the clean graphic lines and pure colors to reflect the purity and innocence of her son in the photo. The photo with the diagonal line created by his eyes breaks up the horizontal and vertical lines of the backdrop, putting the emphasis on his sweet face.

Kathy Fesmire, Athens, Tennessee

Supplies: Letter stickers (Doodlebug Design); cardstock

you are my Sunshine

The vibrancy of youth is celebrated with bright orange and pinks against striking black and white colors on this page. Jill layered patterned paper strips and die-cut shapes for a touch of whimsy. Her handcut title corners her daughter's photo whose face epitomizes youth. Die-cut sticker sentiments on dimensional adhesive pop with expression on a black folio closure envelope.

Jill Jackson-Mills, Roswell, Georgia

Supplies: Patterned papers (Scrapworks); transparency (Magic Scraps); stickers (Creative Imaginations); die-cut shapes (My Mind's Eye); chipboard letters (Making Memories); folio closure envelope (Bazzill); letter buttons (Wal-Mart); cardstock

A young girl gets to meet her favorite Disney character in this heartwarming layout. Trudy captured these great shots of her daughter with Robin Hood on their trip to Disney World. A vertical title and journaling printed on strips balance the photos while striped patterned papers add movement and energy.

Trudy Sigurdson, Victoria, British Columbia, Canada

Supplies: Patterned paper (3 Bugs in a Rug); die-cut letters, brackets, photo turns, index tab (Quic-Kutz); brads (Making Memories); circle punches (Creative Memories); distress ink (Ranger); textured cardstock (Bazzill)

A girl's fun and funky favorites at age 17 are fondly recorded on this page. Cathy lists her daughter's affections on tags dangling from waxed floss tied to a ribbon border. Flip-flops cut from patterned paper and backed with cardboard carry the definition of "favorites" and Mom's handwritten journaling. The black-and-white photo of Cathy's daughter is printed on canvas paper and colored with chalk pencils.

Cathy Lucas, Oro Valley, Arizona

Supplies: Patterned papers, number stencils (Rusty Pickle); ribbon (May Arts); tags (QuicKutz); waxed floss, framed letters (Scrapworks); eyelets, brads, rub-on letters (Making Memories); flip-flop charm; letter stickers (K & Company, Making Memories); chalk pencils (Creatacolor); acrylic paint; cardstock

"When I saw these flip-flops, they reminded me so much of my daughter. It's all she would wear for about nine months. It's funny the places you can find inspiration. It definitely worked for this layout all about her."

These two teens are just too cool for words. Kristy captured this photo of her daughter Jessica and her friend Shelby getting ready in true teen style. The vibrant colors reflect the hip personalities of the two divas. Florals, stripes and polka dots add visual energy and movement to the computer-generated page.

Kristy Nerness, Stanley, North Carolina

Supplies: Image-editing software (Adobe Photoshop); digital papers, letters and number (www.thedigichick.com)

you are my Sunshine

Life as a kid sure can be tough, but Jill encourages her son to go seize the day. She matted his photo over a collage of paper strips in rich colors. Fiber secured with brads and staples frames the photo along with Mom's encouraging words of advice written on the background.

Jill Jackson-Mills, Roswell, Georgia

Supplies: Patterned papers, fibers (Basic Grey); acrylic letters (KI Memories); brads; white pen; cardstock

No matter the score, these sisters on and off the volleyball court are winners in their aunt's eyes. Sporting their uniforms in these photos, Denise plays up the volleyball theme with a painted mesh backdrop to mimic a net. Clip-art volleyballs carry the two's initials encapsulated with watch crystals. The same enlarged image printed onto canvas paper holds journaling and was inked and spray-varnished to emulate a volleyball. See sketch on CD-ROM.

Denise Tucker, Versailles, Indiana

Supplies: Patterned papers (Daisy D's, Rusty Pickle); vellum (The Paper Palette); chipboard letters, jumbo letter brads, epoxy sentiment (Rusty Pickle); mesh, letter eyelets (Making Memories); watch crystals (Deluxe Plastic Arts); ribbon, metal tag (Tapestry); screw brads (Karen Foster Design); acrylic paint; spray varnish (Krylon); stamping ink; foam adhesive; cardstock

They're hip, plugged-in, high-performance and, according to Kris, they're high-maintenance. They're Generation Y. She celebrates the quirks and privileges of her son's generation with a photo and title treatment reflective of Y's bold and funky style—jumbo chipboard letters and a massive bottle cap. Her hinged book defines Generation Y and compares it to her Generation X, showing another photo of the fine modern specimens. See sketch on CD-ROM.

Kris Gillespie, Brandon, Florida

Supplies: Patterned papers (My Mind's Eye); chipboards letters (EK Success, Everlasting Keepsakes, Li'l Davis Designs); chipboard squares (Bazzill); hinges (Making Memories); paint (Krylon); jumbo bottle cap (Scrapbook Creations); label maker (Dymo); cardstock

They're young, smart, brash. They may wear flip-flops to the office or listen to iPods at their desk. They want to work, but they don't want work to be their life. This is Generation Y; the cohort of Americans born immediately after "Generation X", though the term is controversial and is synonymous with several alternative terms including "the net Generation", "Millennials", "the Boomerang Generation" and "the "me" generation". Generation Y includes Americans in the mid-20's, to children over the age of 5 (as of 2006). The size of Gen Y is approximately 76 million. They were the first to grow up with the internet, music downloads, instant messages and cell phones. Even before they could mouse their way thru the internet, they were also th to grow up with media choices; tv remotes, TiVo, DSL, and multiple TV's in the house Gen Y has been pampered, nurtured programmed with a slew of activities since were toddlers, meaning they are both h performance and also high maintenance. They have no doubts in their self worth. Welcome to new generation....

The differences between our generations are night and day. For example, we had one TV in our house; while you were growing up, there was almost one TV in every room of the house (not to mention DVD players, CD players, etc.). When we were kids, fast food restaurants were only for emergencies or a special treat; you eat fast food 2-3 times a week. We were lucky if we ever had a "phone" in our bedrooms; nowadays, it is almost mandatory that everyone has a cellular phone. We learned cursive handwriting in school; you learned computer keyboarding. Enjoying a new movie at the Saturday matinee was a luxury; now you rush out and buy DVD's of new releases every Tuesday to get a deal. It's amazing to see how different "X" and "Y" generations are and how incredibly times have changed. We can't help but wonder what your kids will be like....does that make them the "Z" group?

Black-and-white photos of Kay's daughter and her cool friends are showcased with layered edgy patterned papers. Each girl gets a solo spot in the limelight with her photo framed in a filmstrip accented with ribbon-tied photo turns. A license plate is strung vertically with spunky polka-dot ribbon for a hip title treatment.

Kay Rogers, Midland, Michigan

Supplies: Patterned papers, license plate, filmstrip (Creative Imaginations); brads, photo turns (Making Memories); rub-on stitches, flower and sentiment (Doodlebug Design); silk flowers, ribbon (Michaels); cardstock

you are my Sunshine

The quirky likes and dislikes of Sharon's daughter at age 15 are memorialized to enjoy for years to come. The oh-so-teen shot of the sassy girl is bordered with her list of particulars printed directly on the photo. A funky backdrop of randomly cut purple and brown patterned papers layered over jagged-edge cardstock is accented with brown machine stitching and purple and brown flower clusters.

Sharon Laakkonen, Superior, Wisconsin

Supplies: Patterned papers (Mara Mi); flowers (Prima); mini brads (Queen & Co.); letter stickers; cardstock

brittany...15 years old...goofy...sensitive...artistic...messy...awesome cook

my girl

Thoughts

Chloe' Christine

Are a souls' "Blue prints"

'2005'

Collette caught her daughter in deep thought in these photos. She printed her daughter's name vertically on the focal photo. The small photo demands attention wrapped with twine dangling a flower charm. A whimsically graphic background is distressed a bit with sandpaper and stamping ink. Paper strips flagged with stapled ribbons add simple embellishment.

Collette Osuna, Eastpointe, Michigan

Supplies: Patterned paper (Junkitz); sandpaper; floss; ribbons (SEI); letter rub-ons (Creative Imaginations); cardstock

When even the slightest of humidity hits, Kathy's daughter's hair whirls with curls. Thankfully, the curly cutie has made peace with her unruly hair and smiles in this focal photo. To highlight her girl's gorgeous curls, Kathy cut cardstock into circles and curves and used bouncy flower and swirl patterned papers. The deep reds and shades of brown complement the auburn beauty along with pink flowers that bloom all-girl.

Kathy Laffoley, Riverview, New Brunswick, Canada

Supplies: Patterned papers, rub-ons (Fontwerks); brads (Making Memories); flowers (Prima); cardstock

"I love this photo of Emma because it highlights her beautiful curls. I thought the curve of the paper, the circles as well as the flowers lent themselves to the rounded feel of the layout."

curly girl

All it takes is a touch of humidity and Emma's hair has a party! She has been like this since she first sprouted curls around her first birthday. Big, bouncy curls! Thankfully, she has made peace with her beautiful curls, found a few styling products she likes and doesn't fight them too often! Cape Enrage, August 2005

Wherever you both go in the world your charm, self-confidence and great personalities will make you many friends!!

LOOK OUT WORLD

LUCAS MITCH

be cause (HERE) WE are!

A photo of two handsome boys says it all—look out world! During a beach vacation, Beth had her boys strike a pose, and when she first saw the photo, her title immediately came to mind. Her mix of die-cut and stamped title letters is big and bold to balance the enlarged photo. Brushes of paint lightly soften the photo's edges, and mailbox and epoxy letters identify the boys.

Beth Sears, Quispamsis, New Brunswick, Canada

Supplies: Patterned paper (Junkitz); letter stickers (Basic Grey, Karen Foster Design, Provo Craft); foam letter stamps, mailbox letters (Making Memories); acrylic paint; ribbon; stamping ink; paper clips; pen; cardstock

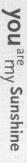

you *are* my Sunshine

Make-up

Kristina

12

eye shadow
lip gloss
mascara
blush
eye liner

NOVEMBER 2005

Simply, become who you are, and remember from where you came. Become more than anyone dreamed, and be an inspiration to many.

Simply Become who you are.

Every girl awaits that rite of passage when she can finally wear makeup. Karen's daughter Kristina is all-girl in this 8½ x 11" layout. Karen chose to place her journaling, a quote, on a large circle under the focal photo. Flowers and the purple-brown color scheme add femininity and charm.

Karen Cobb, Victoria, British Columbia, Canada

Supplies: Patterned paper (3 Bugs in a Rug); coaster cards (The Weathered Door); chipboard, wire flower, twill (Maya Road); craft paint (Plaid); date stamp (CTMH Co.); circle punch (EK Success); die cuts (QuicKutz); floss (DMC); cardstock

Kelli may have a future rock star on her hands as she caught these shots of her teenage son and his friend in a total jam session. Black cardstock combined with funky patterned papers creates a studio feel. Die-cut shapes adhered with dimensional tape accent the page. Punched labels give all the jamming details.

Kelli Noto, Centennial, Colorado

Supplies: Patterned paper (Basic Grey); jumbo chipboard letter (Zsiage); label maker (Dymo); die-cut shapes (QuicKutz); chalk stamping ink; cardstock

Recording

ERIC AND DYLAN DO NOT KNOW HOW LUCKY THEY ARE TO HAVE A RECORDING STUDIO OF THIS CALIBER AT THEIR DISPOSAL. THEY HAVE A BLAST CREATING THEIR OWN CDS. THEY DO COVERS OF THEIR FAVORITE BANDS AND CREATE FUNKY TUNES. RECORDING HAS BROUGHT THEIR MUSIC UP A LEVEL. WE MIGHT HAVE A COUPLE FUTURE ROCK STARS IN OUR MIDST.

warmhearted

independent

patient

s i x t e e n

2004

Time passes quickly when you are growing up. It seems like yesterday I was holding you in my arms admiring your cute little face. Today you are sixteen and not that baby anymore but a beautiful young lady. You are prepared to experience new dreams and create your own memories but for now your next adventure is driving school.
Happy Birthday Tiffany!

Sixteen is an age full of adventure. As the world awaits her daughter Tiffany, Karen wants to capture each precious moment and freeze it in time. She placed her heartfelt journaling on a distressed tag tied with fibers. A watch face and key charm strung from a necklace chain symbolize Tiffany's journey from teen girl to young woman.

Karen Cobb, Victoria,
British Columbia, Canada

Supplies: Patterned paper (Rusty Pickle); date stamp, blossom, eyelet letter (Making Memories); floss (DMC); stickers (Sharon Soneff); stamping ink (Ranger); craft paint (Plaid); frame (Jest Charming); solvent ink (Tsukineko); walnut ink (7 Gypsies); fibers; brads; photo corners; flower; ribbon; cheesecloth; eyelet; watch face; necklace chain

Look at the charming photo of this young teen boy and you can see the future in his eyes. Sandra used a fitting quote for this page about her son Jacob, passing on a piece of wisdom for finding oneself in a big world. The masculine color scheme combined with stripes and geometric shapes makes this page 100 percent boy.

Sandra Ash, Victoria,
British Columbia, Canada

Supplies: Patterned paper, stamps, rub-ons (Carolee's Creations); ribbon (May Arts); stamping ink (Ranger); cardstock

100% BOY

Life isn't about finding yourself
Life is about creating yourself

Sugar and spice and everything nice...this sassy gal looks as if she can't wait to take on the world. Sandra chronicled her daughter Taylor as she embarks upon realizing her dreams and working to accomplish them. A bit of motherly advice sprinkled on a black and pink background make this page all-girl.

Sandra Ash, Victoria, British Columbia

Supplies: Patterned paper, rub-ons, stamps, paper clips, ribbon (Carolee's Creations); punch (EK Success); stamping ink (Ranger); cardstock

Entering the teen years comes with many expectations, but Karen knows her daughter Aleisha is well-prepared. Confident and wise beyond her years, this young woman has the world in front of her. Karen used a pink color scheme to keep the page feminine and graceful while clock hands represent her daughter's rite of passage into this new exciting phase of life.

Karen Cobb, Victoria, British Columbia, Canada

Supplies: Patterned paper, letter stickers, buttons (Chatterbox); metal phrase (Making Memories); clock hands (Jest Charming); maruyama (Magenta); buttons; brad

When a family mourned the loss of their beloved pet, the striking stripes of this shelter cat won their hearts. To play up her cat's coat, Heide placed the photo on striped patterned paper accented with a matching border. A series of brads set on a thin paper strip creates a collar-like accent and is personalized with a monogram paper clip.

Heide Lasher, Englewood, Colorado

Supplies: Patterned paper (source unknown); monogram paper clip (Jo-Ann Stores); brads; cardstock

> **"I love the look of a large circle for a cool focal point so I used a dinner plate to draw a large circle on the back of the patterned paper."**

Caught red-handed is what this title implies. When Michon's daughter discovered her pup had stole one of her stuffed animals to snuggle with, she grabbed her mom to take these photos as evidence. Stamped with paint across the background and onto photos, the bold red title explains the embarrassed look on the dog's face. Michon plays on the red theme with red accents throughout the page. See sketch on CD-ROM.

Michon Kessler, Altura, California

Supplies: Patterned papers, stickers (Karen Foster Design); foam letter stamps (Making Memories); acrylic paint (Delta); ribbon (Offray); cardstock

Good news of a greyhound's happiness and contentment deserves a front page headline as Tristann established on this page with newspaper patterned paper. Pet sentiment patterned papers create a background for the pampered pup story while dog accessory and phrase stickers showcase the photo evidence.

Tristann Graves, Vancouver, Washington

Supplies: Patterned papers, stickers (Karen Foster Design); cardstock

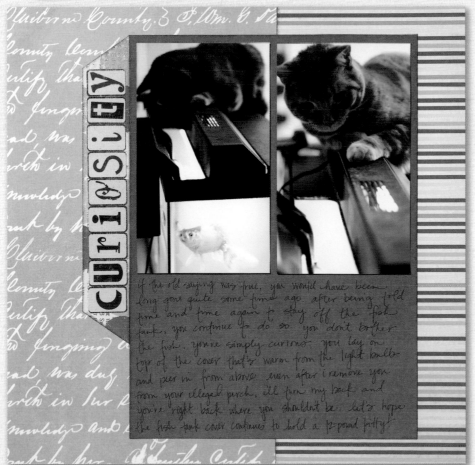

A 12-pound cat perched on a fish tank epitomizes the adage "Curiosity killed the cat." After removing Thomas several times from, as Melanie puts it, his "illegal perch," she finally gave up and grabbed her camera to catch these priceless shots. Patterned papers in shades of orange and red enhance the prey's fins and the predator's mane. Handwritten journaling humorously tells the story while letter stickers sum it up—curiosity.

Melanie Bauer, Columbia, Missouri

Supplies: Patterned paper, letter stickers (Scenic Route Paper Co.); stamping ink; pen; cardstock

There is no better friend than a dog. Pure hearts that know only love. Goofy has always been the perfect example of this. My best friend and constant companion for twelve years. Always there and just happy to be with me, no matter what. I'll never forget our time together.

My little space heater at night, snuggling up under the covers behind my knees or in front of my tummy when I was all curled up.

The way you'd run wildly around the house, over furniture and people and anything else in the way. You always made me laugh.

Playing tug-of-war with a toy, your tough little growl, even though I knew you'd never hurt a soul. The pure joy when the toy finally ripped and you got a hold of the squeaker inside.

Digging madly on the blankets, your nose pressed up against them, like you were searching for some great treasure, then finding my foot underneath sending you off in a happy sprint around and around the bed.

These memories and so many more are the reasons I love you Goofy. You'll be missed more than you'll ever know, but you'll never be forgotten.

forever friend

love

foReVeR

Memories of a 12-year beloved pet help heal a broken heart. Miranda reflects on Goofy's idiosyncrasies and their special relationship in journaling printed on vellum. Rub-on sentiments applied to her favorite photo show his place in her heart—forever friend. Hidden journaling tucked behind the enlarged photo details the companion's unconditional love. Miranda plans to frame and hang this memorial in a place where Goofy can forever look over her.

Miranda Isenberg, Walled Lake, Michigan

Supplies: Patterned paper (KI Memories); zipper pulls (Junkitz); canvas tags (Creative Imaginations); rub-on sentiments (Wordsworth); acrylic letter charms (Doodlebug Design); ribbon; brads; vellum; cardstock

MODEL KITTY

My friend Karen is a manager of a grocery store in North Carolina.

A few months ago, the chain that she works for held a pet photo contest. They were looking for a cat to feature on their new private label cat products - cat food, cat litter, kitty treats, etc.

Karen has several cats and sent in photos of them not ever expecting that they would have a chance to win. Much to her surprise, her fine feline Sadie was selected as the GRAND PRIZE WINNER and now has a new job as kitty supermodel.

Above: Sadies contest entry photo.
Left: Sadie posing with her photo on the scoopable cat litter container.

This prize-winning photo landed a modeling contract for this feline to star on pet products. The small photo shows Sadie posing next to a shot from her modeling debut—the front of a cat litter container. Playing up those irresistible baby-blues, Barb used soft shades of blue and gray distressed papers. A whimsical circle patterned paper coordinates with the focal photo and adds a touch of color.

Barb Hogan, Cincinnati, Ohio

Supplies: Patterned paper (Basic Grey); ribbon (May Arts, Offray); vellum tag (Making Memories); letter stickers (Wordsworth); chipboard letter (Li'l Davis Designs); brads; cardstock

Written in the words of a retired racer, a poem titled "A Greyhound's Prayer" brings heartwarming meaning to these soulful eyes. Tristann scanned a greyhound image and printed it onto a transparency to create a background that complements her photo. Warm plaid patterns coordinate with the photo and create a sense of home—something this greyhound is grateful for.

Tristann Graves, Vancouver, Washington
Image: Greyhound Pets of America newsletter

Supplies: Patterned papers, die-cut letters (Basic Grey); ribbon (Making Memories); transparency; cardstock

A puppy's prayer to be treated with the same love and devotion he gives his master is the journaling on JD's page that serves as the title page to her pet's album. She recites the mantra to her children to help them understand the importance of taking good care of Ginger. JD printed the prayer on a transparency and then painted the back of it to highlight the heartwarming reminder. See sketch on CD-ROM.

JD Richardson, Saint John,
New Brunswick, Canada

Supplies: Patterned paper (Junkitz); corrugated paper; twill letters (Carolee's Creations); jigsaw letter (Making Memories); Scrabble tiles (Hasbro); acrylic paint (Plaid); stamping ink; transparency

Dominique captured this precious moment between her daughter Raphaëll and Toffee, the adorable bundle of fur she gets to see when she visits Grandma. A mixture of patterned papers sits atop a blue background. A vintage purse buckle and a faux price tag add character and charm to the lively pet layout.

Dominique Quintal, Longueuil, Quebec, Canada

Supplies: Patterned paper, cardstock (KI Memories); rub-ons (Arctic Frog, Doodlebug Design, Junkitz); ribbons (American Crafts, May Arts); impress-on (Creative Imaginations); purse buckle; brads

From Bernie's famous head tilt to Spike's bat impersonation, Carolyn has quite the photo collection of her pets' peculiar expressions. Once she captured this photo of Ginger sticking out her tongue, Carolyn says she was ready to make the page. An argyle background adds further spunk to the already funny-faced and slightly overlapped double-matted photos. A perky mix of ribbon and puppy buttons borders the page. See sketch on CD-ROM.

Carolyn Cleveland, Maysville, Georgia

Supplies: Patterned papers (Making Memories, Scenic Route Paper Co.); stickers (Carolee's Creations, EK Success); buttons (Jesse James); flower; ribbon (May Arts); brad; stamping ink; cardstock

"I've been taking photos of my pets for years, but these three have always stood out as the oddest poses of all. When I saw the photo of Ginger sticking out her tongue, I knew I was ready to scrap!"

Ben

A sweet face. Lovely, dark eyes. A wonderful disposition. Ben is a dog that got a second chance in life. Todd brought him home one day, thin and scared, afraid of everything in sight. With time and love, he learned to trust and play. He learned to relax and just be a dog. A great dog.

05·05

One look into these dark brown eyes and it is evident this dog has a story. Though once sad, scared and starving, the story ends happily with Ben's newfound family who loves and adores him. To highlight his big brown eyes, Maria used complementary colors and shades of brown along with minimal page accents. Layered off-centered circles play up the title and add a sense of movement to the page.

Maria Gallardo-Williams, Cary, North Carolina

Supplies: Patterned paper, letter stickers (Imagination Project); brads; pen; cardstock

A good nap may be the only shared passion for these two cats as Kim's fur children are often heard fighting. The more the fur flies, the more Kim appreciates their cat naps—as she caught these deceiving photos of a peaceful moment. Just as the calm cats fool the eye, so does Kim's layered and textural page as it was all created digitally with elements downloaded from the Internet. See sketch on CD-ROM.

Kim Mauch, Portland, Oregon

Supplies: Digital patterned papers, leather letter (www.scrapbook-bytes.com/store); digital staples (www.shabbychicprincess.com)

{ni-night cats}

06 04

Z is testy

H is pesky

Zander and Houdini are both males and both the same age. Houdini loves to play, Zander doesn't. This is very problematic. Houdini chases Zander up and down the stairs and often tackles him. There are times when the fur is literally flying and the house is filled with the sound of cats screaming and fighting. We thought having a child-free house would make for a peaceful and calm environment. We were very wrong. That's why I now say:

Nothing is more *Beautiful* than a sleeping ~~child~~ cat

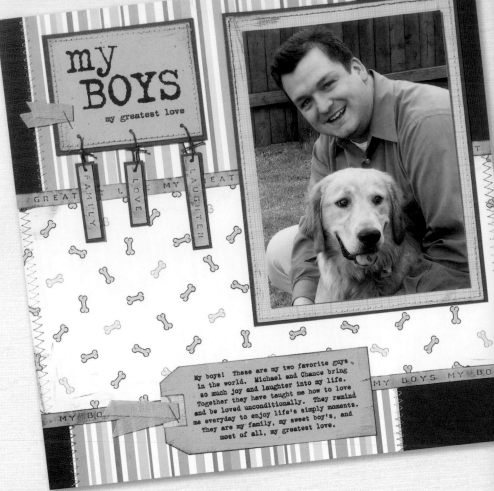

Cindy celebrates her favorite boys in her life, her husband and their dog, with a mix of masculine stripes and dog-bone patterned papers. A double photo mat stitched to the page highlights the featured boys while tag journaling tells how Cindy feels about them. Cindy put cardstock strips through a label maker to create the sentiment borders and thread-dangling words. She then highlighted the embossed words with stamping ink.

Cindy Johnson-Bentley, Allen, Texas

Supplies: Patterned papers (Chatterbox); staple, rub-ons (Making Memories); ribbon; label maker (Dymo); waxed thread; stamping ink; cardstock

The calming effect of bonding with a puppy is captured with quiet lavenders in a monochromatic color scheme. Sheila changed her photos of her children and their new dog to black-and-white to help them better coordinate with her chosen colors. A friendship sentiment washer and letter charms dangling from a beaded hair clip attached to a ribbon make a personalized accent, symbolizing her children with their beloved pup. See sketch on CD-ROM.

Sheila Doherty, Coeur d' Alene, Idaho

Supplies: Patterned papers (Creative Imaginations); ribbon (Michaels); corner-rounder punch (Carl); epoxy letter stickers (MOD); oval cutter (Provo Craft); date stamp (Leisure Arts); metal word, sentiment washer (Making Memories); floss (Two Busy Moms); iron-on flowers (Nunn Designs); cardstock

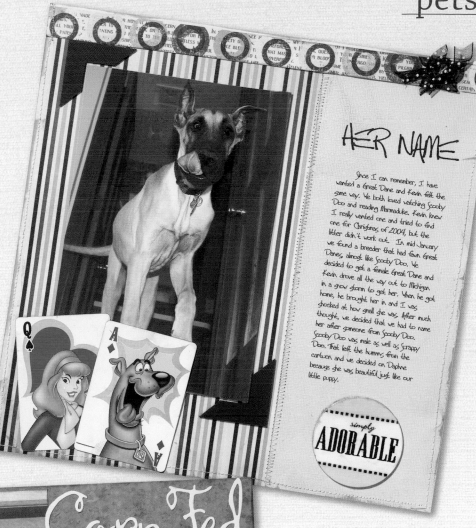

Pam and her husband celebrate their long-awaited Great Dane and the choosing of her name—Daphne. Pam accented Daphne's photo with playing cards sporting the Scooby Doo character with her namesake as well as the cartoon Great Dane. Bold rubber bumper photo corners and vertically striped paper accent the photo of the beloved pup. A chipboard sentiment sums up the photo's subject—simply adorable.

Pam Callaghan, Bowling Green, Ohio

Supplies: Textured cardstock (Bazzill); patterned paper (Scenic Route Paper Co.); photo corners (Scrapworks); chipboard coaster (Li'l Davis Designs); stamping inks (Ranger); ribbon; staples

Turtles love corn on the cob? Who knew? Pam's backyard pet patiently waits for her to put out an ear of corn, and then Dodger attacks it with vigor and devours it without hesitation. She captured these photos of the lively feeding, and tucked a tag with a quick story about it behind the top right photo.

Pam Sivage, Georgetown, Texas

Supplies: Patterned paper (Karen Foster Design); brads; cardstock

It's a bad case of puppy love as Lea made this page just days after welcoming her new dog into her home and straight into her heart. She hints at her love for the adorable pup in the title made from a mix of rub-ons underscored with machine-stitching. A handmade cardstock tag topped with stapled ribbons pulls out from behind the focal photo to reveal she's truly smitten. See sketch on CD-ROM.

Lea Lawson, Missoula, Montana

Supplies: Patterned papers, rub-on heart (KI Memories); rub-on letters (KI Memories, Doodlebug Design, Heidi Swapp); ribbon (American Crafts, May Arts, Offray); label maker (Dymo); stamping ink; staples; pen; cardstock

One quick look into these sweet brown eyes and you might think Morgan's a good dog. But a closer read of the not-so-funny journaling reveals Morgan sure can get into trouble when no one is looking. A vertical paper strip spans the entire page as a photo mat and Kerry's journaling block. A simple acrylic charm adhered with a brad and hints of patterned papers let this pup's photo shine. See sketch on CD-ROM.

Kerry Zerff, Regina, Saskatchewan, Canada

Supplies: Patterned papers (Chatterbox); acrylic charm (KI Memories); brads; cardstock

"My three-year-old daughter fell in love with one of our guinea pigs (most likely her favorite) named Steve French. I wanted to write my journaling almost like a poem. Descriptive words that had a definite beat to them."

Sweet girl, gentle heart. Furry face, twitchy nose. wheek!

piggy love

She calls him "the (little) black & white guy". Always gentle, she loves to hold him, give him vegetables, and chin scratches. There's no doubt - it's piggy love

Summer Lily & Steve French 03.05

The story of a girl's love for her guinea pig is told in a fresh mix of soft and bright colors that complement the page topic as well as the colors in the close-up shots. Ashley offset the photo montage of her daughter and her favorite guinea pig with a stitched border of patterned paper strips. Her stamped background and handwritten journaling accented with stamped letters add a whimsical touch.

Ashley Calder, Dundas, Ontario, Canada

Supplies: Patterned papers (KI Memories, Me & My Big Ideas, Rusty Pickle, SEI); letter stamps (Leave Memories); chalk stamping ink (Clearsnap); solvent ink (Tsukineko); twist tie (Pebbles); spiral clip; safety pin; brads; staples; buttons; ribbon; paper clips; thread; scalloped scissors; cardstock

kick back
RELA

Giggle

Summer 05

let the
Good times
Roll

June 05

Chase just loved splashing around the kiddie pool in the safety of his frog inner tube and his ***FROGGLES***

L IN THE POOL COOL IN THE POOL COOL IN THE PO

FROGGLES

We all seek moments of fun and adventure. The times when we can gather with friends or family to share in life's merriment and joy. Those times when we can just sit back, relax and enjoy each other's company. The perfect mix of activity and relaxation is definately worth recording in your scrapbooks, and since you probably have the camera in hand anyway, capturing the perfect shot is sure to be easy. Whether you are sunning at the beach, frolicking in the snow or just hanging out with the crew, you'll save each moment in time by recording them in your albums.

SKIING

What fun it was to take Rebekah on her first ski trip. I think that has to be one of the best parts about being a parent: teaching your kids new things.

She was a little unsure about moving on skis, especially when she got going too fast. That didn't stop her from wanting to go on the "big hill" – up the lift & down the mountain – right away. Her dad & I thought that, for now, it was best we all stay on the bunny slopes.

During her lessons her instructor taught her several important lessons. First he taught her how to stop by pointing her skis together. Then he taught how to stay upright (kids tend to lean back, making them go faster) by holding her arms in front of her. Lastly he taught her to steer by pointing her arms and looking where she wanted to go. The rope lift was a little tricky too, but after a few falls, she was on it like a pro.

I was so proud of her perseverance as she learned something new. She never cried or got frustrated when she fell, but just kept at it. I know that soon she'll be skiing circles around her dad & me.

Don't worry, Mom, I'm **tough!**

wh

tru

U R

rls

have

fun

PLAY HARD ROB

I LOVE YOU OUTSIDE JUMPING & DOING TRICKS RATHER THAN INDOORS WATCHING T.V. SEE HOW COOL YOU CAN BE.

2005

Traditional Halloween colors combined with purple and green make for a frightfully bright holiday page. Tina used a black photo mat accented with orange patterned paper strips and brightly colored sticker sentiments to showcase her focal photos. A brightly striped ribbon border highlights the third photo while matching stapled ribbon swags light up the sticker title.

Tina Albertson, Harlan, Indiana

Supplies: Patterned papers, sticker sentiments, market tag (Pebbles, Inc.); ribbon (Doodlebug Designs, May Arts, Creative Impressions); fiber (Magic Scraps); washer (Bazzill); rub-ons, eyelet brads (Doodlebug Designs); photo corner punch; staples; stamping ink; cardstock

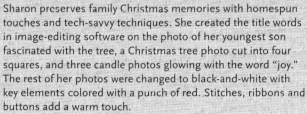

Sharon preserves family Christmas memories with homespun touches and tech-savvy techniques. She created the title words in image-editing software on the photo of her youngest son fascinated with the tree, a Christmas tree photo cut into four squares, and three candle photos glowing with the word "joy." The rest of her photos were changed to black-and-white with key elements colored with a punch of red. Stitches, ribbons and buttons add a warm touch.

Sharon Laakkonen, Superior, Wisconsin

Supplies: Patterned papers (Daisy D's); buttons (Making Memories); ribbon (May Arts, Making Memories); cardstock

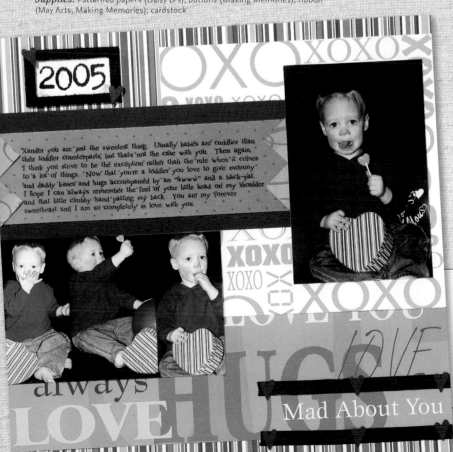

A Valentine photo shoot of a wiggly toddler proved a sweet success with the help of a prop. Carrie captured her son's attention with a heart sucker and held it long enough to get these photos. The photos are set on a backdrop of sweetheart patterned papers. Journaling printed on patterned vellum records this sweet toddler's loving traits. See sketch on CD-ROM.

Carrie Civinskas, Roscommon, Michigan

Supplies: Patterned papers (Reminiscence Papers); patterned vellum; ribbon (Offray); heart punch (EK Success); rub-on numbers, leather label holder (Making Memories); cardstock

> **"When I designed this Valentine's Day layout, I wanted to use many of the photos I had taken. To accomplish this without the layout looking cluttered, I used PhotoSoft Elements to create a three-photo collage."**

A child's wonder and excitement of turning a plain white egg into colorful artwork are captured on this page. Jamie's enlarged photo shows her son's gallery of handiwork while the photo close-ups show his fascinating egg experience. To convey his excitement, Jamie used fun patterned papers and playful epoxy accents under her transparency journaling block. See sketch on CD-ROM.

Jamie Harper, Phoenix, Arizona

Supplies: Patterned papers (American Crafts, KI Memories); die-cut letters (KI Memories); flowers (Prima); ribbon (May Arts); photo turns, word stamps (Making Memories); brads, epoxy stickers (MOD); stamping ink; cardstock

BiRTHdAY TrADiTiON

I feel pretty, oh so pretty. It's alarming how charming I feel.
— STEPHEN SONDHEIM, WEST SIDE STORY

·clara

·sophie

·amber

2005

When Kimberly's sister gets out her face paints, you know it's time to celebrate a birthday. Photo close-ups of Kimberly's daughters' cheeks tout her sister's handiwork. The rounded-edge photos pop against a simple white backdrop cut slightly arced. It is accented with a series of pierced holes and patterned fabric tape. Whimsical coasters add a playful touch to this artsy tradition.

Kimberly Kesti, Phoenix, Arizona

Supplies: Patterned fabric tape, coasters (Imagination Project); letter stickers (Me & My Big Ideas); quote sticker (Autumn Leaves); cardstock

Maegan's daughter has her cake and wears it too in her 1st birthday photos. To mimic the frosting that is all over her girl's face, Maegan coated her title chipboard letters with spackle and then painted them pink. Bright colors and spunky patterned papers add to the party feel. Jumbo chipboard photo turns and flower and circle journaling blocks lend to the fun.

Maegan Hall, Virginia Beach, Virginia

Supplies: Patterned papers, rub-ons, ribbons, acrylic charms (Doodlebug Designs); chipboard letters (Making Memories, Heidi Swapp); chipboard photo turns (Basic Grey); flower brads (Making Memories); chipboard flower (Bazzill); rub-ons (SEI); spackle; acrylic paint (Delta); cardstock

Shannon's sister is wishing hard while she blows out these candles on her 31st-birthday cake. Big sis got her to divulge her wishes and memorialized them all on arched journaling strips. These curvy elements along with a rolling title and flower arches bring movement and excitement to the page. See sketch on CD-ROM.

Shannon Taylor, Bristol, Tennessee

Supplies: Patterned papers (My Mind's Eye, Reminiscence Papers); chipboards, sentiment tab (Heidi Swapp); flowers (Prima); brads (Junkitz); plastic discs (Li'l Davis Designs); modeling paste; acrylic paint; birthday rub-ons (Basic Grey)

> **"I wanted to create an embellishment that looked like cake, so I covered plastic discs with modeling paste and pink paint to create frosting-like embellishments that look good enough to eat."**

Mom's birthday is festively remembered on this page. Rebecca layered colorful patterned paper strips behind the photo of her mom and sister for a confetti effect. A dotted circular pattern stamped in white on a kraft background gives whimsical movement. A bright mix of rub-on letters and fabric letter tabs add fun to the birthday-greeting title.

Rebecca Cantu, Brownwood, Texas

Supplies: Patterned papers (KI Memories, MOD, 7 Gypsies, Daisy D's, Chatterbox, Inspire 2, NRN Designs, Basic Grey); rub-ons (KI Memories, Making Memories); brads (Making Memories); stamps (Fontwerks); fabric letter tabs (Scrapworks); fabric photo corners (Making Memories); white stamping ink; cardstock

fondue*

*an impromptu pre-dinner snack of the beer, cheddar and onion variety. too much fun and laughter amid the dipping of toasting bread pieces: the kind of simple no-fuss fun you can only share with someone you're close to; someone you love. easy to say when you're seen with cheese dripping from your mouth.

april 2005

Sharing hot cheesy goodness with the one you love means only one thing—fond fondue memories. But when Melanie was left with not-so-great photos from this really great night, she didn't let that stop her from recording it. She turned the lesser-quality photos to sepia and then complemented them with a 1970s orange color scheme and funky pattern theme that pays homage to the fondue-trendy era. See sketch on CD-ROM.

Melanie Bauer, Columbia, Missouri
Photo: Andrew Bauer,
Columbia, Missouri

Supplies: Patterned paper, stickers (American Crafts); stamping ink; pen; cardstock

This photo centric page celebrates what teens do best—hang out and eat. Blessed with high metabolisms, Kimberly's daughter and her friends allowed her to snap these shots of them hanging out at their favorite haunts. A hidden tag tucked behind the photo montage tells of the teenage, title-inspiring mantra—"When in doubt, eat." See sketch on CD-ROM.

Kimberly Kesti, Phoenix, Arizona

Supplies: Patterned paper, rub-ons (Scrapworks); chipboard letters (Li'l Davis Designs); tag (American Tag); cardstock

it must be great to have such high metabolism like Meghan and her buddies can often be found at their favorite eating establishments—Starbucks, Panda Express & Quiznos oh—and coldstone for dessert! their official motto: when in doubt- eat!

when in doubt... **eat**

Complete with sombreros and a mariachi band, Susan really lived it up on her 28th birthday. She cropped and stitched around her festive photo, making it pop off the page. Colorful cardstock strips stitched under the photo serve as journaling blocks. Bright flower patterned papers bring the fiesta to her layout.

Susan Weinroth, Centerville, Minnesota

Supplies: Patterned papers (American Crafts, Basic Grey); letter stickers (American Crafts); patterned brads (Queen & Company); cardstock

Courtney's husband and fellow pastors got in touch with their inner child at the Chicago Children's Museum as documented in these photos. To showcase their free-spirited fun, Courtney designed the page around the museum's colorful and playful logo. Printed journaling strips detail the evening's fun. See sketch on CD-ROM.

Courtney Walsh, Winnebago, Illinois

Supplies: Buttons (Foofala); floss (DMC); pen; cardstock

let the **Good** times **Roll**

Courtney designed a simple setting to stage her busy photos of a theater production that she and her husband directed. She created a photo montage in image-editing software and overlayed it with action words spelled with felt, velvet and plastic letters for added texture. Bright buttons add a burst of color and dimension. See sketch on CD-ROM.

Courtney Walsh, Winnebago, Illinois

Supplies: Buttons (Foofala); plastic letters (The Paper Studio); velvet letter stickers (Making Memories); letter stickers (KI Memories); felt letters; cardstock

Kathleen memorializes a Las Vegas vacation with a photo montage of the sites and her friends. The lower portion of the word "Vegas" in her title was created digitally directly on the photo and finished with the top part cut out of cardstock. Handcut scrolls from gold patterned paper are accented with large gems for a touch of Vegas glitz and glamour.

Kathleen Summers, Roseville, California

Supplies: Patterned paper (Basic Grey); gems (Darice); jewelry tag; image-editing software (Adobe Photoshop); cardstock

As a tribute to all things wild and glamorous about the Oscars, Sam and his friends hosted a party, dressing up like the characters from the nominated movies. Sam's montage is photo evidence of the fun had by all. Details of the night's adventures are revealed in his journaling hidden beneath the lift-up title block that is appropriately accented with punched stars and a 3-D director's-chair sticker. See sketch on CD-ROM.

Samuel Cole, Woodbury, Minnesota

Supplies: Patterned papers (Anna Griffin, Déjà Views, Imagination Project, Memories Complete, Reminiscence Papers); chipboard letters (Imagination Project); star punches, dimensional adhesive, 3-D stickers (EK Success); metal photo corners (Making Memories); rub-on word (Karen Foster Design); sandpaper; paper clip; cardstock

Kimberly and her friends got well acquainted with schnapps while feasting on an entire buffet of it in Germany. Her group photos show the happy friends while arrow photo turns point to the before and after photos of the beverage culprit. A mix of tiny geometric patterned papers adds movement and makes one see double, which perhaps visually describes the drink-tasting experience. See sketch on CD-ROM.

Kimberly Moreno, Tucson, Arizona

Supplies: Patterned paper, photo corner punch (EK Success); letter stickers, ribbon (American Crafts); letter stamps (Image Tree, PSX Design); arrow photo turns (7 Gypsies); brads; monogram paper clip, metal-rimmed tag (Nunn Designs); rub-ons (Scrapworks); brown pen; cardstock

the dresses were beautiful. the flowers, exquisite. the cake was delicious. the bride & groom happy. The weather

Cooperated. The details were there. But what made the wedding so special for me was the people, hands- down!

WeDDinG Party

JUL 29 2005

Without the family & friends... it would've been just another wedding. Instead... it w

A blessed wedding day made exquisite by all the details and the participants is celebrated by Courtney with home-spun appeal. She created a quiltlike background with bright patterned paper strips with inked edges. She accented her photo montage on a blue mat with hand-sewn stitches. Handwritten journaling on white paper strips borders the page with a personal touch.

Courtney Walsh, Winnebago, Illinois

Supplies: Patterned papers (KI Memories); floss (DMC); letter stickers (Doodlebug Design, Making Memories); ribbons; stamping ink (Making Memories, May Arts, MJ Trimming); pen; cardstock

A playful candid of her daughter and her bridesmaids proves to be a precious wedding-day memory. Linda enhanced the pink bridesmaid dresses and her daughter's white wedding dress with crisp white and shades of pink accents. Girly stripes and perky daisy patterns play up the fun, labeling the moment with a punchy bold title—girls just wanna have fun.

Linda Garrity, Kingston, Massachusetts

Supplies: Patterned papers (MOD); ribbon (Michaels); brad (K & Company); date stamp (Making Memories); silk flower; cardstock

> "I love this photo because it wasn't posed—they were just fooling around while I was changing the film, and I happened to catch this shot. I chose the bright colors and funky font to convey the sense of fun."

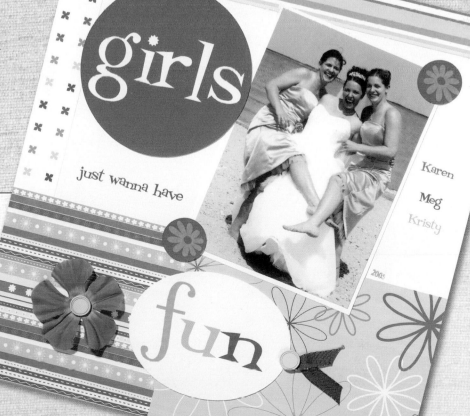

girls just wanna have fun

Karen
Meg
Kristy

2005

With stimulating bold colors and extreme visual attractions, Danielle's page captures the energy of a county fair. She cropped the super-enlarged photo of her husband and son at a slant to mimic the force of a roller coaster ride. To journal with a twist, Danielle wrapped her text around their faces directly on the photo. Glitter letters and jeweled accents capture the amusement-park excitement.

Danielle Thompson, Tucker, Georgia

Supplies: Patterned papers (Basic Grey, Karen Foster Design, Scrappy Cat); label maker (Dymo); glitter (AIC Premier Glitter); letter beads (The Beadery); elastic cord (R.I. Textile Co.); jeweled accents (Jesse James); eyelets (American Tag); chalks (Craf-T); stamping ink; cardstock

A trip to the fair validates a family's decision to move to a small town to escape big-city hustle and bustle. Visually documenting the day's adventures, Sheila pieced together a photo montage much like a puzzle, rounding one corner of each outer photo. The journaling printed directly on the background tells how the small-town fair made the family feel comfortable about their new home choice.

Sheila Doherty, Coeur d'Alene, Idaho

Supplies: Patterned paper (KI Memories); conchos (Scrapworks); ribbon (Michaels); staples; tickets; cardstock

Jennifer created a western stage for her Host a Cowboy Murder Mystery Game photos by stitching together cowboy patterned papers. Copper metal eyelets, a western charm and buckle and a brad add touches of cowboy flair. A sheriff badge and a horse sentiment sticker lend western style. A folio closure envelope holds game and place cards from the fun event.

Jennifer Gallacher, Savannah, Georgia

Supplies: Patterned papers (Chatterbox, Daisy D's, Karen Foster Design); cardstock stickers, copper eyelets, metal charm (Karen Foster Design); dimensional adhesive (All Night Media); foam letter stamps, ribbon, buckles, folio closure envelope (Li'l Davis Designs); acrylic paint; photo corners (Canson); cardstock

Renee's son is a cowboy in the making! She got this shot of her little youngster learning how to use a rope lasso from a real life bona fide cowboy. Large wooden letters and twine tied like a lasso lend themselves to this wild, wild West theme.

Renee Villalobos-Campa,
Winnebago, Illinois

Supplies: Patterned papers (Daisy D's); envelope (Avery); ribbon (SEI); wooden letters (Hobby Lobby); letter stickers, brads (Provo Craft); chalk ink (Clearsnap)

When Dominique's daughter and a friend tried the newest attraction at a waterpark in Montreal, she knew it would be photo-worthy. Circle-cropped photos depict the ride in motion while the focal photo features the smiley faces of these two excited girls. Bright oranges and blues add a splash of color to this vibrant layout. See sketch on CD-ROM.

Dominique Quintal,
Longueuil, Quebec, Canada

Supplies: Patterned papers (Chatterbox); stickers (Arctic Frog, Provo Craft); ribbons (May Arts); brads, anchors (Junkitz); flower; cardstock

ride • joy • wet • high

the splash

July 23, « la Ronde » in Montreal, Dad and both of you went in the new attraction called 'le splash'; Riders board 20-passenger boats for a breathtaking plunge over a 15-meters waterfall. The splashdown creates a 5 meters wave, which may soak passengers as well as some bystanders on the bridge overlooking the ride. Obviously, after the ride, you stayed, with daddy, on the bridge to see THE wave! The only thing I can say... You get out of this ride completely soaked...

ALEXIA • RAPHAELL
july 2005

sun • cool • fun • hot

Best Friends Forever

When we moved from North Carolina, I hoped that you, Rebecca, and Sara would continue your friendship. Not only have you three remained close, but you consider yourselves best friends! This summer was your turn to host the 3rd annual week-long visit. They flew here to Nashville. What an exhausting (but fun) week you had! I planned lots of field trips to show them the best that Nashville has to offer. We went to Nashville Shores Water Park, movies, The Hermitage,

The Aquarium Restaurant and The Wild Horse Saloon for line dancing (what trip to Nashville would be complete without a bit of country music?). You went swimming nearly every day, also. Sleep was NOT on the agenda, though; at least not until the wee hours of the morning. I woke up several times around 3 a.m. and heard giggling coming from your room. Other times I found you in the kitchen playing "name the mystery food" and poker on the dining room table.

I am so happy that you have wonderful, close friends like Rebecca and Sara. You are learning such a valuable lesson in nurturing friendships. Lindsay, I'm very proud of your commitment to stay in touch. B.F.F. is on every letter you send each other. Next year, you will be flying by yourself to North Carolina for the annual visit. I know you three are already planning all sorts of activities. I guarantee that sleep will once again NOT be on the agenda! *Summer '05, age 13*

A fun-filled, sleep-deprived reunion of Jane's daughter and her long-distance friends is relived in color. Jane created a colorful photo montage accented by solid and patterned paper squares all with rounded edges for a soft effect. A handcut curved border travels across the spread accented by a mix of colorful threaded buttons and brads. The faux-dimensional title printed on the background was created with Microsoft's Word Art.

Jane Rife, Collierville, Tennessee

Supplies: Patterned papers (American Crafts); buttons; floss; brads; cardstock

Ah...a day at the beach. What could be more wonderful? A montage of beach umbrellas set against a rick-rack patterned paper would make just about anyone green with envy. The bright orange, pink, green and blue pop right off this vibrant layout. See sketch on CD-ROM.

Barb Hogan, Cincinnati, Ohio

Supplies: Image-editing software (Adobe Photoshop Elements 3.0); patterned paper (T. Cordova)

Brightly painted chipboard letters scream summer against nautical striped paper to set the theme for these water fun photos. Tonia accented her bold title with glossy epoxy stickers to reflect the water theme photos. Her vertically placed journaling block that details the quality time spent with visiting cousins echoes the striped paper. A chipboard sentiment sums up the summer's day spent on the water—kick back and relax. See sketch on CD-ROM.

Tonia Borrosch, Honeoye, New York

Supplies: Patterned paper (American Crafts); chipboard letters, acrylic paint (Making Memories); woven tabs (Scrapworks); chipboard sentiment (Heidi Swapp); ribbon (Michaels); epoxy stickers (Autumn Leaves); cardstock

> "I was so inspired by the bright reds and yellows in the photos that I decided to complement them with bright, fun patterned papers."

The splish splash of summer fun comes alive with vibrant colors and glossy accents. Erin used a quick shutter speed to capture the water droplets mid-air in the focal photo of her husband whisking their daughter down the slide. A printed transparency details the wet adventure and holds her painted title. Stitched patterned paper squares get a wet look with a transparency overlay defining summer. See sketch on CD-ROM.

Erin Campbell-Pope, Petal, Mississippi

Supplies: Patterned papers (Creative Imaginations, KI Memories, Me & My Big Ideas, Paperbilities); rub-ons, photo corners (Making Memories); definition transparency (Daisy D's) paint; ribbon (American Crafts); buckle, frame holders (Jest Charming); jump ring; eyelet; jewelry tag; acrylic charms (KI Memories); bottle cap (Li'l Davis Designs); stamping ink; staples; transparency; thread; cardstock

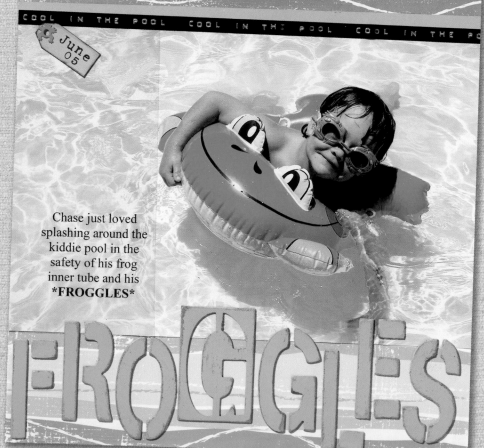

Green and glossy accents set the stage for this water-fun page. Michelle painted her chipboard title in bright green and then applied clear gloss medium for a wet look that complements her photo subject. A frog eyelet secures a green date-stamped tag and plays up the frog-themed water accessories her son sports in the photo.

Michelle Bentley, San Diego, California

Supplies: Patterned paper (Creative Imaginations); label maker (Dymo); chipboard letters (Rusty Pickle); acrylic paint (Making Memories); crystal lacquer clear gloss medium (Sakura); frog eyelet; transparency

Sarah caught her daughter taking a refreshing drink on a warm summer afternoon and couldn't resist the urge to frame it in time. The fresh blue and green color scheme complements the photo and theme while the repeated circle patterns and the curved lines add movement and energy to this mouthwatering layout.

Sarah Mullanix, Anderson, Indiana

Supplies: Patterned paper (Autumn Leaves, Carolee's Creations, MOD); sticker letters (Mustard Moon); die-cut letters (QuickKutz); epoxy circle letter (Foofala); photo anchors (7 Gypsies); ribbon (American Crafts); brads (Making Memories); cardstock

Emily, you must have thought that the Water Looked too good for only the Flowers to enjoy, because when I came Back around the side of the house from Watering the flowers, this is what I found. I caught you mid-drink, refreshing yourself. What better way is there to enjoy this warm Spring day than to indulge yourself with a cool Refreshing drink of water straight from the hose.

water H2O water water water

REFRESH

Freezing cold water hitting your warm body on a hot day. Your expression is priceless as you realize that maybe you should have waited for the water to warm up a bit. All I can think of as I take this picture of you is...

brr.

Icy blue, green and purple contrasted with stark white play up the chilly effect the water had on Celeste's son in this photo. Celeste printed her journaling onto the white background with coordinating purple ink. Die-cut letters make a quick title while patterned paper strips become borders in a snap. See sketch on CD-ROM.

Celeste Smith, West Hartford, Connecticut

Supplies: Patterned papers, die-cut letters (KI Memories); cardstock

These photos prove a chaperoned ski trip can be fun as Deb's sons took an icy snow plunge. The computer-generated page is full of faux texture and dimension with digital patterned papers, gems and staples downloaded from the Internet. Deb used a digital brush to create the distressed effects and whimsical swirls. A digital pen brought Deb's handwriting to the page for a personal touch.

Deb Perry, Newport News, Virginia

Supplies: Digital patterned papers (www.scrapartist .com); digital jewels, staples (www.theshabbyshoppe. com); digital grunge brush by Dianne Rigdon, digital swirl brush by Michelle Coleman (www.scrapartist .com); digital typeset letters by Rhonna Farrer (www .twopeasinabucket.com); image-editing software (Adobe Photoshop); digital pen (Wacom)

A backdrop of icy purples studded with silver creates a wintry backdrop perfect for Samantha's sledding photos. Samantha's swirl patterned background paper lends a sense of fun while purple paper strip borders dipped in silver embossing powder give an icy look. Playful expressions framed in circles add fun and sentiment to the page. See sketch on CD-ROM.

Samantha Walker, Lehi, Utah

Supplies: Patterned paper (American Traditional Designs); metal photo corners (Making Memories); star brads (Provo Craft); circle frames (Scrapworks); letter dies (QuicKutz); silver embossing powder; stamping inks; brads; cardstock

> "I thought the purple would be the perfect complement to the white snow with a blue cast. It truly creates an icy look that pops off the page."

Dressed in icy layered pastels, this winter-frolic page came together quickly with coordinating products. Lisa slipped paper strips through die-cut shapes for a quick border with a layered look. Ribbons tied in knots on die cuts, charms and the journaling block make fast snowflakelike accents. Rub-on letters make custom ribbon in a snap while rub-on snowflakes and stitches added lots of texture in seconds.

Lisa Schmitt, Easton, Connecticut

Supplies: Patterned papers, die cuts (KI Memories); rub-ons (Doodlebug Design, Making Memories); ribbon (Making Memories); acrylic charm (Doodlebug Design); cardstock

Shades of cheery pink accented with white create the perfect backdrop for this story of a girl's perseverance. Sheila tells of her daughter's first ski lesson with pink journaling printed on a light pink journaling block accented with flower eyelets. Her vertical title is highlighted with flower charms strung with pink chain. A brave girl expression is printed on a circle with the keyword "tough" highlighted with a watch crystal. See sketch on CD-ROM.

Sheila Doherty, Coeur d' Alene, Idaho

Supplies: Patterned papers (American Crafts, Chatterbox, Karen Foster Design); flower charms (Nunn Designs); flower brads, paper flowers (Making Memories); watch crystal (Scrapworks); bead chain (Pebbles); rhinestone eyelet (SEI); circle punch (Carl); cardstock

Sam plays up a retro bowling theme with starburst- and circle-punched shapes. The starbursts accent the photos that coordinate perfectly with the funky patterned paper. Juxtaposed die-cut letters on punchy circles spell out bowling lingo with a playful spin. Black circle punches placed on a red sticker strip borders the journaling and mimics bowling balls cruising down the lane. See sketch on CD-ROM.

Samuel Cole, Woodbury, Minnesota

Supplies: Patterned papers, stickers (Karen Foster Design); starburst and circle punches (EK Success); letter dies (QuicKutz); circle cutter (Creative Memories); stamping ink; sandpaper; acrylic paint; cardstock

Black and white squares emulate a chessboard, setting the stage for Christine's son in his favorite pastime—playing chess. Whether it's a winning success or a losing distress, the photos show him reveling in studying the board and strategizing to someday beat the computer game. The color photos stand out against neutral supplies. Symbols on chipboard squares serve as bullet points to journaling strips and add bold expression to the page.

Christine Brown, Hanover, Minnesota

Supplies: Textured cardstock (Canson, Prism); epoxy letter stickers (Creative Imaginations); chipboard letter and squares (Heidi Swapp); acrylic paint (Making Memories); magnet squares (Target)

OUT TO PLAY

I HAD A HARD TIME GETTING TANYA TO LEAVE THE PARK WHEN I TOOK THEM OUT TO PLAY. OH, HOW SHE LOVES THE SWING

A series of photos matted on gray cardstock with dimensional adhesive capture this girl's glee of swinging at the park. Thomisia enlarged a shot of her youngest daughter with her expressive grin. The small shots show her big sister pushing the swing and explain why Mom, as her journaling says, had a hard time getting little sister to leave the park.

Thomisia Francois, Duncanville, Texas

Supplies: Patterned papers (KI Memories); mailbox letters (Making Memories); ribbon (Offray); buttons; stamping ink; cardstock

Earthy rust colors bring the outdoors to this page while punchy oranges magnify the sense of fun Shannon's son is having in these photos. Orange rubber letters boldly spell out the title. Rust painted corrugated cardboard mimics the bricks in the focal photo and adds rugged texture. A painted and stamped wooden tag holds a cropped close-up of her son. Twine adds a boyish touch to Shannon's letter-stamped journaling. See sketch on CD-ROM.

Shannon Taylor, Bristol, Tennessee

Supplies: Patterned papers (Scenic Route Paper Co.); textured paper (Artistic Scrapper); corrugated cardboard; acrylic paint; stamps (Hero Arts, Inkadinkdo); jute; acrylic charm (Junkitz); wood tag (Chatterbox); rubber letters (Scrapworks); chalk; cardstock

PLAY HARD ROB

I LOVE YOU OUTSIDE JUMPING & DOING TRICKS RATHER THAN INDOORS WATCHING T.V. SEE HOW COOL YOU CAN BE.

A favorite Christmas gift is remembered playfully with funky patterned papers and slightly untraditional holiday colors. The black-and-white photos of Libby's daughter sporting her new moon shoes bounce against citrus green layered over seasonally striped patterned papers. Libby cut out punchy patterned paper flowers and continued the squiggly line design onto the background with a pen. Eclectic mixes of letter stickers make a spunky title.

Libby Weifenbach, Van Buren, Arkansas

Supplies: Patterned papers (Imagination Project); letter stickers (American Crafts, Doodlebug Designs); epoxy letter stickers (Sulyn Industries); label maker (Dymo); photo corner punch (EK Success); number dies (QuicKutz); stitching; pen; cardstock

> **"My inspiration came from the patterned paper. I loved the bright colors...Christmaslike with a funky edge. What could be more perfect for Christmas morning photos of a cool toy like moon shoes?"**

An enlarged vertical photo plays up Terri's son's passion for climbing. She printed her journaling about his climbing talent on the same block as his close-up photo. Letter stickers spell out the title and are purposely stacked to play up the title's message—climb on. Colorful square patterned paper is the perfect playground for this playful topic. See sketch on CD-ROM.

Terri Davenport, Toledo, Ohio

Supply List: Patterned paper, stickers (American Crafts)

let the **Good** times **Roll**

"Ok girls, let's get some photos. Smile pretty. Uhh...that's not quite what I meant. You girls are so goofy!"

GOOFY GIRLS

JOY

These photos weren't quite what Thomisia had in mind when she set up a photo shoot with her daughters. But she followed their playfulness, creating this lighthearted spread that showcases her girls' silly side. She enhances their sassy faces with bright colors and playful patterned papers. A vertical series of black-and-white photos shines on a purple paper strip while circle-cropped photos on dimensional adhesive seem to float playfully on the page.

Thomisia Francois, Duncanville, Texas

Supplies: Patterned papers, letter stickers (Basic Grey); letter stickers (K & Company); fabric tab (Scrapworks); silk flower; transparency; cardstock

The constant movement of a 4-year-old is captured with photos and design on this page. Lisa cut a Hula-Hoop-like accent from green cardstock to surround her photo montage of her daughter in action. A die-cut circular journaling block and embellishment set on a patterned background add to the theme of nonstop movement. Dots of pearly dimensional paint form another circle, highlighting the slightly curved title. See sketch on CD-ROM.

Lisa Dorsey, Westfield, Indiana

Supplies: Patterned paper (MOD, Treehouse Memories); word charm (Li'l Davis Designs); flowers (Prima); dimensional paint (Duncan); acrylic paint (Delta); stamping ink; cardstock

warm summer day energetic 4 year old one hula hoop lots of fun

HULA HOOP

PLaY

While outside for a serious photo shoot, Linda captured these joyous shots of her son oozing with happiness. The three photos are bound with the perfect twill tape sentiment. A large circle works as both a photo mat and a journaling block. It is set on spunky polka-dot patterned paper stitched to the background for movement and texture. See sketch on CD-ROM.

Linda Harrison, Sarasota, Florida

Supplies: Patterned paper (K & Company); letter stickers (Arctic Frog); flowers (Prima); brads; chalk stamping ink; thread; circle punch; hole punch; cardstock

JOY Captured

CAPTURE the joy

There is extreme happiness and inner joy which absolutely oozes out of you. You have always been a very content little guy, but as you grow, your contentedness has become so much more. It is a happy little soul that I see within you. I hope nothing or no one ever dims that light inside of you. May the joy within you never, ever fade.

let the **Good** times **Roll**

Black-and-white photos pop so infectiously against this girly backdrop that you can practically hear the giggle of Tina's daughter. Très-chic touches play up the feminine theme with patterned papers in fresh colors, ink smudges, stitched borders, tied ribbons and flower clusters. Tina accented a large die-cut monogram letter that labels the page along with a rub-on sentiment that embraces her daughter's giggling personality.

Tina Albertson, Harlan, Indiana

Supplies: Patterned papers (Fontwerks); flowers (Doodlebug Designs, Prima); ribbon (May Arts); rub-on sentiment (Scenic Route Paper Co.); photo corners (Chatterbox); brads; thread; stamping ink; cardstock

giggle

Summer 05

To convey her son's glee, Vicki used playful circle shapes in boyish colors set at fun angles on this page. Whimsical circle patterned paper cut at extreme angles and stitched to the background is echoed in a cut cardstock circle title block. Ribbon strung through loop brads on chipboard circles draws attention to her smiling son's photo and adds visual interest.

Vicki Boutin, Burlington, Ontario, Canada

Supplies: Patterned paper (Die Cuts With a View); letter stamps (Scraptivity); loop brads (Karen Foster Design); typewriter letter stickers (EK Success); chipboard circles (Bazzill); flower brad (Making Memories); ribbon; staples; embossing powder; cardstock

What a **happy** kid! You **laugh** and **smile** often which cause **others** to **laugh** right along with you. **Riley**, you fill our lives with **GLEE**!!

G L E E

A dad being goofy with his kids is the theme of this fun layout. Striped and dotted paper combined with a blue and green color scheme give this page a masculine feel.

Phillipa Campbell, Jerrabomberra, New South Wales, Australia

Supplies: Patterned paper, die cuts, buttons, tags (Chatterbox); letter stickers (Creative Imaginations); letter "f" (Making Memories); ribbon; denim

"My husband is a big kid at heart. The kids love to spend time with him because he is so much fun. This layout represents their relationship."

45

going on

f i v e

David you are such a big kid at heart. You may now be forty five but you never stop having fun. I love to watch you with all our nieces and nephews. They cant get enough of your fun loving nature. Sticking tongues out, playing practical jokes, tearing through the house at 100 miles an hour, it is all just part and parcel of Uncle David. One of the qualities I love most about you if your effervescent, happy go lucky attitude. Spending time with you is always fun! Photos April 2005, Journaling November 2005

FUN
enthusiasm

That grin is infectious!!

When you were a baby it was rare

to see it. As you grow so does that smile.

It gets bigger and brighter everyday.

Baby, I love that grin!

GRIN GRIN GRIN grin GRIN GRIN grin GRIN GRIN GRIN grin GRIN GRIN grin

When Vicki's girl was a baby, it was rare to see her grin, but as she grows, so does her smile, making Mom very happy. A close-up photo shows Vicki and her daughter both with cheeky grins. A spunky but muted backdrop highlights their faces. Vicki stamped "grin" on a series of torn patterned paper pieces stapled to the page. The theme is further played up with a label border.

Vicki Boutin, Burlington, Ontario, Canada

Supplies: Patterned papers (Carolee's Creations, K & Company, SEI); letter stamps (Scraptivity); metal word (Making Memories); label maker (Dymo); rickrack; staples; stamping ink; cardstock

let the **Good** times **Roll**

In playful girly fashion, Kristen used bright colors and punchy accents to enhance this best-friend story. The hammy grins of Kristen's daughter and her friend pop against a Day-Glo mat. The mix of neon-green rickrack, bright plaid patterns and big flower patterned paper brings girl power to this page.

Kristen Swain, Bear, Delaware

Supplies: Patterned papers, buckle (Junkitz); ribbons; rub-on letters (Making Memories); brads; black pen

Lisa captured these candid photos of her daughter and her friends—the girls of Eighth Street. She turned the photos black-and-white and used products in the same color scheme to give the layout a cohesive look.

Lisa Risser, Buffalo, Minnesota

Supplies: Patterned paper, trim, blossoms, brads (Making Memories); flowers (Prima); chipboard letters (Heidi Swapp); corner punch (EK Success); white pen

serenity

Ah, the sweet serenity of an early morning low tide on the Brewster Flats. Solitude for miles, just us and the small sea creatures waiting to be discovered. This lonely sailboat temporarily landlocked inviting you to climb aboard – the sound of the surf in the distance and the quiet punctuated with the sounds of your delight of discovery – a perfectly serene morning. Cape Cod ~ June 2005

An 11 x 8½" layout packs a lot of punch with a simple yet bold page design. Celeste represents the serenity of the photo's beach setting with neutral and bright nautical paper strips set on crisp summer white. She details her and her son's waterside adventure with journaling printed in reverse type on glossy paper. Letter stickers spell out the title, describing the serene beach experience. See sketch on CD-ROM.

Celeste Smith, West Hartford, Connecticut

Supplies: Patterned paper (Arctic Frog); letter sticker (American Crafts); cardstock

Though Colleen lives near the ocean, she never takes for granted the serenity of a walk on a sandy beach. And though her rat terrier hates water, he loves chasing seagulls as captured in this photo. Colleen uses one large focal photo to convey the excitement and beauty of the day. Striped patterned paper and acrylic accents enhance the nautical theme.

Colleen Adams, Huntington Beach, California

Supplies: Patterned paper (Daisy D's); acrylic charms (MOD); cardstock

Savor this day because it will be gone tomorrow

It's a cliché because it's true: the simple things are often the most cherished pleasures. A walk by the sea before the summer crowds arrive is one of the joys of living near the beach. We are so lucky to live here. Sand in my shoes, beach glass in my pocket – life is very good indeed.

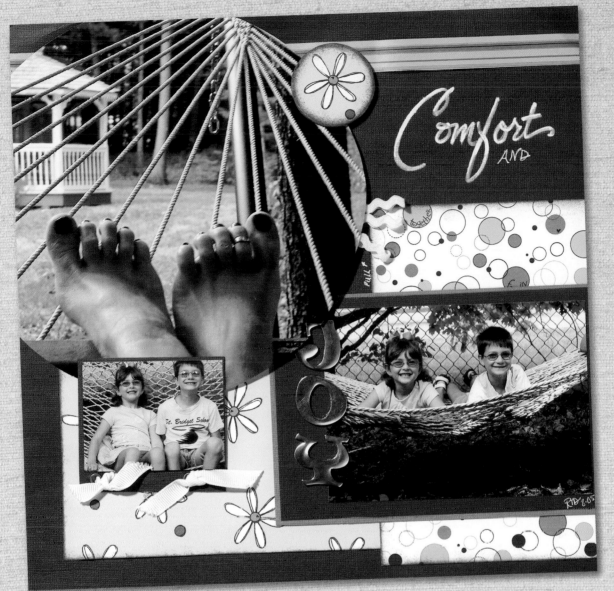

Comfort AND

joy

How can one item bring both COMFORT and JOY? If you take one beautifully supportive rope hammock and place it in a shaded enclave with a view, of both the flower garden and the pool, you end up with an area of serenity and calm. Add one mom (who like most moms) does not usually sit (until she has all the items checked off her "to do list") and you give her a wonderfully delicious COMFORT; imparting her with the feeling that "all is right" with her world and that she is living the "dream" ... the "lush life". The intensity of this feeling is as strong as the smell of the summer blooms that surround her; washing over her and enfolding her in complete COMFORT.

An enlarged shot cropped from a creative perspective shows the resting feet of Mom that's in great contrast to the children playing in the same hammock. From the perspectives of both comfort and pure joy, Reneè journals on a circular tag tucked behind the focal photo about the family's hammock and the purposes it serves. A complementary color scheme in a playful mix of patterned papers enhances the backyard photos.

Reneè Thomson DiNardi, Glastonbury, Connecticut

Supplies: Patterned papers (Heidi Grace Designs); metal letters (Scrap Metal); rickrack (May Arts); chipboard (Bazzill); eyelets; stamping ink; white gel pen; cardstock

This spread documents a special place for Marie and her husband—the California beach where he proposed 10 years prior. She arranged her 11 beachscape photos with the sky in shades of blue on the left side of the spread to photos with shades of orange on the other, representing the midday moving to the setting sun. A monochromatic collage of tags, die cuts, charms and sticker sentiments accents each page. Marie's handwritten memoirs cross both sides of the spread.

Marie Pilgrim, Banning, California

Supplies: Tags (Target); die-cut sentiment tags, stickers, rub-on letters (Chatterbox); buttons (Junkitz); mini transparencies (EK Success); printed twill stickers (Paper House Productions); chalk (Craf-T); metal word (Jo-Ann Stores); pen; cardstock

Vicki credits her good sense of humor to her parents, seen cracking up in these photos. The sense of fun of the giggling pair is enhanced against a perky backdrop of pink flowers and green stripes. A semicircle in a contrasting stripe encompasses Vicki's mixed media title for even more fun on this page.

Vicki Boutin, Burlington, Ontario, Canada

Supplies: Patterned papers, rub-on letters, stickers (Scenic Route Paper Co.); letter stamps (Scraptivity); brads (Queen & Co.); pen; cardstock

Holly and her husband celebrated their 11th anniversary at their beach house with no one around but the camera's self-timer and a tripod to capture these photos. Sticker letters spell out the title on the couple's focal photo with an emphasis on the word "private" stamped on a mini tag. The tag dangles from a whimsical collage of a chipboard heart, chipboard circle, stamped acrylic flower and a ribbon. See sketch on CD-ROM.

Holly Corbett, Central, South Carolina

Supplies: Patterned papers, rub-ons, cardstock sticker (KI Memories); chipboard shapes, rub-ons, acrylic flowers (Heidi Swapp); tag (QuicKutz); mini brads; acrylic paint, floss (Making Memories); ribbon (Li'l Davis Design); stamps (Hero Arts, PSX Design); solvent stamping ink; cardstock

The sound of two little beeps make Kelly's heart go pitter-patter, signaling digital love notes on her phone from her boyfriend. The two are addicted to text messaging, sending and receiving notes to brighten one another's day. Small snapshots show the modern-day Romeo and Juliet while photo close-ups show Kelly's texting fingers and her phone's outbox. Geometric patterns, acrylic tiles and extreme angles create a contemporary feel.

Kelly Purkey, Chicago, Illinois

Supplies: Patterned papers (Doodlebug Design); stickers (American Crafts, Doodlebug Design, KI Memories); acrylic tiles (KI Memories); brads; pen; cardstock

> "We live in such a technology-driven era, and it's funny how it works its way into our everyday lives. Getting text messages from my boyfriend became a great highlight of my day."

For Mary and her husband, this mid-air pose captured with a self-timer and her running and jumping into his arms is a travel standard. This time it takes place on a beach, and she transfers the setting to her page with cheesecloth for a fisherman's net effect, nautical striped patterned paper, rope and seashells. A quote printed directly onto the photo is framed with a brush tool in image-editing software.

Mary MacAskill, Calgary, Alberta, Canada

Supplies: Patterned papers (Arctic Frog); page pebble, brads (Making Memories); seashells; cheesecloth; hemp rope; silk flower; circle punch; image-editing brush tool (source unknown); cardstock

"The sea! the sea! the open sea! The blue, the fresh, the ever free!"
Bryan W. Procter

"There's a lot of sand. It could get inside the camera, you know. Well, ok. I can use the backpack. Yeah, if I prop it on the backpack, it should be okay. Very, very carefully. (Looking through the viewfinder) Oh, could you move over there a little bit? No, over there. Okay, good. Ready? 10 seconds..."

Our standard self-timed photo pose. Only this time, it's by the sea.

Newport Beach, California
April 2005

Some must search their whole lives through to find a love that is pure and true. But we were blessed beyond compare to find the love that we now share

Kimberly says her inspiration for this layout came straight from her heart. A large focal photo of her and her husband nearly spans the page and holds Kimberly's grateful words for her marriage printed directly onto it. A close-up shot of the couple corners the page next to her title punched slightly off-center from letter patterned paper.

Kimberly Garofolo, Phoenix, Arizona

Supplies: Patterned papers (Urban Lily); stamping ink; cardstock

U R mine

After looking at a photo her daughter took while their family was vacationing at Cape Cod, Linda was pleasantly surprised to see how happy, relaxed and in love she and her husband are. She chose a cheery light green background and used mini flowers and a heart embellishment to accent.

Linda Sobolewski, Guilford, Connecticut

Supplies: Patterned paper (Carolee's Creations); rub-ons (Basic Grey); paper flowers (Doodlebug Design); heart (Heidi Swapp); paint (Making Memories); letter stickers (Chatterbox); ribbon (May Arts); cardstock

When Hera's parents came to visit from New Zealand, she worked on an anniversary album for them every night after they went to bed. In this page from the album, the photo of her parents is hinged and the journaling on the back expresses Hera's hopes and wishes. The story is set in happy patterned papers with a slight worn look accented with buttons. An anniversary wish is printed directly onto the background.

Hera Frei, Kusnacht, Zurich, Switzerland

Supplies: Patterned papers (Daisy D's); rub-on word (Making Memories); buttons (Bazzill); metal hinges; cardstock

In July, 2005 Nan and Koro came to Switzerland to spend the Summer with us. We were very worried as to how they would manage the 24 hour flight as Koro has a quadruple heart by-pass and is a diabetic and both are in their mid -70's. During their six week stay, we will celebrate their golden wedding anniversary, Nan's birthday, Mummy's birthday and Koro will perform Mika's christening. This photo was taken 3 days after they arrived, at the Zurichberg Restaurant, overlooking the Lake of Zurich. Whilst trying to create a "wedding anniversary gift" album of their stay (after they have gone to bed every evening!) I also wanted to use this opportunity to journal my wishes for you and your grandparents during this time. I hope that in the next six weeks you will come to know your grandparents, as the wonderful, caring people that they truly are, My Mum and Dad. I hope that Koro will pass on some of his family history, stories of his childhood, teach you to sing as he does and that both of you will be blessed with his strong but gentle nature. I have no fear that Nan will run after you hand and foot. She will read you books. She will get you a jumper just in case it turns cold. She will cook you 'my' favourite childhood dishes. She will stand beside you in case you fall from a tree. I hope they will be proud grandparents, on your first day at school, Tane and as you start your first full day at spielgruppe, Mika. I hope they will enjoy the European culture. I hope everyday is not 30 degrees. I hope they will return to New Zealand with many lasting memories, not only of landscapes and cuisines but also of their two precious grandsons. I hope this will be a time of love, learning and laughter for all four, a very special JOURNEY!

Je t'aime un peu, beaucoup, passionnément, à la folie !

Declaring her love for her husband, Gislaine's French title is translated to say "I love you a little, a lot, passionately, madly." French scripted papers in warm reds and aged creams help tell the relationship story that began with love letters represented with stamped images and the couple's initials. Silk flowers and scattered petals mimic the old adage "He loves me, he loves me not."

Gislaine Vincent, Dorval, Quebec, Canada

Supplies: Patterned papers (DDDesigns); stamps (My Sentiments Exactly, Magenta); word washers (Making Memories); ribbon (May Arts); stencil letters; rosebud lace; silk flowers; stamping ink; cardstock

"This layout was inspired by the French patterned paper. It reminded me how I used to remove the petals on daisies one by one and repeat those words 'He loves me a little, he loves me a lot.'"

Heather created this heartwarming layout reaffirming her everlasting love to her husband of three years. She mixed striped and floral patterned papers over a brick red background and added brown ribbons to accent. The close-up photo reveals the passion that is alive in this young couple's eyes.

Heather Taylor, Logan, Utah

Supplies: Patterned paper (Chatterbox); ribbon (May Arts); chipboard (Li'l Davis Designs); cardstock stickers (Doodlebug Design); photo turns (Making Memories); cardstock

you're still THE ONE

TRUE LOVE

together

Sure, we've only been married for a little over three years, but it seems like we've always been together, and I don't remember what life was like before you. I love that we have fun together, and that we look forward to the future. Babe, you're still the one, and you always will be. —March 2005

A fold-out album jampacked with love tributes Suzy's husband on Father's Day. Chipboard covers with punched holes are covered in patterned papers and bound with tied fabric strips. As the album completely unfolds, the double-sided pages are filled with family photos and sentiments to this loving dad. The album fits neatly into a four-flap cardstock holder.

Suzy Plantamura, Laguna Niguel, California

Supplies: Patterned papers (7 Gypsies, Autumn Leaves, Carolee's Creations, Li'l Davis Designs, My Mind's Eye, Rusty Pickle); ribbon rings, metal key (7 Gypsies); brads, staples, eyelets (Making Memories); photo sleeves, letter stickers, black trim (MAMBI); envelope, red ribbon, library pocket, epoxy word (Li'l Davis Designs); stamps (Basic Grey, Paper Inspirations, Stampin' Up!, Stampotique); metal-rimmed tags, shipping tags (Staples); label maker, tape (Dymo); stamping ink; flowers; fabric; vellum envelope; black marker

MOUNT ST HELE

of our mini road trips last summer, we drove to Mount St Helens, which is about 2½ hour
wanting to go every since the visitors center opened about 10 years ago. I was seven years
s erupted. I vaguely remember the eruption and the ash that covered everything for days a
ors center, we would get glimpses of the mountain as we got closer and closer. It was an
ast zone". As we made the drive, I could see not only the destruction caused by nature, bu

WEDDING
The day we were married

I love you.
Not only for what
But for what I a
When I am with
I love you.
Not only for wha

Reme

Dan & Meg
5.28.06

you
&
be

I love you

Spectacular FALL colors

Surf

AUSTIN
7

MACKENZIE
5

Austin just missed the cutoff date to advance to the next league
made the cutoff date. The end result is that the three of you are a
year. We have only had 2 games so far and you are all so much
starting to "get" the game. Lauren tries her hardest but jus
Mackenzie likes to throw his glove up in the air and sit down

TEAMMA

BOYS & TOYS

Summer rejuvenate

Ride hard boys! Although the signs around say "no wake," "slow speeds.," I couldn't help it! I encouraged it! Do donuts, throw water, dunk the jet ski! Why you ask.... For the perfect picture!

Enjoy
THE JOURNEY

GALLAWAY

seize
the Day

family

visiting DC
Washington

37

Vacation 2005
Steve, Catherine
Ellis, Emmy,
Sam, William
and
Pete

ADORABLE

2005

US Capitol

What triggers you to follow your wanderlust? Is it traveling to foreign or exotic locales, participating in the dynamism of competitive sports, discovering the beauty in nature or falling into total bliss on the day of your wedding? These are the moments we thirst for; the times we are completely and utterly captivated by the shot of adreline surging through our veins. We can't freeze these moments in time no matter how hard we try, but it is possible to relive them through the pages of our scrapbooks. So take hold of each captivating moment and remember it forever in your albums.

Pam used colors, textures and symbols true to Native American culture to commemorate Mesa Verde. Her adobe pink torn and chalked photo mats and background aged with webbing spray create a distressed backdrop to these photos of ancient ruins. Mica lends an earthy backdrop to the stone-textured title and kokopellis. A dream catcher hints at cultural spiritualism. Inspired by pottery, Pam painted a border rich in symbolism and traditional colors.

Pamela James, Ventura, California

Supplies: Webbing and stone spray paints (Krylon); mica; watercolor paints; elastic cord; eyelets; dream catcher charm (Lakota); transparencies; brads; stamping ink; chalk; pen; cardstock

The beauty of wildlife seen at a desert museum is relived with Sherry's photos. A mountain lion focal photo jumps off the page accompanied by cropped close-ups of other desert animals. Sherry punched paper strips with a label maker to identify each animal and inked all the page elements for a sandy-desert effect.

Sherry Wright, West Branch, Michigan

Supplies: Patterned papers, stencil letter (Kopp Design); label holder (Li'l Davis Designs); mailbox letter, ribbon charm (Making Memories); transparency; ribbon; label maker (Dymo); corner rounder (EK Success); stamping ink

one of these things
is not like the other

Many traveled from continents afar to admire the amazing view of Sydney Harbour.

May 2005

A giraffe enjoying a city view is the ironic inspiration for Jennifer's page. Intending to get a shot of this beautiful creature at the Sydney zoo resulted in this photo showing a dichotomy of cultures. African patterned paper strips and framed squares play up the giraffe's heritage. Jennifer's journaling hints at her distant travels as well as the giraffe's journey.

Jennifer Moody, Lewisville, Texas

Supplies: Patterned paper (Grass Roots); conchos (Scrapworks); cardstock

"While taking photos at the Taronga Zoo in Sydney, I realized my viewfinder was "seeing" more than just the animals. I loved the irony—a giraffe from Africa enjoying the same view as a tourist from the United States."

A trip back to Alaska where Courtney and her husband once called home proved nostalgic and inspired this cover page to their travel album. A photo montage shows a glimpse of the many adventures they squeezed in during their two-week trip. Patterned paper strips make subtle borders that coordinate with her simple letter-sticker title.

Courtney Kelly, Colorado Springs, Colorado

Supplies: Patterned paper, letter stickers (American Crafts); cardstock

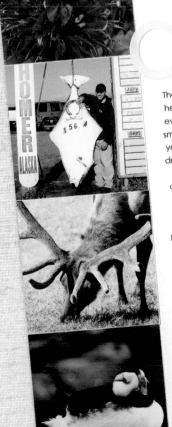

alaska

There is nothing like home. Sure there is "home is where your heart is", but there is still nothing like returning to your home, everything being familiar, having memories everywhere, the smells, the sights, the activities, the feelings. It's been almost 3 years since we were last in Alaska, since we were last fishing, driving down the Seward highway, since we were looking out our window at the mountains in our home every day. And although those memories are all in the past it felt so good to be adding new ones. With only two weeks to visit we crammed every day with something, and not tackling near enough on our to do list either. Things like: Halibut fishing, Botanical Gardens, Big Game Alaska, Seward, Homer, Kasilof, Seward Sea-life Center, a Resurrection Bay Wildlife Cruise, and much much more! Feeding and petting reindeer, visiting favorite restaurants like Sourdough Mining company for their corn fritters or the Moose is Loose bakery in Soldotna. We did drive-bys of so many places that brought back memories, went to a PLDC graduation of an old buddy we knew back when we were stationed at Ft. Richardson. Two weeks was not nearly enough time to enjoy all the things we miss, but, there is always next year's salmon season.

August 2-15, 2005

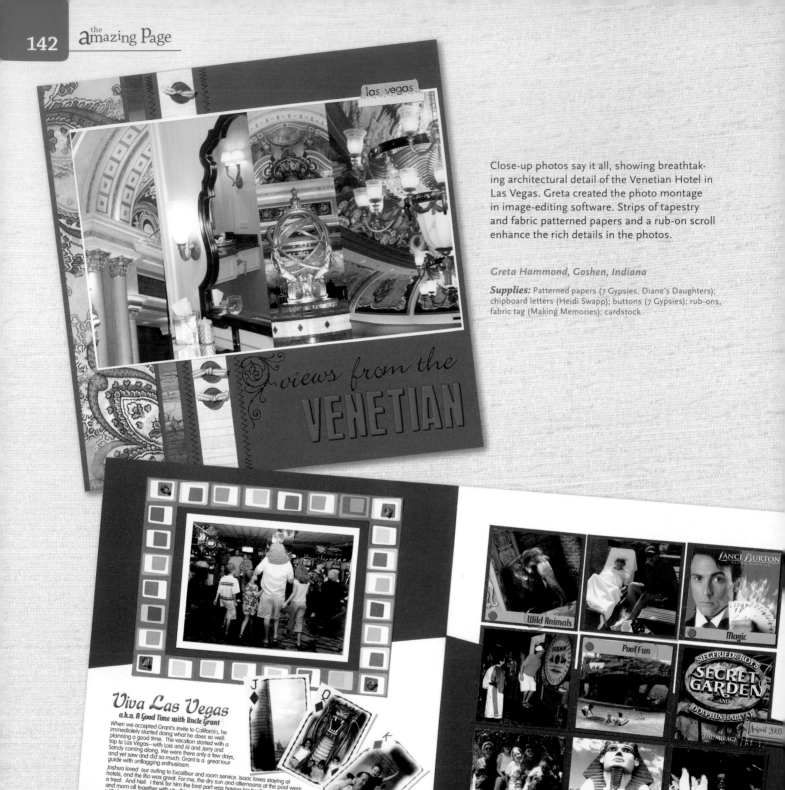

Close-up photos say it all, showing breathtaking architectural detail of the Venetian Hotel in Las Vegas. Greta created the photo montage in image-editing software. Strips of tapestry and fabric patterned papers and a rub-on scroll enhance the rich details in the photos.

Greta Hammond, Goshen, Indiana

Supplies: Patterned papers (7 Gypsies, Diane's Daughters); chipboard letters (Heidi Swapp); buttons (7 Gypsies); rub-ons, fabric tag (Making Memories); cardstock

A family getaway is relived with vivid imagery and fond journaling on Deborah's spread. A focal photo shows the entire gang walking through a casino. The triple-matted photo was enhanced with threaded beads in the corners tied with French knots. Deborah created custom playing card frames for three of her photos by scanning the cards and then importing the photos onto them in image-editing software. A feather filter was applied to softly fade the edges of the images.

Deborah Hodge, Durham, New Hampshire

Supplies: Patterned paper (Karen Foster Design); glass beads (Bead Bin); floss (DMC); label holder (KI Memories); snaps (Making Memories); cardstock

A picture-perfect family photo set in front of the U.S. Capitol graces this fun and funky digital page. Barb used an array of shapes and swirls mixed with retro background papers to compose a vacation page with a twist. She added an image resembling a postal stamp in the lower right corner of the photo to give the impression of a postcard.

Barb Hogan, Cincinnati, Ohio

Supplies: Image-editing software (Adobe Photoshop Elements 3.0); digital kit (www.shabbyprincess.com)

Strategic stitching allowed Oksanna to include memorabilia as well as more photos from Paris on this spread. She stitched three sides of two photos to the background and left the tops open as pockets to hold a map and a room-key folder both topped with a stamped and stapled pull-tab. Two stitch-bound albums made with folded-edge cardstock hold photo stacks. Decorative punches, stamped images and silk ribbons add Parisian flair.

Oksanna Pope, Las Gatos, California

Supplies: Patterned paper (Karen Foster Design); tag (DMD); stamps, embossing powder, stamping ink (All Night Media); decorative corner punch (EK Success); metal sentiment (Paper Bliss); glitter spray (Tulip); cardstock

Black-and-white travel photos with rounded corners look like postcards. The photos really stand out on a bright pink background to which Barb stamped a leaf design and inked the edges for a foggy effect reflective of the photos. The black accents and title block tie the photos to the page. Rub-on stitches on the title block and a spray of ribbons tucked behind add a sprig of color and dimension.

Barb Hogan, Cincinnati, Ohio

Supplies: Patterned paper (Junkitz); rub-ons (Wordsworth); brads, button, flower (Making Memories); letter stickers, punch label die cut (Pebbles); ribbon (Michaels, Offray, Stampin' Up!); slide frame (Boxer Scrapbooks); stamp (Stampin' Up!); stamping ink; pen; cardstock

Oksanna had the perfect striped, patterned paper for her photos, but she only had one sheet and wanted to make a spread. For an imitation, Oksanna cut a square of the striped portion of the patterned paper (from behind her building photo) and then adhered it to white cardstock and dry-brushed blue paint around the edges. To tie in both pages, she accented them with punched and painted red flowers with handcut stems.

Oksanna Pope, Las Gatos, California

Supplies: Patterned paper (Scrappy Cat); metal sentiment (Paper Bliss); fence sticker, oval punch, flower punch (EK Success); acrylic paint; star punch; cardstock

"I wanted to make a patterned paper that matched the one I was using. I simply placed a smaller square on a white 12 x 12" background, brushed paint out to the edge and then removed the square."

This 5 x 7" two-ring binder album is covered in tropical colors and prints to take you on Suzy and her husband's island getaway. Interactive tags, file folders, pockets and cardlike mats curiously engage the reader to pull, lift or open to discover detailed journaling and more photos. Colorful staples, rickrack, ribbons, flowers and sticker sentiments dress the pages with beachy flair. The last pages are 5 x 7" postcardlike photos.

Suzy Plantamura, Laguna Niguel, California

Supplies: Patterned paper, tags, letter stickers (Basic Grey); shipping tag, coin envelope, white tags (Staples); rickrack (MAMBI); staples, eyelets (Making Memories); letter stickers (Creative Imaginations); stamps (EK Success, Hero Arts, Limited Edition Rubber Stamps, Paper Inspirations); ribbon, mini book, bubble letters, ticket stub letters, mini file folder, bubble word, metal frame, wooden flower, label holder, green envelop (Li'l Davis Designs); fabric, ribbon, flowers, brads, Scrabble letters

Standing in the doorway of the plane, I still felt grounded. My jump master asked me, "Do you want to do a BACK FLIP out of the plane?" How could I resist? Six seconds and one flip later, I was touching nothing but air. I felt the exhilarating rush of ADRENALINE as I soared through the sky at 120mph. Within seconds, me and this INVISIBLE element seemed perfectly in tune, yet the thrill of danger sharpened my FOCUS. Somehow, it slowed down time and heightened my senses.

With less than a mile left to fall, the earth quickly EXPANDED, rushing to meet me. I was so aware of the immense SPEED at which I was travelling. At 5,100 feet, the chute expanded and the mad rush of wind suddenly transformed into PEACEFUL calm. Slowly, my ears adjusted to the new volume and I could hear the parachute fabric flapping above my head. GRAVITY reasserted itself as I floated gently to the earth. With a pull of the toggles, my descent slowed and I felt the GROUND under my feet again. The first words out of my mouth were, "Let's do it again!"

If you don't get an exhilarating sense of adventure from Becky's close-ups, her detailed journaling will take you there. Printed on vellum and cropped at an angle as if to float across the page, Becky's expressive journaling takes you on her 5,100 foot freefall. Key words are highlighted with capital letters and ink. The bold bright title and the printed statistics explain the circumstances of her 120 mph adventure. See sketch on CD-ROM.

Becky Fleck, Columbus, Montana
Photo: Chris Fleck, Columbus, Missouri

Supplies: Patterned papers, monogram letters (Basic Grey); vellum; chipboard letters (Heidi Swapp); jigsaw letters, date stamp (Making Memories); stamping ink; cardstock

JUMP elevation: 10,500 ft
free FALL 5,100 ft
speed: 120 MPH

{freefall}

MAR 3 2001

up, up up & {away}

The alarm went off at 5:00 am. I thought I was crazy. But we had to be out the door by 6:00. There was no time to waste. So I hurried into the shower, and then woke Hoyte to do the same. I snuck upstairs and gently got up Ethan, who was much more eager than I to be up at that time. I brought him down to get dressed in the clothes that were already waiting for him and then did the same for his brothers. I finished packing the jackets, blankets and cups and we were out the door into the cold morning for our ride into Louisville, about 30 minutes or so away.

We pulled into the parking lot at the Fairgrounds and the entire place was already abuzz. People were walking quickly toward the gate as there were only a few minutes left until it started. We joined in with the crowd and as we got closer we heard the announcer say it was time to begin. A loud gunshot fired. We rounded the corner and stood transfixed. Out there in a field of the Kentucky State Fairgrounds, over 50 hot air balloons were starting to inflate to participate in the Great Balloon Race - one of the most colorful events of the Kentucky Derby Festival.

The boys just stopped and stared. We all did. It was a breathtaking site. As far as we could see and for more than we could count, balloons kept filling up the sky. Big bursts of flame would shoot up right by us as the pilots were readying their balloons for flight. Ethan and Turner ran from one to another as fast as they could with delight and awe in their faces. We were able to be close enough to any one of them that we actually had to move our stroller as a balloon was lifting off or it would have run into us! The boys had to stay and watch until the last balloon drifted into the sunrise to chase the hare balloon that began the race.

And I knew in that moment that next year, I wouldn't even blink twice when the alarm went off on a cold May morning...

May 1, 2005

When Kelly grudgingly got up early one chilly May morning to go see an air balloon race, all regret quickly lifted when she saw this breathtaking sight. The vivid photos take flight against a simple black background and a rainbow of paper strips. Her upward-moving title adds motion and ties in both sides of the spread.

Kelly Goree, Shelbyville, Kentucky

Supplies: Letter stickers (American Crafts); die-cut symbols (A2Z Essentials); pen; cardstock

Susan used colors and shapes indicative of how her family felt during an amazing Sea World show. A bright backdrop complements the photos while spherical patterns mimic the motion of the action-packed water show. Susan begins her journaling with large letter stickers spelling "fun" and continues the adventure story on a printed transparency. Colorful juxtaposed letter stickers form the title that in French means "circus of the sea."

Susan Easely, Hernando, Mississippi

Supplies: Patterned paper, cardstock stickers, ribbon (Doodlebug Design); rub-ons (All My Memories, MOD); cardstock

ride hard

Tropical Fun

{Hero} [HEE-ROH] 1. UNCONQUERABLE 2. ONE WHO SPENDS TIME IN TELEPHONE BOOTHS PARTIALLY CLAD 3. CHAMPION

BOYS & TOYS

Ride hard boys! Although the signs around say "no wake," "slow speeds." I couldn't help it! I encouraged it! Do donuts, throw water, dunk the jet ski! Why you ask.... For the perfect picture!

Enjoy THE JOURNEY

There is no harm in breaking a few rules to capture the perfect shot. That's what Julie thought when she told her husband and son to kick up the waves and create a wake to catch this action photo. Super enlarged to sport the page, Julie accented the focal photo with a nautical stripe ribbon. Masculine colors and metal accents lend a bit of brawn to the layout.

Julie Johnson, Seabrook, Texas

Supplies: Rub ons (Basic Grey); metal sentiment plaque (Making Memories); wooden tag (Go West Studios); sticker (7 Gypsies); ribbon (May Arts); chalk stamping ink; transparency; cardstock

> **"I wanted to use very few embellishments or color on the layout. I wanted the photo to be the main focus."**

Creating this page was as big of an adventure for Angie as her family rafting excursion. Inspired by the colors in the family photos, Angie digitally created nautical patterned paper with image-editing software along with the rest of the elements. A faux grosgrain ribbon borders the photo accented with a digital word pebble. Stapled ribbon anchored to a metal tag draws the eye as well as fools it with its faux dimension.

*Angie Svoboda, Ord, Nebraska
Photo: Rapid Image LLC, Idaho
Springs, Colorado*

Supplies: Digital patterned papers, ribbons, word pebbles, metal tag, staple by Angie Svoboda (www .computerscrapbookdesigns.com); image-editing software (Adobe Photoshop)

rafting- a family adventure

thrill

FAMILY ADVENTURE ON THE CLEAR CREEK RIVER IN COLORADO. WE WERE THE LAST RAFT OUT FOR THE DAY SO OUR TOUR GUIDE LET US HAVE PLENTY OF TIME TO PLAY. WE SPUN COOKIES AND THE KIDS ALL JUMPED OUT TO GET WET AT ONE POINT. JULY 2005

Shuri rose to an online scrapbook challenge to use the numbers 1, 2 and 3 on a layout. She used clear number stickers on journaling strips to provide the water adventure's statistics. The strips were placed over the enlarged photo of her husband and son canoeing the rapids. Jumbo chipboard letters and stickers on a tag sum up the river experience—wild ride.

Shuri Orr, Dawsonville, Georgia
Photo: Sarah Beth Orr, Dawsonville, Georgia

Supplies: Patterned papers, word stickers, definition overlay, brads, staples (Making Memories); number stickers (SEI); chipboard letters (Li'l Davis Designs); ribbon (American Crafts); stamping ink; cardstock

Patterned papers in bold nautical themes look as though they were made for this water sport photo. When Carrie saw them, she says she just knew she had to create this layout about her son on his wakeboard. The funky papers cut into strips pop against a crisp white backdrop. Staggered ribbons secured with brads provide minimal embellishment to let the photo speak for itself—Dan's a wakeboard master.

Carrie Ferrier, Fort Wayne, Indiana

Supplies: Patterned papers, rub-on letters (Arctic Frog); brads (Creative Imaginations, Karen Foster Design); ribbon (May Arts, My Mind's Eye); cardstock

Looking down from a fourteener gives the phrase "being on top of the world" a whole new meaning. Laura has climbed five of the 53 mountains whose minimal height is quantified in her die-cut title. She backed it with custom-printed cardstock that lists the prestigious peaks and highlights the ones she's conquered. Letter stamps spell out the towering mountains and borders Laura's photographic proof of her big adventures.

Laura Achilles, Littleton, Colorado
Photos: David Achilles, Littleton, Colorado

Supplies: Patterned papers, word sticker (KI Memories); letter stamps (PSX Design); metal-rimmed tag (Avery); metal clips (Rob & Bob); ribbons (Offray, May Arts); photo corners (Heidi Swapp); stamping ink; cardstock

A breathtaking photo of the famous Mount St. Helens takes center stage on this striking computer-generated layout. Kim chose to keep her digital embellishments to a minimum to allow the photo to be the main focal point of the page. Her journaling tells the story of her fascination with the natural wonder and the question left in her mind of what will happen next.

Kim Mauch, Portland, Oregon

Supplies: Image-editing software (source unknown); patterned paper (www.hollymccaigdesigns.com, www.jenwilsondesigns.com); bookplate, stitching (www.shabbyprincess.com)

MY flying lesson

Find *what* brings you *joy* and go there.

To say it was a tough year for me emotionally is an understatement. When dad had his health problems . . . I was an emotional wreck. My hero, the person who instilled a love of teaching in me, was hurting. When dad got really bad, I would constantly question my teaching abilities, and I struggled to keep my emotions together enough to teach. I seriously considered taking a leave of absence so I could focus on my dad and my family. It was this day, however, when we finished the kites and went outside to fly them that I had my "AHA" moment. I realized then that my students had actually helped me get through my trying time. Seeing them every day and keeping it together for them was my therapy. And that day, out flying kites with my kids, I felt joy. For the first time in a long time. My students taught me all about flying on this day. And it's a lesson I'll never forget.

A teacher weathers a life storm, realizing a life lesson came from her students. Both symbolically and literally, Kay's students taught her to fly. Symbolically speaking, her commitment to teaching proved therapeutic, helping her soar through a difficult time. Literally speaking, the class made kites and taught Miss Rogers all about flying them. The story comes to life with colorful paper strips and black accents that complement the photos. See sketch on CD-ROM.

Kay Rogers, Midland, Michigan

Supplies: Patterned papers, acrylic accents, die cuts, rub-ons, buckles (KI Memories); brads (Making Memories); letter stickers (Mrs. Grossman's); photo corners (Canson); cardstock

Long Run Adrenaline Kick The Course Mile Race Pace Distance Medley Outdoor Recovery

2005 RUN 10K

Rebecca's sister and aunt have a shared passion for running. Pictured here at an annual marathon, cool image-editing effects creatively zoom in on the running photo subjects by softly blurring the crowd. Rebecca scanned the logo from the run's T-shirt to create a photo overlay in image-editing software. Because the photos are busy, a neutral background and minimal use of pattern and color help balance this layout.

Rebecca Cantu, Brownwood, Texas

Supplies: Patterned papers (Déjà Views); patterned accents, letter stickers (KI Memories); epoxy sticker (Autumn Leaves); clear sticker (Jock Talk Phrases); rub-ons, metal-rimmed tag, brad (Making Memories); cardstock

Tricia caught this photo with her little "tough guy" donning his dad's high school football jersey like a true pro. She set the photo of Ben atop the 1988 photo of her husband to show the striking similarities. Foam stamps make up the title while handwritten journaling adds a personal touch.

Tricia Kruse, Cedar Bluffs, Nebraska
Photo: Patti Kruse, Eagle, Nebraska

Supplies: Patterned paper, stickers (Scenic Route Paper Co.); stamps (Making Memories, Stampcraft); rub-ons, photo turns (Making Memories); washers (Bazzill); bottle cap; ribbon; staples; cardstock

Patti's son pictured here in the center of the huddle listens intently with his teammates to the coach's game plan. It must have been a good one as the team won this state championship game. Patti journals about the season of hard work on vellum secured with brads. A jumbo chipboard title and a ribbon charm sentiment sums up the group's winning attitude—team spirit.

Patti Hamil, Dawsonville, Georgia

Supplies: Patterned paper, chipboard letters (Zsiage); vellum (Close To My Heart); metal ribbon charm, acrylic paint, staples (Making Memories); mini brads; cardstock

> "During my son's state playoffs, I caught this photo of him kneeling in the center of the group listening intently to the coach. It just captured the moment so perfectly I had to put it front and center on this page."

North Forsyth Lynx
Georgia State Champions

Patrick's team had an excellent season, even topping it off by winning the State Title! The boys worked so hard all season and really played as a team. This was the best group of boys, they were all polite, they got along great together and played well together. We had a wonderful and supportive group of parents too. This picture is between games during the playoffs, Patrick was kneeling down in the center of all they boys. Everyone teased him because he was the smallest player on the team but had the loudest voice. You could hear him in the dugout above all the other boys! This was a great experience for him!   July 2003

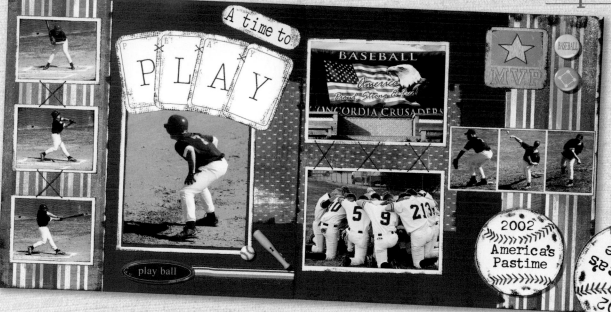

There's a time to play and a time to pray, and for Denise's son there is time for both during baseball season as seen in these photos. She preserved the faith-in-action photos on masculine papers with ink-smudged edges to reflect the played-hard season. A playing-card title adds to the game theme. Floss stitches mimic a baseball. A baseball sticker secured with a brad swings open to reveal Mom's season statistics.

Denise Whittaker, Tomball, Texas

Supplies: Patterned papers (Junkitz); shaker box sentiment sticker (Carolee's Creations); buttons (Hobby Lobby); rub-ons (Imagination Project, Making Memories); 3-D baseball sticker (EK Success); floss; ribbon; stamping ink; cardstock

Karen shows her superstar son in action on the field during his first soccer season. To symbolize his many winning shots, she used patterned tape with jumbo-sized numbers to border the right of the page. Black-and-white letter stickers paired with ink-edged clear letters spell out her super title. Punch labels provide season statistics. See sketch on CD-ROM.

Karen Pedwell, Arana Hills, Queensland, Australia

Supplies: Patterned paper (7 Gypsies); letter stickers (American Crafts, Sticker Studio); patterned tape, clear letters, chipboard label holder, chipboard stars (Heidi Swapp); mailbox letters, staples, acrylic paint (Making Memories); label maker (Dymo); brads; cardstock

SOCCER

FUTBOL

Ben's favorite sport is SOCCER!

TOUGH STUFF

2005

Tricia's son loves the game of soccer, as is evident in the photos of the youngster in action. A green and black color scheme lends a masculine touch while hidden journaling tucked on a tag behind the title details her son's determination for this competitive sport.

Tricia Kruse, Cedar Bluffs, Nebraska

Supplies: Patterned paper (7 Gypsies, Karen Foster Design, Paperbilities); stickers (Karen Foster Design); foam stamps (Making Memories); silver brads; ribbon; fibers; charm; white mesh; acrylic paint

Ben's favorite sport is SOCCER! He does a wonderful job keeping his eye on the ball. He chases the ball at top speed and isn't afraid to have a collision!!

A losing football season is victorious nonetheless for the hard work and character that went into it. Suzy printed her photos of the Seahawks in action with white borders and then tore them for a rugged effect. The mix of black-and-white and color photos pops against the neutral playing ground. Label sentiments add team spirit to the page.

Suzy Plantamura, Laguna Niguel, California

Supplies: Label sentiments (Me & My Big Ideas); vintage ephemera; cardstock

THE SEAHAWKS
Thane Hanson

FOOTBALL PUNCH

CHAMPIONS

COMPETITION

VICTORY

HERO

Thane played football for the Laguna Beach Seahawks in the fall of 2001. He was one of the team captains and the starting quarterback. He also played Linebacker which he enjoyed the most as he loved to tackle. He had a weak offensive line which made it tough to be a quarterback as he was always being tackled before he could pass the ball. The team did not have a very good season, but they had fun. This was probably his last year to play football. Atleast he never got a bad injury!

Tricia's son's first season of tackle football was more than eventful, as is evident in the series of photos on this action-packed layout. A large number "37" identifies who the star athlete is while additional photos tucked in an envelope on the lower right retell other season highlights. Hidden journaling behind the bottom left photo plays off a popular ad campaign.

One season, six games, 7 team touchdowns, 12 announcements of your name, 15 amazing tackles and tons of new friends. Your first year of tackle football. Priceless

Tricia Kruse, Cedar Bluffs, Nebraska

Supplies: Patterned paper (Junkitz); letter stamps (Stampabilities); pull tab (7 Gypsies); number stickers (Scenic Route Paper Co.); ribbon (Hot Off the Press); rub-ons (Chatterbox); sport stickers (Making Memories); stickers (Karen Foster Design); white mesh; twill; staples; key ring; spiral clip; acrylic paint

After a frustrating baseball season spent watching her son through a fence, Christy decided to scrapbook her Mom's-eye view. Metal mesh accents mimic the obtrusive fence while a peeled-back mesh frame reveals the photo Mom sneaked into the dugout to catch. Hand-stitched floss represents a baseball's stitching.

Christy McKay Peake, Elgin, South Carolina

Supplies: Patterned papers (Junkitz); mesh (Paragona); screw eyelet, ball chain (Making Memories); number rub-ons (Heidi Swapp); metal-rimmed tag (Avery); floss (DMC); stamping ink; cardstock

An oversized photo against sporty stripes makes for a quick masculine page. Petra complements the vivid photo with orange and brown accents. Her chipboard title emphasizes the golf cue "fore" while rub-on letters finish the title vertically to say "forever." Acrylic letters brushed with orange paint spell out "golf." A vertical quote from a famous golfer sums up her husband's favorite sport, "the greatest game mankind has ever invented."

Petra Muetzel, Garfield Heights, Ohio

Supplies: Patterned paper (Chatterbox); tab die-cutting tool (Sizzix); chipboard, rub-on letters, acrylic letters (Heidi Swapp); acrylic paint; brads; cardstock

Photos of Linda's raceway visit burst with color in a well-planned design. A 3 x 12" tire pit photo bumps a large red semi-circle as the base of the design. Linda's centered candid portrait creates a focal point for the eye, which is then directed to a triangle of gold found in the sticker title, pit pass and bottom photo mat. The pit pass adds authenticity and dimension to the savvy design.

Linda Harrison, Sarasota, Florida
Photos: Robert Harrison, Sarasota, Florida

Supplies: Letter stickers (Sticker Studio); chipboard letters (Li'l Davis Designs); pit pass (EK Success); corner punch (Marvy); hole punch (Fiskars); cardstock

"I started this page with a white background because I knew it was going to be loaded with color. I put the photo of me in the center so the eye doesn't get lost moving around the page."

A missed deadline results in a team of siblings playing in the same T-ball league. The serendipitous mistake turned to lots of family fun especially for Mom watching from the sidelines. A backside photo of Robyn's children in their jerseys is merged with a smaller posed shot in image-editing software. Robyn also digitally created her journaling and varsitylike title over the focal photo.

Robyn England, Mansfield, Texas

Supplies: Image-editing software (Adobe Photoshop)

Austin just missed the cutoff date to advance to the next league. Lauren and Mackenzie just made the cutoff date. The end result is that the three of you are all on the same t-ball team this year. We have only had 2 games so far and you are all so much fun to watch. Austin is really starting to "get" the game. Lauren tries her hardest but just can't hit the ball very far. Mackenzie likes to throw his glove up in the air and sit down in the outfield. ~April 2005

TEAMMATES

Baseball rivals they may be, but that doesn't stop these two sports enthusiasts from being good friends. Barb placed the striking focal photo on the right side of the layout and used her journaling to balance the left. Repeated circles add unity and rhythm to this fun computer-generated layout.

Barb Hogan, Cincinnati, Ohio

Supplies: Image-editing software (Adobe Photoshop Elements 3.0); patterned paper (source unknown); ribbon, monograph letters (www.shabbyprincess.com); metal rings (www.twopeasinabucket.com)

Friendly Rivals

Daniel and Ryan have been best pals for quite a few years now. they might go to rival schools, but they have a whole lot in common! they are both BLACK BELTS and they even look a whole lot alike!

Daniel & Ryan

spring 05

It's hard to get a good face shot of a moving hockey player, so Amber had her son gear up and pose in front of a black sheet to get this muggy shot. The others were captured by his coach dad from the bench. Amber's handcut title frames the enlarged shot while sporting the team's colors. A quote from a hockey pro overlays the photo printed on a transparency. See sketch on CD-ROM.

Amber Baley, Waupun, Wisconsin
Photos: Warren Baley, Waupun, Wisconsin

Supplies: Patterned paper (Creative Imaginations); transparency; stamping ink; cardstock

Living in the state of the winning Super Bowl team proved pure excitement for Renee's family. By throwing a game-day party complete with snacks and team jerseys, Renee's family showed team pride. She preserves the event with fun photos and journaling housed inside a foldout crowned with a woven Steelers patch. Names of the football players are printed on gold cardstock strips in black for a custom border in team colors.

Reneè Foss, Seven Fields, Pennsylvania

Supplies: Steelers patch (EK Success); ribbon (Offray); rub-on letters (Déjà Views, Doodlebug Design, KI Memories); metal-rimmed tag (Making Memories); cardstock

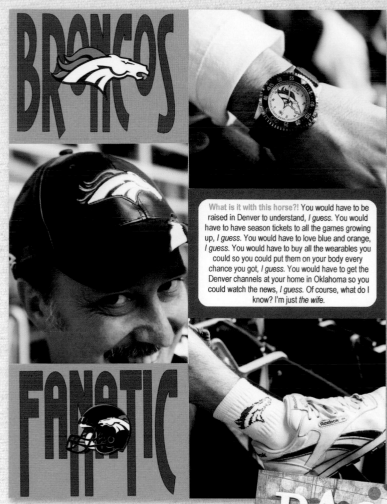

What is it with this horse?! You would have to be raised in Denver to understand, *I guess*. You would have to have season tickets to all the games growing up, *I guess*. You would have to love blue and orange, *I guess*. You would have to buy all the wearables you could so you could put them on your body every chance you got, *I guess*. You would have to get the Denver channels at your home in Oklahoma so you could watch the news, *I guess*. Of course, what do I know? I'm just *the wife*.

With joking sarcasm, Charrie documents her husband's obsession with the Denver Broncos football team despite the fact that they live in Oklahoma. Close-up shots of his logo-driven wardrobe are a dead giveaway that he truly, as her title suggests, is a Broncos fanatic. A blue handcut title accented with the horse logo and a Broncos helmet is blocked with orange in the spirit of the team's colors.

Charrie Shockey, Ardmore, Oklahoma

Supplies: 3-D stickers (EK Success); cardstock

When Amber's family was offered tickets to see a preseason Green Bay Packers game without the harsh Wisconsin weather, they jumped at the chance and had a great time as seen in these photos. Amber used patterned papers with a gritty, dirt-smudged look to match the rugged sport theme. An embossed chipboard star shines for the winning team. Amber's paper strip journaling recalls the exciting experience.

Amber Baley, Waupun, Wisconsin

Supplies: Patterned papers, chipboard star (Basic Grey); star brads (Queen & Co.); star silhouettes, chipboard letters (Heidi Swapp); embossing powder (Scraptivity); stamping ink; watermark ink (Tsukineko); cardstock

When we were offered tickets to a preseason football game, we jumped at the opportunity to give the boys their first Packer experience in comfort. No snow...no layers upon layers of clothing...no hand warmers tucked inside their mitten and boots... Instead, we would cheer on our team under the warmth of the sun. We were disappointed to watch Brett Favre from the sidelines as a spectator of the game, rather than the future Hall of Fame Quarterback in action. But still, we were surrounded by the roar of the crowd, and we left the stadium victorious. We couldn't offer the boys a TRUE Packer Experience, but we hope the memories of this day in Lambeau Field stay with them a lifetime.

The score, the crowd, the hecklers, the entertainment, the near-catch of a fly ball—these are all reasons Angela's family enjoyed their day at the ball field. Sporty stripe patterns layered with circle die cuts and brads emulate the rowdy spirit of excitement at a baseball game. The scoreboard and smiling sports fans shine against the bright backdrop. Rub-on letters sum up the tradition—American pastime.

Angela Walker-Morgan, Findlay, Ohio

Supplies: Patterned papers (Imagination Project); rub-ons (Royal Manufacturing); brads (American Crafts)

Though Melissa documents her daughter's field trip with this page, she also recalls her own childhood memories combing that same bay for treasures. Grainy earth tone patterned papers entwined with netting capture the gritty feel of the beach and echo the net fishermen in the photo. Sporting oversized waders, Melissa's daughter with her shining smile is evidence of the day's adventures.

Melissa Ackerman, Princeton, New Jersey

Supplies: Patterned papers, folio closures (Basic Grey); epoxy phrase and letter stickers, cardstock letter stickers, rub-on phrases (K & Company); netting; transparency; cardstock

"This layout holds a special place in my heart. I thought the papers and netting captured the feel of the beach in the bay on a somewhat cloudy but exciting day."

Everything is fascinating through the eyes of a child, even a simple leaf. Samantha dedicates this page to precious moments spent with her son and uses his photo as a focal piece. A small close-up of his hand is framed and pops against an orange mat. An orange paper strip borders the page and holds fabric letter tabs spelling out his name.

Samantha Walker, Lehi, Utah

Supplies: Patterned papers (American Traditional Designs, Karen Foster Design, Scrapworks); fabric letter tabs (Scrapworks); brads (Making Memories); clear frame (American Traditional Designs)

Watching the movie *It's a Bug's Life* on screen is cool, but coming face to face with a neon green bug in your back yard is downright surreal. To document her children's fascinated faces as they study the bug, Jessie super-enlarged the focal photo for a larger-than-life effect much like the experience itself. The backyard adventure unfolds in a photo montage complemented by hand-painted title blocks and a vertical border.

Jessie Baldwin, Las Vegas, Nevada

Supplies: Fabric (Michael Miller); metal accents (Magenta); pigment paints (Plaid); cardstock

A garden tour provided great adventure for Danielle's family. Her boy's intrigue with the surrounding beauty is highlighted as the focal photo while a photo montage of the samples of nature was made more vivid with increased saturation. A dry-embossed and sanded flower with a butterfly pendant gracing the center accents the page. For a soft effect to the 8½ x 11" spread, Danielle rounded the outer corners.

Danielle Thompson, Tucker, Georgia

Supplies: Patterned papers (Chatterbox, Scrapworks); embossing template (Lasting Impressions); stylus; sanding block (Scrapper's Block); fibers (Maya Road); butterfly pendant; gold paint pen (Marvy); cardstock

Ever since I was a little girl, I have eagerly anticipated the change of seasons. There is something magical as the cycle of nature makes its course each year. I love witnessing the birth of nature each spring, followed by the lazy days of summer where flowers bloom into maturity and the world is filled with green. Then there is nothing quite like the first crisp fall day, where you can literally smell the change of season in the air. I love at the end of fall, when nature winds down for its long winters nap. I look forward to bundling up in sweaters and scarves anxiously awaiting the first snow fall as if it is baptizing the earth and making it clean once again.

While many prefer the more moderate climates that many places on the earth has to offer, I consider myself very lucky to live in Utah, where I am blessed to witness the change of seasons, year after year after year.

Kristi loves the changing of the seasons and salutes each one on this page. Vivid close-ups celebrate each seasonal best with simple solid mats. Behind Kristi's favorite season, fall, is hidden journaling. On the adjoining page, Kristi defines the seasons and explains her favorite aspects of each.

Kristi Lee, Alpine, Utah

Supplies: Photo corners; dot eyelets (Doodlebug Designs); rub-on letters (Chatterbox); chalk stamping ink; cardstock

Winter

win·ter (wĭn′tər). The usually coldest season of the year, occurring between autumn and spring, extending in the Northern Hemisphere from the winter solstice to the vernal equinox, and popularly considered to be constituted by December, January, and February.

Winter will always bring happy memories to me. If you take one look in my closet, you will clearly see that winter is one of my favorite seasons to dress for. There is almost nothing more exciting for me than going to the store and picking out a new sweater, or long sleeved shirt to wear during the chilly months.

Winter will always bring fond memories of my childhood, spending many hours playing in the snow with my brothers. I remember distinctly making sure that there were enough Wonderbread bags for each of us to line the insides of our boots with to help prevent our feet from getting wet. I even recall (now don't quote me on this) one year there being enough snow that we piled it up and actually jumped off of the roof of the house and slid down the slope to the ground.

It's fun to watch my children eagerly anticipate the snow much as I did as a child. Its fun to watch them build snowmen, and snow forts, throw snowballs, and sled, exactly as I did as a kid. But you know what, it's even more fun to join them and be a kid again myself!

Spring

spring (sprĭng). The season of the year, occurring between winter and summer, during which the weather becomes warmer and plants revive, extending in the Northern Hemisphere from the vernal equinox to the summer solstice and popularly considered to comprise March, April, and May; a time of growth and renewal.

After a long winter, spring is exactly what my soul needs. I eagerly greet each spring with wonder as I watch the world turn into bloom. It is amazing to me as the miracle of re-birth is evident everywhere you look! I can't wait for the first signs of daffodils to greet me with their cheery yellow. What more could one possibly need than a world covered in color!

Spring is also home to one of my favorite holidays – Easter. Not only do I look forward to my favorite chocolate; Cadbury's Mini-Eggs, (which you simply cannot feel guilty about eating around that time of year), but I look forward to celebrating the resurrection of our Lord and Savior, Jesus Christ, for without his sacrifice we would not live with our Father in Heaven once again.

Summer

sum·mer (sŭm′ər). The usually warmest season of the year, occurring between spring and autumn and constituting June, July, and August in the Northern Hemisphere, or, as calculated astronomically, extending from the summer solstice to the autumnal equinox; A period of fruition, fulfillment, happiness, or beauty.

Ahhhhhhhhh Summer. I LOVE the lazy days of summer. I love the kids being out of school, and lounging around in our jammies until noon if we so desire. I love not having a thing to do or a care in the world other than just being with my children. I love a picnic in the park or a swim in the pool. I love the taste of a butterscotch- apple- crisp. I love the smell of hamburgers cooking on the grill. I love staying outside in until dark and feeling the left over warmth of the day still lingering in the cement. I love celebrating the birth of our nation with family, food and fireworks! I even love taking a break from civilization and spending a few days camping in the mountains.

Oh and did I mention that I love lounging around in my jammies until noon??? I love those lazy, lazy days of summer!

Autumn

au·tumn (ô′təm). The season of the year between summer and winter, lasting from the autumnal equinox to the winter solstice and from September to December in the Northern Hemisphere; fall.

It's true! Fall is and always has been my favorite season of the year. There is something truly magical to me as the smell of autumn creeps into the air. So many wonderful things in my life have occurred in the fall, and as the leaves change their colors, I am always reminded of the many happy memories that autumn holds such as meeting my best friend Tracey, marrying him, giving birth to our first child, moving to Germany, and most recently giving birth to our precious baby boy.

I have nearly as much fun helping my girls select Halloween costumes as they do, and I eagerly look forward to spending time with family on Thanksgiving and eating at least one slice of Pecan Pie and not even feeling guilty about it.

I marvel as the world turns ablaze with color and love the joy that a simple pile of leaves can bring to my girls.

Autumn is and always will be my favorite season of the year.

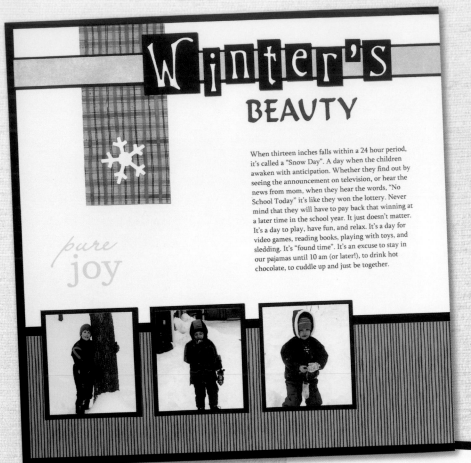

Winter's BEAUTY

When thirteen inches falls within a 24 hour period, it's called a "Snow Day". A day when the children awaken with anticipation. Whether they find out by seeing the announcement on television, or hear the news from mom, when they hear the words, "No School Today" it's like they won the lottery. Never mind that they will have to pay back that winning at a later time in the school year. It just doesn't matter. It's a day to play, have fun, and relax. It's a day for video games, reading books, playing with toys, and sledding. It's "found time". It's an excuse to stay in our pajamas until 10 am (or later!), to drink hot chocolate, to cuddle up and just be together.

pure joy

Michelle's title has double meaning as a blanket of snow is beautiful and as a fresh abundant covering may bring a "snow day" to spend with her children. She journaled about the blessed event on a white background with printed sentiments. Small photos show her kids bundled up for adventure. The focal photo of the snow-covered landscape, silhouetted and then layered with craft foam, pops with dimension.

Michelle Maret, South Bend, Indiana

Supplies: Patterned papers (Bo-Bunny Press); metallic paper (Tree House Designs); letter dies and snowflake (QuicKutz); craft foam; cardstock

"I wanted to create my own paper, so I combined multiple fonts onto a white background and printed it. It was easy and fun and took almost no time to do."

together

play   fun

sledding

winter   time

beautiful

By creating a photo montage in image-editing software, Christine managed to get eight small snapshots plus one focal photo on her winter wonderland page. Patterned papers in icy blues and lavenders accented with glass pebbles and a silver metal title mimic the beauty of snow and ice sculptures as seen in Christine's photos. She printed her journaling on a soft blue in a contrasting indigo, detailing the chilly day's heartwarming adventures.

Christine Stoneman, Cumberland, Ontario, Canada

Supplies: Patterned papers (K & Company); metal stencil letters (Clearsnap); glass pebbles (EK Success); cardstock

snow and ice sculptures

We like to get down to see the snow and ice sculptures every year. It is important to go see the ice sculptures on the first weekend, before the inevitable warm spell melts some of them! This year we were early enough that we saw the artists making a lot of the ice sculptures. We were going to go for a skate on the canal, but I need new skates and we never think of this until we are standing beside the canal saying, oh yeah, I need skates ☺. So we walked on the ice instead, watching the crowds and stopping for a hot chocolate. We went for lunch at a little restaurant and then headed home. The following week we went across to Hull to see the snow sculptures. They were spectacular. There were also several snow slide areas and a wonderful display by some Inuit dancers. Both days that we went were beautiful and sunny and the festival was a big hit.

WINTERLUDE

Kathleen moved into her new home in the dead of winter, and was greatly surprised when spring awakened a botanical paradise in her back yard. A photo sampling of the blooming surprises form a colorful montage on a rounded photo mat. The beautiful flowers need no embellishment, but they share a mat with a painted and gloss-coated chipboard title and Kathleen's printed journaling telling of all her nature discoveries. See sketch on CD-ROM.

Kathleen Summers, Roseville, California

Supplies: Patterned paper (Chatterbox); chipboard letters (Heidi Swapp); acrylic paint; clear gloss medium (Ranger); acrylic tag (Queen & Co.); flower brad; transparency; pen; cardstock

at our new house

When we made the offer on the house in February, many of the trees were bare, the wisteria was just a mass of tangled sticks, and the rose bushes were small things with nubby branches. What surprises Spring brought! After we moved in we were so surprised at all the beautiful things blooming and all the incredible colors. As if our new home wasn't lovely enough before, now it was a botanical paradise too! All of these photos are flowers and blooms from our very own yard. And I didn't even get the tulips, freesia, cherry blossoms… the list goes on! I'm already looking forward to next Spring.

Bloom

I wouldn't choose pink to decorate my home and it's not a shade of lipstick that I would wear. It's not the colour that I would choose as my favorite and I don't have a daughter who wears pink frilly clothes.

But in my gardens, pink dominates. It is the colour of rebirth and new beginnings. It symbolizes nature and perpetual bloom. In my gardens.

PINK
pink
pink rules

Katrina is not a girly-girl, but when it comes to her garden, she expresses her feminine side with a sea of pink. Vibrant flower close-ups bloom with detail and are boldly contrasted with a citrus green background. Katrina printed her journaling in coordinating green and emphasized the word "pink" with varying fonts and shades of pink. A gem-centered flower adds frill while rounded corners lend a soft touch.

**Katrina Murphy,
Petersborough, Ontario, Canada**

Supplies: Patterned paper (KI Memories); flower (Prima); corner rounder (EK Success); cardstock

Seize the Day

[beau·ti·ful]

Like in a fine painting each single stroke is neccesary. You would not see the beauty of a single stroke, but all together they create a beautiful work of art. I am a single stroke in God's beautiful work of Art this canvas we call life.

~ Quote by Bob Perks/life ~

34 years old

Heather 1971

A pensive photo and a favorite poem give insight into Heather's depth of heart. Her black-and-white portrait positioned as though she is peering off the page is layered over an enlarged rose photo with the poem printed directly on it. A row of tied ribbons provides a border to the beautiful photo. Hints of paisley patterned paper shine from beneath the transparency title.

Heather Preckel,
Swannanoa, North Carolina

Supplies: Patterned paper (My Mind's Eye); printed transparency (Creative Imaginations); frame charms (Nunn Design); brads; bead; pen; cardstock

Spring has sprung on Angelia's page with citrus green, fresh yellow and pretty pink papers. Angelia cut the patterned papers into wavy strips and pieced them together as a bright backdrop with rounded corners. A row of brad-center flowers bloom beneath the photos of Angelia's daughters posing with a sure sign of spring—tulips.

Angelia Wigginton, Belmont, Mississippi

Supplies: Patterned papers (Anna Griffin); rub-on seal (Basic Grey); flowers (Prima); mini brads; epoxy stickers (Provo Craft); cardstock

bumble bee · bumble bee

butterflies and blossom

FLOWERS & SHOWERS
THE FLOWERS OF SPRING OCCUPY PLACES IN OUR HEARTS WELL OUT OF PROPORTION TO THEIR SIZE ~ Gertrude S. Wister
SPRING
SPRING WET SHOWERS
FLOWERS MILLIONS BLOOMING
BIRDS SWEET SINGING
MEMORIES IN BLOOM

I simply could not resist these tulips blooming in a friend's yard up the road from us. It seemed the perfect spot to take some spring photos, and you two were happy to pose, as long as you could run barefoot for a few minutes. Tulips just say "spring" to me. April, 2004

Lisa's daughter, pictured posing in a sunflower field, glows amongst a sea of gold and brown papers and custom accents. Lisa double matted the photos with yellow and brown cardstock and set them against a mazelike patterned paper indicative of the sunflower field. Stamped sunflower images in brown ink come to life with watercolor pencils and are blended with a brush of water.

Lisa Turley, Chesapeake, Virginia

Supplies: Patterned papers (KI Memories); chipboard title (Li'l Davis Designs); sunflower stamp; watercolor pencils, paintbrush (Royal & Langnickel); brown stamping ink; cardstock

Sunflowers symbolize the passage of time in this touching computer-generated layout. Kim chose two striking close-up photos to place at the top of her page, while floral patterned papers, the title and journaling balance out the bottom. The yellow and green color palette evokes a feeling of sunny warmth.

Kim Mauch, Portland, Oregon

Supplies: Image-editing software (source unknown); letter tiles (www.digitaldesignessentials.com); bookplate, striped paper, stitches (www.hollymccaigdesigns.com); word paper (www.jenwilsondesigns.com)

sunset
Sunset
sunset

Sunset
OVER THE
sound

The sunset over the sound in the Outer Banks is beautiful. I love the sense of peace I feel listening to the soft lapping sound the waves make on the sound shoreline while the sun slowly sinks to the water.
August 2005

A serene sunset basks on a simple background. Lisa used black cardstock as a contrasting photo mat and block for her title and journaling. Watercolor patterned paper reflective of the setting sun's colors complements the photos. Thin patterned paper strips anchored with brads are indicative of the sun's rays.

Lisa Turley, Chesapeake, Virginia

Supplies: Patterned paper (Murdock County Creations); rub-on letters (KI Memories); mini brads; white gel pen (Sakura); cardstock

"These photos were taken during a vacation in the Outer Banks of North Carolina. It's so peaceful to watch the sunset over the sound. I kept my page simple to keep the focus on these amazing photographs."

Kelie created a tropical backdrop with layered strips of summery papers to complement her daughter's photo. A ribbon bunch centered with a summer-sentiment bottle cap borders the photo with bright color and texture. For added beachy- and girly-flair, Kelie slid summer charms onto colored bobby pins and then secured them to the photo. A printed transparency begins her title, then letter beads strung on spiral clips finish it with fun.

Kelie Myers Brown, Tahlequah, Oklahoma

Supplies: Patterned papers, die-cut letter (Basic Grey); ribbons; bottle cap (Li'l Davis Designs); brads; bobby pin; charms; letter beads; spiral clips; label holder; dimensional-glue pen (Sakura); transparency; stamping ink; cardstock

Susan captured this autumn splendor while driving through her neighborhood one Sunday morning. She created a complementing backdrop to the rich foliage with brown cardstock and earth tone patterned papers. Fibers delicately outline a photo on each page while hand-stitching adheres her journaling block.

Susan Kohlman, Maynard, Massachusetts

Supplies: Patterned papers, letter stickers (Arctic Frog); fiber (www.farflungcraft.com); cardstock

A series of fall photos graces this computer-generated page expressing gratitude for the colorful season. Denine wanted to use black-and-white photos but didn't want to lose the color of the leaves. She choose to combine both color and black-and-white in her focal photo. Stitching and mini polka dots on a rust background add a finishing touch to this colorful layout.

Denine Zielinski, Nanticoke, Pennsylvania

Supplies: Image-editing software (source unknown); patterned paper (www.jenwilsondesigns.com); brads, stitches (www.shabbyprincess.com); frame (source unknown)

Lisa captures the warm colors of her favorite season with patterned papers in orange, gold and brown. She outlines the patterned photo mats of her daughter surrounded with fall harvest with a black glaze pen for dimension. Flowers cut from patterned papers are accented with the glaze pen as well as sparkly jewels.

Lisa Turley, Chesapeake, Virginia

Supplies: Patterned paper, rub-on letters, letter stickers (Scenic Route Paper Co.); flower jewels (Heidi Swapp); 3-D glaze pen (Sakura); cardstock

The adventures and encounters of Maegan's son and his friends while at a pumpkin patch are captured in these photos. She came up with the words to her chipboard title from her daughter's science book. Geometric and daisy patterns add a fresh spin to the seasonal experience while earth tones hint at fall.

Maegan Hall, Virginia Beach, Virginia

Supplies: Patterned papers, stickers (KI Memories); chipboard letters (Scenic Route Paper Co.); frame kit (Heidi Swapp); rub-ons (Chatterbox); cardstock

Kim's black-and-white wedding photo is the star of the page graced upon pink patterned papers. Black ribbons, stamped stitches and black-inked edges tie the photo to the page. A stamped acetate heart slightly overlays the photo while a clear definition sticker borders it.

Kim Kesti, Phoenix, Arizona

Supplies: Patterned papers (Anna Griffin, The Paper Co., Memory Lane); definition sticker (Making Memories); ribbon (May Arts); stamps (Hero Arts); acetate hearts (Heidi Grace); stamping ink; cardstock

This black-and-white photo, snapped just after the bride and groom were pronounced husband and wife and before the awaited kiss, blissfully pops against hot pink floral papers. Susan boldly displays the chipboard, letter rub-ons and letter brad title to her cousin's wedding page on a large pink circle with stitched edges.

Susan Weinroth, Centerville, Minnesota

Supplies: Patterned paper (Urban Lily); letter brads (Queen & Co.); chipboard letter (Basic Grey); chipboard flowers (Maya Road); rub-on letters (Making Memories); cardstock

> "I wanted to use bright pink, black and white to contrast with the photo. I placed everything in the center of the page to help draw attention to the photo."

For a soft, muted effect, Linda changed her daughter's wedding photo to black-and-white and then slightly sanded and inked the edges. A dreamy mix of pink patterned papers against a wine background sets the stage for this formal affair while a white satin ribbon underscores a love sentiment whispered in light pink.

Linda Garrity, Kingston, Massachusetts

Supplies: Patterned papers (7 Gypsies, Anna Griffin, Autumn Leaves, Colorbök); preprinted transparency (Karen Foster Design); die-cut sticker sentiment (Making Memories); stamping ink; sandpaper; cardstock

The preparations leading up to a bride's big moment of walking down the aisle are captured on this page. Leilani used a colored focal photo and a series of wallet-sized black-and-whites to show the details. A vellum printed title and journaling block add to the bridal setting and tell Leilani's secret hair battle that no one would have ever known otherwise. A beaded flower and satin ribbon add bridal elegance. See sketch on CD-ROM.

Leilani Brooks, Encino, California

Supplies: Beaded flower (Leeza Gibbons); ribbon; date stamp (Making Memories); vellum; cardstock

Look at the photo and walk alongside this happy bride and groom. The black-and-white focal photo takes center stage on the blissful wedding layout. Dominique added a harlequin border to the top and bottom while two touching quotes perfectly encapsulate the journey ahead of this lucky couple in love.

Dominique Quintal,
Longueuil, Quebec, Canada
Photo: Julie Robillard,
Granby, Quebec, Canada

Supplies: Patterned paper (Basic Grey, Chatterbox); ribbons, fibers (Wal-Mart); rub-ons (Autumn Leaves); fasteners (Junkitz); stamps (source unknown); fabric; stamping ink

BRIDE & GROOM

A great marriage is not when the 'perfect couple' comes together. It is when an imperfect couple learns to enjoy their differences.

Dave Meurer

Love makes our house a home

A striking use of black and white supplies sets a formal stage for Jamie's sister's wedding photos. The black-and-white bridal close-up accented by a series of cardstock stickers stands timelessly against a black mat and white cardstock distressed with gray paint. The eye is then drawn to a punch of color in the small photo, revealing a secret moment between the bride and groom.

Jamie Harper, Phoenix, Arizona

Supplies: Cardstock stickers (Pebbles); acrylic paint, word stamp (Making Memories); cardstock

experience

True love

Love

Togetherness

love n. endea... ness, affection, wa... closeness, intimacy, attachment sion, infatuation, crush, e amour, ardor, rapture, desire "Our highest word, and God." — Ralph Waldo E... ance of friendship an... Colton. "Frien... "The h...

[ad·ven·ture]   [mem·o·ries]   fa·mi·ly

I love you

MAY 22 2003

Prisca created this wedding tag book as a precious keepsake for her sister. Black-and-white photos tell the story of the momentous day. Prisca captured everything from the exchanging of the rings to candid moments of laughter. She added an abundance of lace, tulle, ribbons and machine-stitching to add a feminine air and grace.

Prisca Jockovic, Morestel, France

Supplies: Patterned paper (Daisy D's); ribbons (May Arts); flowers, brads (Making Memories); stamps (Fontwerks, PSX Design); stickers (Anna Griffin, K & Company); rub-ons (Heidi Swapp); lace; strass; pearl string; tulle

IT'S TIME TO GO!

let's get this show on the road.

Candid snapshots capture the anticipation and excitement of a wedding, from the bridal party primping to the farewell at the reception's end. Cammie created a clocklike embellishment from punched squares set in a circle and angle cut ribbon for the clock's hands. The accent begins the photo series of her friend's wedding and supports her time-theme die-cut title. Simple circle and half-circle accents play up the excitement.

Cammie Churdar, Greenville, South Carolina

Supplies: Letter dies (QuickKutz); ribbon; circle cutter (EK Success); stamping ink; cardstock

MADE FOR LOVE

Sara and Joe had a fairy tale wedding. You can almost hear Sara giggling, her eyes sparkling. They recited their vows beneath the shelter of the trees, letting their promises lift to the sky, where I am sure God was smiling upon them. Their son, Bailey, had enough of the photo shoot and insisted on being held in his mother's arms. Of all the glamorous photos, these candid ones are my most favorite, showing their love for each other and Bailey. They were meant to be a family, to be together forever. Maya Angelou wrote about love, "Each of us is created of it, and I suspect, each of us is created for it." On that fine day, Sara, Joe, and Bailey were living her poem. May they continue and write their own. They were made for this, made for love.

This bride and groom truly were made to be in love. Jennifer used floral embellishments, swirls and retro patterned papers to add a sense of fun to the page. A fitting quote from poet Maya Angelou perfectly encapsulates the story of this couple in love, while the repeated circular elements add unity to the page.

Jennifer Santos-Hamer, Virginia Beach, Virginia
Photos: Robert B. Hamer, Virginia Beach, Virginia

Supplies: Patterned paper (Fontwerks); chipboard letters, ghost flowers (Heidi Swapp); flowers (Prima); foam stamps (Heidi Swapp, Making Memories); brads (Making Memories); acrylic paint; brad; cardstock

Sherry caught this candid shot of her kid brother with his new bride after all the formalities. She super-enlarged the photo to be the page focus and accented it with a large jeweled-heart buckle and frayed fabric strips. Sherry fondly reflects on the beginning of young love on her transparency journaling and includes wise wedding wishes for the couple's future.

Sherry Wright, West Branch, Michigan

Supplies: Patterned papers, epoxy stickers (Autumn Leaves); transparency sentiment (Daisy D's); transparency; fabric strips; jeweled heart buckle (Dritz)

> **"When I saw this photo I knew it captured the true essence of the love between my brother and his wife. I think these are the moments we must always remember."**

Creative photo treatments focus on wedding-day details on this page. Sherry altered the photo of the bride's bouquet and then used it as a backdrop to her transparency title overlay. An ornate circle frame placed over a photo zooms in on the groom placing the ring on his bride's finger. A succession of flowers and hearts stamped in pearly paints dress the page in bridal elegance.

Sherry Wright, West Branch, Michigan

Supplies: Patterned paper, epoxy sentiment sticker (Autumn Leaves); heart stamp, pearly acrylic paint (Heidi Swapp); flowers (Prima); metal frame (Nunn Designs); cardstock

dream *in color*

discover your inner artist...

SAM

up
close and personal

I lift up my eyes

to the hills where does my help come from?

My help comes from the LORD,

the Maker of heaven and earth.

He will not let your foot slip

He who watches over you will not slumber;

indeed, He who watches over Israel

will neither slumber nor sleep.

The LORD watches over you –

the LORD is your shade at your right hand;

the sun will not harm you by day,

The LORD will keep you from all harm

He will watch over your life;

the LORD will watch over your coming and going

both now and forever more.

What is the true essence of the creative soul that lives within you? Do you record your personal characteristics, quirks and idiosyncrasies? Perhaps your hopes, dreams, passions, pleasures and even longtime favorite hobbies make a presence on your scrapbook pages. All these things make up the person that is uniquely you, and taking time to chronicle them is not only an exercise in self-discovery but in self-expression. So look deep within yourself or those you love, and record the true fibers that make that special person timeless in your heart.

HEART LIKE

Blessings

...are precious in His sight...

Jesus loves the little children

"Hermie the Common Caterpillar" by Max Lucado. Oh how I love that book! The story is about a _____ that continues to ask God why He made him so common. God's reply, "I'm not finished with you _____ giving you a heart like mine." We read this story before bed the other night. Afterwards I asked you _____ thought God was finished with you yet. You replied, "No, He's giving me a heart like His." God has _____ already started. You are one of the kindest, most gentle hearted girls I know. You see people for wh_____ are on the inside, not what's on the outside. The perfect example would be your new friend Michael _____ came home the first day of school and told me about this nice boy who sat at your table. It wasn't _____ lunch with you later that week that I learned that Michael was in a wheelchair and physically challe_____ you, it didn't matter that he couldn't walk. You looked beyond his physical appearance to see wh_____ the inside. Yes, God has already started giving you a heart like His.

I am so blessed.
I praise God every morning for the blessings that he has given me. Blessings like food, a good home, warmth, the lack of financial stresses. But more importantly, I praise him for the blessings of love, family and forgiveness. You see, I don't deserve to have a baby so wonderful, or a husband for that matter. But my God is an amazing, forgiving, loving God. He can forgive someone who has sinned as much as I have sinned and turn around and bless them one hundredfold. Noah is our little angel. Swinging. Smiling. Just happy. Always. What an amazing blessing he is to Kris and I. I thank God for him and Kris everyday. Today, I was just hanging out at the park... in Awe of my blessing.

Celebration Park
March 9, 2005

i have been...

faith
confidence
wisdom
grace
trust
selflessness
humility
gentleness
patience
self-control

I want to be a better mother, a better wife and companion, a better me. I want to care about the things that really matter. I want to leave behind insecurity and fear and let go of the _____ that i rely too

_____ess when you get to a certai_____ _____int in your life, you begin _____ _____tion if you are the per_____ th_____ _____t to be. I do. It's _____ ea_____

An honest self-assessment led to this reflective, completely digital page. Josie created a layered collage of patterns, text and photos to represent the many improved facets she strives for. Her focal self-portrait is feathered into the collage accompanied to the side by the list of traits she hopes to gain. Her title is on the top layer of the collage and overlaps her introspective journaling.

Josie Celio, Diamond Springs, California

Supplies: Image-editing software (Adobe Photoshop Creative Suite)

Jayne created this touching computer-generated layout on the eve of her 35th birthday to celebrate the rite of passage to the next exciting stage of life. Youth may be slipping away in the eyes of others, but Jayne sees that being "middle-aged" holds many promises. The close-up photo is the focal point of the page while swirls and patterns lend a bohemian look.

Jayne Richards, Wayne, New Jersey
Photo: Helen O'Daniel, Prineville, Oregon

Supplies: Image-editing software (Adobe Photoshop); digitial kit (www.jenwilsondesigns.com); frame (www.scrapbook-elements.com)

After seeing this photo of herself taken by her husband, Linda decided to use it on an "all-about-me" page, documenting her current phase in life. She lists her circumstances and wishes on journaling strips bullet-pointed with brad-centered flowers. She chose a mostly monochromatic color scheme to give a serene focused feel. The punch of color adds femininity and ties her photo to the page.

Linda Harrison, Sarasota, Florida
Photo: Robert Harrison, Sarasota, Florida

Supplies: Patterned paper (Arctic Frog); die-cut letters (QuicKutz); fabric letter tab (Scrapworks); flowers (Prima); brads; circle punches; cardstock

> "When I saw this photo, I realized I should not only document what I look like at this moment, but also what my focuses are. These are the types of pages I would love to have been able to see about my mother and grandmother as they were going through life."

My **FOCUSES** Right Now

- To play with Robby every chance possible.
- To make sure Rob is doing what he loves.
- To continue to feed my soul by creating.
- To pamper myself more.
- To have another child.
- To laugh often.

2005

I've been thinking a lot lately about gratitude and how important it is to have a grateful heart. One of the most important things that I want my girls to learn from me is thankfulness. We are all blessed in so many ways and we need to reflect on our blessings and truly be thankful for them. It's easy to be thankful when everything is going great and you're coasting along, but it's especially important to have a grateful heart when things are going wrong, when life seems to be turning you upside down. It's times like that when we need to remember our blessings and choose to be happy.

written: december 2005

give thanks

count your blessings

Maria created this page to pass on a legacy of thankfulness to her daughters. Her gratitude journaling on torn paper is accented with stitching and a ribbon tab. A digital swirl graphic is printed on the kraft background and highlights her rub-on title.

Maria Burke, Steinbach, Manitoba, Canada
Photo: Howard Doerksen, Steinbach, Manitoba, Canada

Supplies: Patterned paper (Provo Craft, SEI); brads, rub-ons (SEI); digital swirl graphic (Rhonna Farrer); cardstock

Colleen discovered she symbolically used color on her layouts to reflect her life issues. Once sticking to dark shades to reflect sadness and confusion, Colleen is now renewed, moving past difficult issues and reacquainting herself with bright colors and happy page topics. She celebrates this milestone with a self-portrait on a spunky floral patterned paper coupled with bright stripes. A wooden frame with Colleen's initial further personalizes the page.

Colleen Stearns, Natrona Heights, Pennsylvania

Supplies: Patterned papers, cardstock stickers, wooden frame, wooden tag (Chatterbox); ribbons and fibers (Chatterbox, May Arts); letter buttons (Junkitz); stamping ink; cardstock

A self-portrait set against rich saturated colors and a mix of funky patterns results in a hip all-about-me page. Liana changed her photo to black-and-white and then added touches of color using image-editing software. The photo is further highlighted with a decorative corner punch pierced through the mat as well as the photo. Liana's self-proclaimed descriptive words are printed on coin envelopes bound with a paper fastener.

Liana Suwandi, Wylie, Texas

Supplies: Patterned papers (Basic Grey); chipboard letter (Heidi Swapp); decorative punch (Anna Griffin); ribbon (KI Memories, Making Memories); flower (Michaels); coin envelopes; paper fastener; staples; brad; acrylic paint; library card; cardstock

pieces...

...of me

The Story of:
WIFE/DIL/SIL
BEST FRIEND
COLLEAGUE
PHOTOGRAPHER
ARTIST
DAUGHTER
MOTHER
INDIVIDUAL

A photo montage of interests and a self-portrait hint at the many facets of Rachel. She details the "hats" she wears in a handwritten list aged with one of her shown favorites—distress ink. A scrolly yet whimsical hand-drawn border inspired by an online store is evidence of one of Rachel's many listed talents—art.

Rachel Carlson, Highlands Ranch, Colorado

Supplies: Patterned paper (Daisy D's); rub-on stitches (Autumn Leaves); stickers, "The Story of" card (7 Gypsies); letter stamps (Fontwerks); antique floral brads (Making Memories); flowers (Prima); leaf punch; stamping ink; pen; cardstock

Amy savors the best aspects of motherhood on printed journaling strips outlined with faux stitches and highlighted with jumbo brads. A backdrop of heart and striped patterned papers creates a warm setting for the heartfelt sentiments. Amy's self-portrait reveals her sheer joy in being a mom and is wrapped with a grosgrain ribbon on love sentiment papers accented with a hugs-and-kisses charm.

Amy Brown, Eclectic, Alabama

Supplies: Patterned papers (Rusty Pickle); rub-ons (Making Memories); brads (All My Memories, Making Memories); acrylic letter (LazerLetterz); hugs-and-kisses charm (Go West Studios); cardstock

Cradling my baby in my arms, comforting her

Following her every move a step behind, catching her if she falls, encouraging her if she is unsure

Feeling every cry of pain etched in my heart when she hurts herself

Hearing the name Mommy in the sweetest voice possible, bringing tears to my eyes

Little moments becoming surreal, and realizing that some moments are more important than anything

Knowing that I would give up anything and everything for her

BEING MOM

sunday

It has not always been easy being a single Mom and working full-time outside of the home. The weekdays are hectic to say the least. Balancing a job, motherhood, and housekeeping never left me much time to myself. Sure, I have always had a half an hour here and an hour there, but that was just not enough to satisfy me. So, Sundays were born. Sunday became a day for me...a day for Denine. Ryan now leaves me every Sunday to spend some quality time with his Dad, and I am left to myself. I am left to do whatever it is that I want to do or not do. The day revolves around me. I can choose to clean the house if that is what I want. Or, I can choose not to. I can talk on the telephone to friends, or I can take a nap. It's my call...all day long. I am not one to sit idle, so most Sundays are busy; but busy with things that I love. Scrapping (while watching television), playing on the computer, gardening, or reading are some of the things that often fill my "me" days. Sundays go by fast, but I enjoy every minute. These days bring me joy. These days help me to regroup. These days help me to find satisfaction for myself. The satisfaction that in turn helps me to be a better Mom, worker, and housekeeper. These days help me to be a better "me."

gardening

talking

eye *reading* 250 for ideas for scrapbook 15 hot cards it

computing

scrapping

just for me

Denine celebrates her favorite day of the week—Sunday—her "do whatever I want to" day with a design emulating a sunburst. Her semicircle journaling block forms the sun's center, and an arced title shines like rays set against a sunflower backdrop. A series of photos of Denine's hobbies were labeled with text in image-editing software and show how she loves to spend her "just-for-me" day. See sketch on CD-ROM.

Denine Zielinksi, Nanticoke, Pennsylvania

Supplies: Patterned paper (Basic Grey, KI Memories); tags (EK Success); cardstock

A reflective look at life's choices led to this pensive page by Annette. Her self-portrait shines against bright patterned paper. She symbolically created a path through her journaling with two colors of pieced-together cardstock on which she printed the details of her life's path. The rub-on and chipboard title is underscored with a knot-tied ribbon.

Annette Pixley, Scappoose, Oregon

Supplies: Patterned paper (MOD); flowers (Prima); chipboard letters; ghost flower (Heidi Swapp); rub-on letters (KI Memories); brads; cardstock

the path

We all travel a path in life. Each path is different – different obstacles, different choices, different outcomes. And it is those things that make us who we are.

I can look back now and see the points in my path that have made the difference, the times when the choices or obstacles made a large impact on my life today. My parents divorce was a determining factor in my path, for in choosing to live my own life and not follow in theirs I was choosing to start a path all my own. The choice to end an old relationship and start a new one with Brian was an important decision – one that has made the largest (and happiest) difference in my life. The choice to stay at home with Chase when he was born has made me into the mother I am today and contributed to the love and happiness in our family. And by choosing to move to Scappoose we have found a community that we happily call home.

I don't know where my path will lead me next. I don't know what choices or obstacles lie ahead. And I can't tell you the outcome. But I do know that wherever the path leads me next, I am blessed to have a loving family by my side.

Annette, 8/9/006, age 31

With a husband and a son to usually scrapbook about, Danielle relished in the opportunity to make a girly "all-about-me" page. She printed the grayscale childhood self-portrait in three different sizes on blue cardstock and then cut and layered them with dimensional adhesive. The funky large graphics were made by enlarging symbols from a dingbat font and then printing them on green and pink cardstock. Hand-drawn scribbles add further whimsy.

Danielle Thompson, Tucker, Georgia

Supplies: Patterned papers, letter stickers (American Crafts); buttons (Bazzill); paper flowers (Prima); fun foam; rub-on flowers (KI Memories); pink acrylic paint; white gel pen; decorative scissors; cardstock

You may think this page is an "all-about-me" with Kimberly's title and self-portrait. But her hidden journaling tucked inside a file folder reveals she believes it's ultimately all about God and who he created her to be. She shares a few insightful details about her life in her own handwriting. A bucklelike accent made from notched paper and photo turns secured with brads draw attention to her stamped title.

Kimberly Garofolo, Phoenix, Arizona

Supplies: Patterned paper (Me & My Big Ideas); letter stamps (Wendy Speciale Designs); velvet letter stickers (Making Memories); file folder, stamping ink; cardstock

As though a yearly account of his life, Sam begins his journaling with the year then reiterates his title and page theme throughout his journaling with "I am being Sam." Sam's introspective story is as bright as his backdrop of patterned paper strips. A mix of inspiring woven thread sentiments hint at Sam's attitude on life while rub-on numbers document his age.

Samuel Cole, Woodbury, Minnesota

Supplies: Patterned paper (Daisy D's, Imagination Project, KI Memories, Paperfever); rub ons (Déjà Views, Imagination Project); letter stickers (Imagination Project); woven thread sentiments (Me & My Big Ideas); star punch (Emagination); circle punch; stamping ink; staples; cardstock

Minimal accents on neutral cardstock create a tranquil retreat for Linda's self-portrait from a vacation. Centered on the page, the photo is delicately cornered with a silk flower secured with a decorative brad and scrolly rub-ons. Gingham ribbon underscores the photo and journaling, adding subtle texture. Printed in a simple font directly on the background, the journaling, destination and date memorialize the peaceful getaway.

Linda Harrison, Sarasota, Florida
Photo: Robert Harrison: Sarasota, Florida

Supplies: Rub-ons (Foofala); ribbon (Offray); decorative brads, silk flower (Jo-Ann Stores); die-cut letters (QuicKutz); cardstock

Ambitious
Bold
Caring
Devoted
Easy going
Friendly
Giving
Humorous
Inspiring
Joyful
Kind
Loving
Motivated
Nice
Organized
Patient
Quick~Witted
Relaxed
Special
Ticklish
Uplifting
Vivacious
Wise Cracker
X~tra Special
Youthful
Zestful

Now You Know My

Kim shares a glimpse of herself with this self-portrait and list of self-proclaimed descriptive words on tags. The tags of printed adjectives are strung with ribbon through eyelets and are listed alphabetically, giving playful meaning to her chipboard ABC title.

Kim Hughes, Roy, Utah
Photo: Sunset Photos, Binghamton, New York

Supplies: Patterned papers (ChatterBox, Memories Complete); self-adhesive vellum; decorative brad, rub-on letters, chipboard letters, acrylic paint, stamping ink, sanding block, eyelets (Making Memories); ribbon (Offray); corner rounder (Creative Memories); cardstock

Having achieved great personal growth, Amy journals about the freeing experience on a circle-cut transparency outlined with machine-stitching. Chipboard letters with button centers are accented with a trail of stitching as though they are dancing across the page. A circle cut into strips becomes a flower accent to highlight her self-portrait. A torn patterned paper strip adds a splash of pattern and color.

Amy Howe, Frisco, Texas

Supplies: Patterned paper, letter stickers, rub-ons (Basic Grey); chipboard flowers (Making Memories); acrylic paint; stamping ink; cardstock

to be me.

free

all of my life i have been afraid to be myself- afraid of people not liking the real me. i don't know if it's age or life experience, but i am finally at a point in my life where i just don't want to live trying to be someone or something that i am just not. i do want people to like me; to have friends. but i want them to like me because i am real & genuine. i have to say that after 27 years of trying to be the person that others want me to be, i feel so happy & free just being the person that i know i am. it feels good to be me.

A poem Dee found in a catalog inspired this reflective self-validating page. Dee printed the poem directly onto the background. Her portrait, taken by her husband, is framed with polka-dot photo corners, white distressed rub-ons, pink gems and a heart with a stapled "me" sentiment.

Dee Gallimore-Perry, Griswold, Connecticut

Supplies: Patterned papers (Autumn Leaves); rub-ons (Heidi Swapp, Li'l Davis Designs, My Mind's Eye); heart accent (KI Memories); poem (Female Creations Catalog); button (Making Memories); photo turn (7 Gypsies); preprinted transparency (Autumn Leaves); ribbon, photo corners, gems (Heidi Swapp); die-cut flower (Sizzix); word sticker (American Crafts); definitions (Embellish It); clear decorative sticker (Creative Imaginations); sandpaper; thread; staple

A mom's admission of being unhip to fashion sets the humorous tone for this page. With a bold mix of contemporary patterns and funky fonts, you wouldn't guess the page artist herself is the one claiming to be fashion-challenged. From the trendy barcode date to the arrow that points directly to her forehead, Jodi creates a cool page that contradicts her self-confessed title.

Jodi Heinen, Sartell, Minnesota

Supplies: Patterned paper (KI Memories); letter stickers (KI Memories, Sticker Studio); rub-ons (My Mind's Eye); cardstock

"When I think about being cool or hip, I always think of black and white. This color scheme worked perfectly to match the theme of my layout."

UP CLOSE AND PERSONAL

journey

I CAN HEAR AND I CAN LISTEN. I CAN HEAR AND HAVE WONDERFUL TALKS WITH MY GIRLS. I CAN HEAR THE WORLD AROUND ME. I CAN HEAR MUSIC, I CAN HEAR LAUGHTER, I CAN HEAR SORROW. I AM FOREVER GRATEFUL.

gift

RICH discover me value PONDER

Laura created this gratitude journal for abilities easily taken for granted. A black-and-white close-up of each celebrated body part accompanies Laura's thankfulness. Coordinating patterned papers, stickers and tags along with a mix of stapled ribbons, flowers and brads accent the pages. The book is made of three folded 10 x 4" cardstock sheets adhered back-to-back. A patterned paper strip secured with stapled ribbons forms a fauxbinding on the cover.

words cannot express how grateful...

Laura Achilles, Littleton, Colorado
Photos: David Achilles, Littleton, Colorado

Supplies: Patterned papers (Basic Grey, Chatterbox, Die Cuts With a View); stickers, tacks (Chatterbox); ribbon (May Arts); paper flowers (Prima); mini brads (Karen Foster Design); rub-ons, staples (Making Memories); stamping ink; cardstock

As a pledge to self, Sharon vows to be more optimistic about all aspects of her life in her handwritten journaling on this page. Her pensive self-portrait shares the journaling block as a photo mat. Bright pink geometric and floral patterned paper strips stitched to the background set a positive stage for this renewal page. Pink daisies accented with page pebbles add a happy touch.

Sharon Laakkonen, Superior, Wisconsin

Supplies: Patterned papers (Imagination Project); acrylic flowers (Heidi Swapp); page pebbles (KI Memories); letter stickers (Chatterbox); letter tiles (Michaels); ribbon (May Arts); staples; stamping ink; pen; cardstock

Fast

F O R W A R D

Looking Ahead & Having Hope. Instead of dwelling on the past, I have decided to focus on the future. To me the future always looks brighter... It is filled with promise. Who knows what great things are in store for me? If I can turn myself away from the "What if's" and think about the "What May Bes", I see a year that could be the best yet! So, this is my goal for myself. I want to see the positive in every area of my life. I want to think about good things. I want to do good things for others and I want to truly be happy no matter what comes my way.

This is me, Julie Johnson. Pure & Uncut. Up until 2000, I had a pretty normal life. I got married in 1999, bought a house, and had a baby on the way. I was labeled normal. I led a normal life, drove a normal car, lived in a normal house, and worked a normal job. In March of 2000, my world came crashing down. My husband was in an accident, he was in a coma and fighting for his life. I was no longer normal. I was devastated, stressed, sad, alone, but I was also strong, courageous, and faithful. For two months while my husband was in a coma, we were fighters, him for his life, and me for my unborn child. I listened to everyone tell me how to feel, what to eat, not to cry, to go home and get sleep. I just wanted to be normal again, to be average, to be normal, to be unnoticed, to be a normal person and to return to my normal life. Months past and Darryl got better, my life was normal again. Two weeks later I lost my job because I had made the decision to take care of my husband and child. Again I was labeled, unemployed, devastated, broke. This spiraled me down into depression. Yet another label. Lucky for me, life started to become normal again. Finally. Normal is good, normal is great. I am happy with normal. Darryl started to become more independent and I was no longer pregnant. Then all the sudden it came down like a ton of bricks.. I wasn't normal at all, I beat this, I won. I fought the beast, I fought the devil. I am a strong person, I am a good person. I am me, Julie Johnson, mother, wife, daughter, and friend. I am EXTRAORDINARY.

La eLeD

Pulling through very difficult circumstances in her life found Julie redefining the label "normal." She underscored the word several times in her printed journaling that splits the page with an enlarged photo of herself pensively looking at the water reflecting on the revolutionary experience. Simple patterned paper strips and handcut hearts accent the moving story.

Julie Johnson, Seabrook, Texas

Supplies: Patterned papers, sticker strip (Autumn Leaves); buttons (SEI); ribbon (Making Memories); chipboard sentiment (EK Success); cardstock

Heather documents her New Year's resolutions with an optimistic backdrop of bright colors and fun shapes to mat her extreme photo close-up. The patterned paper is actually wrapping paper that inspired the circle theme that brings movement to the page. Heather printed her resolutions on paper strips stapled to the background. Letter stickers in a mix of colors spell out her title along with letter buttons secured with brads.

Heather Preckel, Swannanoa, North Carolina

Supplies: Patterned wrapping paper (Target); letter stickers (American Crafts); brads, letter button (Junkitz); photo corners (Heidi Swapp); ribbon (May Arts); staples; cardstock

A mom's hopes for her daughter to dream big come to life in color on this page. Courtney created a watercolor mural on notebook paper to vividly play up her dreamy childlike theme. Coordinating daisy patterned paper continues the youthful theme and allows the black-and-white photo of Courtney's daughter to stand out. Handwritten sentiments add personal touches to Mom's wishes for her daughter.

Courtney Walsh, Winnebago, Illinois

Supplies: Patterned paper (KI Memories); notebook papers; letter stickers (source unknown); rub-on flowers (KI Memories); watercolors; pen; cardstock

in Shoes

Courage

Hope

There is comfort to be found in a new pair of sneakers, the hope and promise of a new beginning. They represent change a new goal and challenge that goal to be healthy-to be more active. They represent the desire to be the perfect size 10 even when you know that is not possible. The joy comes in the first step taken and becomes increased with each pound lost. The comfort found in that moment is priceless and for that is what I continually strive for in each new pair of sneakers.

dream

Shiny new sneakers have big dreams to fulfill as Chiara uses them symbolically as the wind beneath her wings. A focal photo shows her inspiration source along with smaller close-ups. The shoes' sporty stripes are played up with touches of teal awakened by bold yellow. Her heartfelt journaling printed directly on geometric patterned paper is supported with inspirational sticker sentiments.

Chiara Osborne, Bayside, New York

Supplies: Patterned paper, sticker sentiments (Arctic Frog); letter stickers (source unknown); cardstock

dream as big as the ocean blue big

The first time I heard the song "Dream Big" by Ryan Shupe & the Rubberband, I thought of you instantly. You and that raggedy old dolphin you sleep with every night. Dolphy has seen better days – he used to be pink and he used to have 2 eyes. None of that matters to you though. I just wanted you to know that each night as you drift off to sleep with your ocean companion – I watch you and hope that you will have a fabulous life.

"cause when you dream it might come true. So when you dream, dream big." Ryan Shupe

Sweet dreams.

Whisper-soft monochromatic colors create a pillowy setting for this dreamy photo. Jodi changed the photo of her daughter to black-and-white to cure an otherwise busy background and then added a yellowish hue with image-editing software. A collection of gold-tone charms makes an eclectic border, emulating perhaps the visions dancing in this sleepy girl's head. A song quote plays up Jodi's "dream big" theme.

Jodi Heinen, Sartell, Minnesota

Supplies: Metal charms (Nunn Design); acrylic letters (Jo-Ann Stores); chipboard stars (Making Memories); buttons (Buttons Galore, Making Memories); flowers (Making Memories, Prima); wooden frame (Chatterbox); acrylic sentiments (KI Memories); watch charms; metal photo corners; brad; cardstock

"Yellow has always been a color that reminds me of sleep and dreams. I wanted the layout to have a soft, dreamy feel to it."

Life isn't always a series of perfectly straight edges, lined up in neat rows.

No, sometimes it's ChaOs defined by torn strips and crooked paths.

I guess the trick is to remember where you're going and hope that you don't accidentally stray from your intended direction.

I find myself getting lost sometimes. Don't know where it is I'm going, or where I came from. Just wandering, seemingly aimlessly.

Then I remember the reasons why I'm here. The blessings of a family who loves me. The things that really matter. Suddenly, the path appears....and I am

home again.

LOST & found

Becky's thoughtful journaling articulately expresses the sometimes-confusing path we all follow on the journey of life. But she's reaffirmed that in the end we find ourselves on the path that brings us home. A mixture of fonts adds impact to the words, while a pensive black-and-white photo of Becky gleans insight into her inner self.

Becky Thompson,
Fruitland, Idaho

Supplies: Patterned paper, fabric (Imagi-nation Project); rub-on letters, brads (Making Memories); stamping ink

my

Going back to college at the age of 40 takes a lot of determination and courage! Even though my hubby Bill has a college degree and a job that he loves, he has always wanted an engineering degree. Through the years, the timing never seemed right for him to go back to school.

Finally, shortly after his 40th birthday, Bill took the plunge to fulfill this life-long dream. He enrolled in two difficult classes and he now spends evenings and weekends studying. I know it will take awhile before he graduates, but I truly admire him for taking the first step towards fulfilling his dream. Besides, I cannot stop smiling when I think that I am married to a HOT college boy, again!

COLLEGE

boy

At the age of 40, Sharon's husband is college bound and, boy, is she proud. She celebrates his fulfilling of a lifelong dream with a masculine mix of retro-patterned papers that complement his photo. Paper flowers add rhythm to circles, while thin black paper strips stitched between each patterned strip give the eye a rest. Stamped letters on handcut tags and jumbo letter brads spell out the title.

Sharon Laakkonen, Superior, Wisconsin

Supplies: Patterned papers (A2Z Essentials); letter brads, mini brads, photo turns (Queen & Company); flowers (Prima); letter stamps (Fontwerks); stamping ink; cardstock

A woman's tremendous strength and faith while battling breast cancer inspired this page. To convey Joanne's grace, strength and elegance, Courtney chose a timeless color palette in rich tapestry patterns. The story is printed on cardstock with rounded corners for a soft effect. Courtney says the photo of Joanne without hair is the only evidence of her battle. "She is now completely healthy and out there changing the world."

Courtney Walsh, Winnebago, Illinois

Supplies: Patterned papers (Daisy D's); rub-ons (Chatterbox); ribbon (EK Success, May Arts); brads (Basic Grey, Making Memories); cardstock

The wait to adopt a baby seemed like an eternity for Melodee and her husband. And now that they've been parents to a precious son for 5½ years, the time is flying by. Melodee printed the entire adoption story from anticipation to the arrival on vintage patterned paper. A photo shows Mom feeding her blessed son. Rub-on sentiments and die-cut definitions bring added meaning to the heartfelt page.

Melodee Langworthy, Rockford, Michigan

Supplies: Patterned papers (Autumn Leaves, My Mind's Eye); die-cut definitions (My Mind's Eye); rub-on sentiments (7 Gypsies, Scenic Route Paper Co., Making Memories); epoxy (Creative Imaginations); charm (7 Gypsies); chalk stamping ink

Lisa savors the moments of motherhood and realizes her great blessing even if she only has one child. She created a clocklike element with circle-cut paper, number stickers and a clock hand anchored by a button. The clock points to the photo of her and her miracle daughter, and the chipboard fairy signifies her dreams as a child to be a mother. See sketch on CD-ROM.

Lisa VanderVeen, Mendham, New Jersey

Supplies: Patterned paper, stickers (Basic Grey); chipboard fairy, chipboard words (Provo Craft); button (Foofala); circle cutter (Creative Memories); clock hand; cardstock

Leora admires her daughter's passion for living life to the absolute fullest. She chose this analogy to perfectly articulate her desire for her daughter to continue to live a life full of "color." She cropped the paper in Photoshop to create a curve for added visual interest.

Leora Sanford, Pocatello, Idaho

Supplies: Image-editing software (Adobe Photoshop); Mocha Sunshine kit digital paper (www.thedigichick.com); Gina Cabrera flower (www.scrapbook-bytes.com); brad (www.shabbyprincess.com)

God's Presence

Every day as I look around, I am comforted by the presence of God. He is my source of joy. Every earthly thing that I feel could give me even an ounce of comfort or joy is nothing compared to being in God's presence. His joy is everlasting; eternal. I could not fathom a life without Him. Nor could I go one day without giving Him the praise He is worthy of. His love for me is so great and His mercy endureth forever. As I see the wonder of His creations, it's just that much more of a reminder of how much He actually loves me. In the quiet times of the day when He shows me the beauty in the little things, I feel the comfort He provides for me. His gift for me is the breath of life. He gives me a chance every day to come into His presence and feel His blessings. For that I am very thankful; and although I am grateful for my family, friends and the material possessions that He has allowed me to possess, they could never provide for me the everlasting comfort and joy that being in His presence provides for me. He is the ultimate source of my *comfort and joy* . . .

A montage of stunning photos graces Marsha's computer-generated page about her appreciation and recognition of God's presence in her life. Impactful journaling expresses her gratitude for all her earthly blessings and her utlimate comfort and joy she finds in her steady walk of faith. See sketch on CD-ROM.

Marsha Zepeda, Bakersfield, California

Supplies: Image-editing software (Adobe Photoshop CS2); digital papers (www.scrapbook elements.com)

AMAZING Grace

By grace you have been saved, through faith – and this not from yourselves, it is the gift of God.
Ephesians 2:8

When you were a baby you were never one to just fall asleep on your own. You always required nursing to calm your spirited body into slumber. When you grew into toddlerhood and gave up nursing, I would rock you in the rocking chair and sing to you. Most of the time I was happy to oblige. You were not much into cuddling as a baby or toddler so I enjoyed our quiet time together. This was virtually the only time I got to hold you.

Our routine would go something like this. We would get into the rocking chair in your room. You liked to be held like a baby, the back of your head in the crook of my left arm and your legs draped over my right arm. Over time, I settled on the same songs to sing. I would start with "Jesus Love Me", go into "Jesus Loves the Little Children", then "I Am So Glad that Jesus Loves Me", and finish with "Everybody Ought to Know" (learned that one from your Daddy). That was our little medley. You usually fell asleep after several rounds of "Everybody Ought to Know". But, if you were still stubbornly awake I would add "Amazing Grace", the only hymn I know by heart. Sometimes I would have to sing the whole song, sometimes you'd be out before I finished the first verse.

You are now 4 years old and I haven't rocked you to sleep for almost 2 years. I often miss that quiet closeness we shared when you would fall asleep to the sounds of my voice and the powerful truths of God's Word. I hope that those truths have been etched into your heart forever. I will always treasure those precious moments we spent together.

A bedtime ritual of a mother singing her toddler to sleep with spiritual songs is sweetly preserved. If Mimi's boy wasn't asleep after several songs, she moved into "Amazing Grace." This memory inspired her title that begins with a stamp word and moves into a die-cut Bible verse. The edges of the verse, sleepy photo and bold patterned paper are lightly sanded and quieted with a soft blue backdrop.

Mimi Schramm, Colton, California

Supplies: Patterned paper; die-cut Bible verse (Crossed Paths); transparency; letter stamps (River City Rubber Works); beaded flowers (Xyron); brads; stamping ink; cardstock

STOP and BREATHE

Stop and breathe, I have to tell myself daily. I have changed so much since having children, better in some ways and still need a lot of work in others. I have never been a laid-back type of person. I have always been more of an outgoing in your face, out spoken type. Somehow, with children, that is not such a great mix. I pray everyday for strength and guidance to make this trip on earth a good one, to love my husband with a pure and compassionate heart, to love my children with gentle but firm guidance and somewhere in the middle still love myself and go to bed with a clear conscience That is what I pray, however, that is not how most of my days Go in the real world, so I will continue to pray.

Becky takes a moment to stop and smell the flowers in the photo on this page, but as a busy wife and mother, she strives daily to find balance and peace. A flower transparency placed over yellow cardstock ties in her photo. Ribbons stitched and gathered form a custom flower accent.

Becky Heisler, Waupaca, Wisconsin

Supplies: Patterned paper, letter stickers (Basic Grey); transparency (KI Memories); chipboard; ribbon (May Arts, Offray); stamping ink; cardstock

> "I wanted to symbolize the circle of life, so I printed my journaling on the lower half of the large circular block."

When Maegan heard the words to her inspired title while listening to Christian radio, she decided to instill an attitude of gratitude in her daughter with this page. Her daughter's photo is accompanied by her handwritten list on cardstock strips of everything she is thankful for at her young age. A gratitude charm dangles from a girly ribbon bordering her photo while Bible verse reminders to give thanks are printed on tags.

Maegan Hall, Virginia Beach, Virginia

Supplies: Patterned papers (Daisy D's, Mustard Moon; Scenic Route Paper Co.); ribbon (American Crafts); word charm (All My Memories); chipboard letters (Heidi Swapp, Making Memories); sentiment sticker (EK Success); silk flower; acrylic paint; stamping ink; sandpaper; cardstock

I am Thankful for:
God
food
family
Shelter
drink

"Giving thanks always and for everything to God the Father in the name of our Lord Jesus Christ." Ephesians 5:20

"You are my God, and I will give you thanks; you are my God and I will exalt you. Give thanks to the Lord, for he is good; his love endures forever." Psalm 118:28,29

"And whatever you do, in word or deed, do everything in the name of the Lord Jesus, giving thanks to God the Father through him." Colossians 3:17

"Be joyful always; pray continually, give thanks in all circumstances, for this is God's will for you in Christ Jesus." 1 Thessalonians 5:16-18

"Don't worry about anything; instead, pray about everything. Tell God what you need and thank him for all he has done." Philippians 4:6

Gratitude

attiTuDe

Faith-based wisdom is at the heart of this page, supported by layers of patterned paper and black-and-white symbolic photos. As encouraging as a psalm, Sharon's inspirational journaling and handcut title assures, "choose joy, receive comfort." Handwritten on premade tags, the journaling is accented with stamped faith images. Topped with fibers and secured with a black hair fastener that slides off, the tag book opens to reveal Sharon's faith journey.

Sharon Bissett O'Neal, Dunedin, Florida

Supplies: Patterned papers, fibers (Basic Grey); metal plaque (Making Memories); acrylic paint (Delta); faith stamps (Blue Hand Stamps, Greenbrier, Hero Arts, Inkadinkado, Limited Edition Rubberstamps, Paper Inspirations, PSX Design, Rubber Stampede, River City Rubber Works, Wendi Speciale); scalloped scissors; stamping ink; hair fastener; pen; cardstock

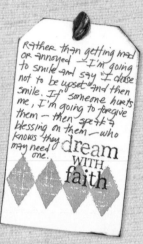

A message to walk by faith even through the most difficult circumstances is instilled by Christine on this page. A mixed-media title begins her testimony, accompanied by the words to a Christian pop song to support the faith-walk theme. Christine recorded her struggles and inspired strength in a hinged book with a photo of her in prayer on the cover. Dark and light colors symbolize despair and hope.

Christine Brown, Hanover, Minnesota

Supplies: Patterned paper (Chatterbox); mesh (Magic Mesh); faith sentiment (Reminders of Faith); paper flowers (Prism); ribbon snap (Melissa Frances); chipboard circle (Bazzill); chipboard letters (Heidi Swapp, Making Memories); metal accents (Paper Bliss); crystal lacquer (Sakura); metal letters, hinges, metal word, date stamp, definition (Making Memories); printed twill (7 Gypsies); cross charm (Westrim); tags; stamping ink; transparency; ribbon; acrylic paint; pen; cardstock

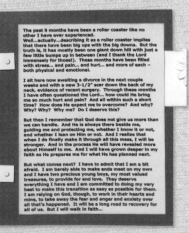

Maria wanted to capture the precious evidence of her young daughter's faith before these stories are forgotten. A black-and-white photo may give a small glimpse of Maria's daughter's young face at age 3, but stories on three journaling blocks give great insight into her faithful heart, old beyond her years. A mix of patterned papers and ribbons in ruby red, brown and cream are rich accents to the heartfelt story.

Maria Burke, Steinbach, Manitoba, Canada
Photo: Frieda Doerksen,
Steinbach, Manitoba, Canada

Supplies: Patterned papers (Making Memories, Scenic Route Paper Co., Scrapworks); letter stickers (Basic Grey); ribbon (May Arts); cardstock

CHILDLiKe FAiTH

NAME _____ FOLIO 7

Sarah, you make me so proud! At the young age of 3 you already have an understanding of God. Sometimes when we make crafts or color pictures, you tell me, "this one I'm making for God".

A couple mornings ago you said to me, "Mommy, I want to die". Needless to say, that took me by surprise. When I asked you why, you said, "so I can go to Heaven and be with Jesus".

Last week when we had to have Joey put down, I explained to you that Joey was a very old cat and that he was really sick and that he had died. I told you that Joey was gone and we wouldn't be able to see him again. You simply smiled and said, "Joey's not gone Mom, he's in Heaven flying with Jesus". Your simple childlike faith is so beautiful. I just know that God looks down on you with such joy. You are a daily inspiration to me Sarah!
March 2005

Out of the mouth of a babe came the convicting question, "Who are you talking to?" Embarrassed that her daughter didn't recognize what it meant to pray, Laura says she realized her family needed to go to church. She printed the life-changing moment on a transparency. It overlays a photo of her daughters doing what they now remind the family to do each night—bow in prayer.

Laura Swinson, Pearland, Texas

Supplies: Patterned paper (KI Memories); letter stickers (Arctic Frog, Li'l Davis); wire loop (Westrim); black halo eyelets (Cloud 9 Design); beads; ribbon; charm; transparency; cardstock

It Took my child's words

I had the best of intentions. I mean, I was raised in church and had always just assumed that my children would be, too. After Mackenzie was born we kept going to church pretty regularly. She went to Sunday school just like I did, learned all of the same songs that I learned as a child, and heard the same bible stories that I had heard. But then when Cassidy was born it just got harder to make it to church and easier to come up with excuses. When we did make it there she would cry when we dropped her off, and would still be crying when we picked her back up. Eventually, we just quit going. Oh, how easy it was to fall into that trap. We'll just go back someday I kept thinking to myself. Well little did I know, I would get a huge wake-up call. And it probably came straight from the BIG MAN himself. One afternoon we met up with my sister, her husband, and their youngest daughter at a restaurant. Upon getting our food, my brother-in-law suggested that we pray. I urged the girls to bow their heads and close their eyes. Cassidy looked at me like I had two heads. (Major foreshadowing as to what was about to happen). She was sitting next to my brother-in-law and had been playing with him since we got there. He started with the prayer. I looked over to see how she was behaving, and noticed that she was looking from person to person wondering why we were all looking down with our eyes closed. Then she turned her head to my brother-in-law, listened to him for a second with a puzzled look on her face, and to my total embarrassment she loudly asks, "Who are you talking to?" He finishes the prayer and says, "I'm talking to God, don't you even pray at home?" We all laughed it off, but it was a big deal to me. I felt like a huge failure of a mom. Here I was supposed to be a Christian, and my youngest daughter didn't even know what it was to bow your head and talk to God. I knew then that things had to change. I told my husband that we needed to go and visit that church that we had been talking about visiting forever, and we did. We started praying before dinner and at bedtime. (We're working on that one) I guess as embarrassing as it was, I needed to hear my daughter ask that question to make me realize I wasn't raising her the way that I needed to. She now reminds us to pray before we eat. Hearing her talk about it and seeing my two girls talk to God gives me so much comfort and joy. I'm comforted in the fact that they are living in a household that praises God, and so joyful that they know how precious they are in HIS eyes.

A gorgeous spring day spent swinging with her son at the park put Paula's blessings in perspective as she records on this page. Circular patterned paper with a spiritual message adds movement and meaning to enhance the page theme. Paula's heartfelt journaling printed on a transparency is cut to fit and adhered with paint on the circular background. Sentiment labels and threaded buttons highlight the photo of her blessed son.

Paula Barber, Allen, Texas

Supplies: Patterned papers, sentiment labels (Crossed Paths); letter stickers, buttons (Chatterbox); floss (DMC); concho (Scrapworks); transparency; paint (Making Memories); stamping ink

After a beach vacation spent with family, thoughts of blessings were on Melanie's mind, inspiring this gratitude page. She celebrates her love for faith and family with an upbeat color scheme of blue and brown. The soft colors complement her triple-matted desaturated family photo. Stitched borders and inked edges add a comforting down-home feel.

Melanie Douthit, West Monroe, Louisiana

Supplies: Patterned papers (Scenic Route Paper Co., SEI); stickers (American Crafts, KI Memories); ribbon, epoxy charm (Crossed Paths); chipboard letters, decorative tape (Heidi Swapp); decorative brad, date stamp (Making Memories); chalk (Craf-T); cardstock

The wisdom and unconditional love of a child is revealed in a conversation with her mother. Lisa documents her daughter's compassionate heart on the journaling block shared with the photo mat. A complementary color scheme coordinates with the photo. Lisa handcut flowers from patterned paper to accent the photo and cut hearts from the same flower design. A handcut majestic font adds meaning to the spiritual title.

Lisa Dorsey, Westfield, Indiana

Supplies: Patterned papers (Arctic Frog); cardstock

"I am always inspired by my daughter's gentle and giving nature. I wanted this layout to document her sweet disposition."

Michelle hopes to pass on a legacy of faith to her daughters and for them to take it into the world. Her prayers are printed on a tag hidden behind the photo of her daughters. Printed on textured cardstock with inked edges, the photo takes on a heritage look. Map patterned paper cut into a circle creates a globelike title backdrop. Metal letters and stamps spell out the commandment.

Michelle Layman, Raymond, Washington

Supplies: Patterned paper (Karen Foster Design); textured cardstock (Bazzill); metal letters (Jo-Ann Stores); foam letter stamps, acrylic paint (Making Memories); small letter stamps; photo turns (7 Gypsies); ribbon; paper clip (EK Success); library card (Brodart.com); stamping ink; twill tape; staples; cardstock

Time alone is the coveted thing Vicki's title alludes to. As a busy wife and mother, this once social butterfly now really cherishes a moment to herself. She matted her pensive self-portrait on a collage of patterned paper squares. Ribbons and daisy trim adhered to the back of the page burst to a frilly daisy overlapping her photo for a feminine touch.

Vicki Boutin, Burlington, Ontario, Canada

Supplies: Patterned papers, ribbon (Making Memories); chipboard (Imagination Project, Pressed Petals); letter stickers (EK Success); pen; cardstock

It never used to be something I gave much thought. In fact, it was the exact opposite. In the past I loved to be surrounded by people and be busy all of the time. These days I want it. I crave it. I require it! That ever elusive thing of which I speak--- time to myself; a stolen moment away from my current life as wife and mother.

These moments of solitude can be found in the simplest of forms, like doing the laundry, taking a walk to the mail box and hopping in to the shower! I have even been known to get excited about a visit to the dentist. The common thread that weaves these things together is taking a break from it all; some time to hear myself think.

It doesn't take much, just a minute to draw back and regroup. I return rejuvenated and ready to conquer it all with my sanity restored! I am mommy, wife and keeper of all that is good in our little world.

It may seem small to some but most mother's can relate. A moment alone is my saving grace!

my saving GRACE

Child of God-Wife-Mother-Friend-Daughter-Sister-Artist

O Lord, you have searched me and you know me. You know when I sit and when I rise you precieve my thoughts from afar.   ~Psalms 139:1-2

October 2005

Kelly created this computer-generated layout listing the many roles she takes on in both her life and her daily walk of faith. She included a Bible verse to express her personal relationship with God. The large focal photo shows a peaceful yet strong woman. A buckle combined with harlequin and brown papers lends a western feel.

Kelly Shults, Tulsa, Oklahoma

Supplies: Image-editing software (Photoshop CS2); digital kit (www.scrapbook-elements.com)

A man visiting from Africa touched Kathleen with his moving message on revival and their common ground of faith. Images from a church brochure show the inspiring speaker and the poignant graphic of joining hands. Ribbons tied to spiral clips border the brochure. Kathleen's handwritten journaling and Bible verse share hopes of revival with a personal touch.

**Kathleen Summers,
Roseville, California**

Supplies: Patterned paper; letter stamps (Leave Memories); stamping ink; tag (Crossed Paths); spiral clips (Making Memories); ribbon; pen; cardstock

A simple psalm gives inspiration to this page that defines what Laura believes—her help comes from the Lord. With her eyes lifted upward, the enlarged cropped photo echoes the first words of Laura's favorite Psalm. She printed the verse onto cardstock and then cut the sentences into journaling strips. Patterned sticker squares create a backdrop for her painted chipboard title. Rub-on stitches accent both the title and the journaling strips.

**Laura Achilles, Littleton, Colorado
Photo: David Achilles, Littleton, Colorado**

Supplies: Patterned papers, patterned sticker squares (Basic Grey); ribbon (Shoebox Trims); rub-on stitches (Doodlebug Design); chipboard letters (Pressed Petals); tacks (Chatterbox)

DReam BiG

Nothing is impossible in Him

Dare to give new things a try, to press beyond the boundaries
of the establishment, follow your heart and His Word.
Challenge those around you to be men and women of character
and integrity ...and you set the example
in your public & private life
and your faith.

You're granted this one life to live
fully so have fun, enjoy the journey
and make it count!

Laugh Often,
Live Well
Love Much

Soar like Eagles

love peace
joy self control

When you pull the covers of this book back-to-back, it forms a beautiful
star. But what's inside the book is the real treasure. Mandi and her husband
filled the pages with words of spiritual and practical truths to pass on to
their children, offering life lessons in dating, marriage, handling disappoint-
ments, faithfulness, self-esteem and contentment. Metal accents, punch
labels and ribbons accent the story, which ends with a family photo.

Mandi Haynes, Rangiora, New Zealand

Supplies: Star album; patterned papers, tags, stickers (Crossed Paths); handle, key lock, paper
clips (7 Gypsies); charms, printed twill tape (All My Memories); label maker (Dymo); stamping
ink; letter dies (Sizzix); stamps (Hero Arts, Inkadinkado, Making Memories, Montarga, Paperbag
Studios); liquid appliqué; letter stickers (Me & My Big Ideas); word tag (Junkitz); buckles, letter
eyelets, metal frame (Making Memories); ribbons (Doodlebug Design, Strano Designs); rub-ons
(Doodlebug Design, Making Memories); lace; elastic; stamping inks; cardstock

Mighty Pearl, Victorious Spirit
Isaiah 2.5

Strength of God, God is Gracious
Psalm 118.14

Handmade touches personalize this page along with Gwen's rhyming poem of her favorite things. She printed her poem on custom cardstock stamped with fleur-de-lis designs in watermark ink. Small black-and-white photos show her favorites with one of them called out, her garden, with a bottle cap charm created with clear gloss medium over a canvas flower.

Gwen Dye, Enterprise, Alabama
Photo: Gary Dye, Enterprise, Alabama

Supplies: Patterned papers (Basic Grey); ribbon (Offray); letter stamps (PSX Design, Stampcraft); ghost letters (Heidi Swapp); chipboard tag (7 Gypsies); bottle cap (Li'l Davis Designs); clear gloss medium (Ranger); brads, rub-ons, metal photo corners, eyelet phrase, fleur-de-lis foam stamp (Making Memories); hinge, canvas flower (Foofala); eyelet key; domino game piece; alcohol inks (Ranger); watermark and solvent inks (Tsukineko); stamping ink; cardstock

A few of **My Favorite Things**

Little boys' kisses and hugs from my man,
Ice-cold Dr. Peppers in a bottle, not a can,
Hummingbirds that flutter on their tiny wings,
These are a few of my favorite things.

Walks on the beach finding perfect seashells,
Friends reuniting with stories to tell,
Flowers that bloom in my gardens in spring,
These are a few of my favorite things.

Being a night owl and staying up too late,
Hoping the boys will let me sleep past eight,
Feeling love when I glance at my wedding rings,
These are a few of my favorite things.

I'm a simple girl. I've never needed all the latest gadgets or trendy styles to make me happy. Maybe it's part of my Southern heritage or maybe it's something I haven't keyed in on at this point in my life. I do know one thing is for sure....

Simple pleasures bring me the most joy!

> "I was inspired by the feel of the outdoors and wanted to bring that natural feel to my page through colors and texture."

A wooded cemetery is Shannon's thinking spot, and she memorializes it in this layout. Her title set on leaf embedded paper combines cork stamped letters with cardstock letters covered in green gloss medium. Twine and raffia wrapped around the title block bind a statue close-up covered in mica. The background photo was cut for inset journaling bordered with copper foil tape and green gloss medium.

Shannon Taylor, Bristol, Tennessee

Supplies: Handmade paper; corrugated paper; cork, handmade paper (Anima Designs); letter stamps (Stamp Craft); mica (USArtQuest); square page pebble (Making Memories); foil tape; metallic rub-ons (Craf-T); green gloss medium (Judikins); raffia; twine; cardstock

There is nothing so decadent to me as chocolate and peanut butter together. It could be construed as something so simple as a glass of water. I like my chocolate chilled in the fridge (like a great crisp apple) with a mound of creamy peanut butter on top. Dark chocolate, milk chocolate, white chocolate, it doesn't matter. But Jif is my peanut butter of choice. The crown jewel if you will. Sometimes I can just nibble it, try to savor each little bite. Other times I can't get enough and just shove the whole thing in my mouth. The pair is a cheap thrill for me. No matter how I feel or what kind of mood I am in, it always brings me comfort and joy. I've tried to give it up before, this addiction of mine . . . it lasted one week and then all I could think of was "bring it on!" It just sucked me back in. My husband always tells me you're addicted, and that's not good for you. He says "Those checkout isles at the grocery store that have no candy in them were made for you!" But I can't control myself. I am like a kid in a candy store. When I opened one of my Dove chocolates and the wrapper said "Do what feels right." . . I knew, I just knew this was to be my expression of Joy and Comfort.

Chocolate and Peanut Butter

A chocolate and peanut butter addiction is confessed with humor and photo evidence. Wendy's journaling printed on vellum jokingly boasts about the combo she calls "a cheap thrill." A focal photo shows the addictive duo and is repeated, printed on the backside of the vellum journaling block. When a chocolate wrapper commanded "Do what feels right," Wendy saved the foil license-to-indulge on a metal-rimmed tag coated with clear gloss medium.

Wendy Reed, Henderson, Nevada

Supplies: Patterned paper (Close to My Heart); chipboard letters, acrylic paints (Making Memories); ultra thick embossing powder (Ranger); silver paint pen (Krylon); label maker (Dymo); tag (Jo-Ann Stores); chocolate wrapper; ribbon; embossing ink; stamping ink; vellum; cardstock

I will use any excuse to justify a big bowl of ice cream! After a hard day, or in celebration of something good, or just because — I have to have it! Cold, creamy and sweet! Ice cream is my all time favorite treat. It is inexpensive and readily available for instant gratification. There are always 2 or 3 flavors in my refrigerator. I know exactly where all the local ice cream parlors are. And I have the local frozen custard place on speed dial so I can check the flavor of the day. Unfortunately ice cream loves me right back!

Playful pinks set the stage for this lighthearted story about a passion for ice cream. Tricia's self-portrait showing her about to indulge in her ultimate comfort food, is secured with hinges and matted on patterned paper torn to look like melting ice cream. Small photos help tell the story from the sundae being created to the delicious masterpiece to, ultimately, the empty bowl.

Tricia Rubens, Castle Rock, Colorado

Supplies: Patterned papers (Junkitz, Rusty Pickle); die cuts (QuicKutz); stamps (Inkadinkado, Scrappy Cat); brads, hinges, tags (Making Memories); photo corners (Daisy D's); floss (DMC); twill tape; stamping ink

The moment Vicki's daughter first tasted chocolate, she was hooked, wearing it all over her face in this photo. Vicki playfully preserves the Easter moment with a collage of patterned paper squares in bright pastels for the holiday and touches of brown to infuse the chocolate theme. The stamped and embossed title mimics chocolaty goodness. Brown ribbon layered with pink lace through a buckle makes for an ultra girly border.

Vicki Boutin, Burlington, Ontario, Canada

Supplies: Patterned papers (Scenic Route Paper Co.); letter stamps (Scraptivity); rub-on letters (Autumn Leaves); label holder (Jo-Ann Stores); stickers (Colorbök); brads; embossing powder; ribbon; buckle; lace; stamping ink; cardstock

Sporting Ghirardelli chocolate hats and ear-to-ear grins, Lily's page topic needs no further explanation than women with a passion for chocolate. Lily pays homage to the favorite treat with rich shades of brown and burgundy accented with fresh yellow. A playful stamp of faux nutritional facts gives license to indulge guilt-free.

Lily Goldsmith, Orlando, Florida

Supplies: Patterned paper (Diane's Daughter); stickers (American Crafts, SEI); stamps (Club Scrap); mailbox letters (Making Memories); rub-ons (Me & My Big Ideas); washers (Bazzill); circle cutter (Provo Craft); stamping ink; cardstock

coffee talk

ritual

"Going to coffee" is usually a ritual that I share with my closest girlfriends, but one morning Jessica asked if I would take her to coffee instead. We went to my favorite local coffee shop and shared coffee (hot chocolate for her), conversation and laughs...just like I do with my friends. This time was even better because I was sharing an experience with my daughter that brought us closer to each other. I discovered that a little "coffee talk" is not just for girlfriends.

What was a ritual with girlfriends, a mother and daughter now share—conversation over coffee for Leora and hot chocolate for her daughter. Leora printed journaling about the new ritual onto the black-and-white photo touting her drink of choice. Flowers cut from patterned paper, coated with gloss and secured with jumbo brads add girly punch to the stamped background. See sketch on CD-ROM.

Leora Sanford, Pocatello, Idaho

Supplies: Patterned papers (Chatterbox, Junkitz); foam stamps (Making Memories); jumbo brads (Karen Foster Design); letter stickers (American Crafts); clear gloss finish (Plaid); stamping ink; cardstock

One must be careful with his or her coffee cup at the Minchuk household. If you look away for even one second, Madison will steal a sip. She was even caught downing chocolate-covered coffee beans once. Sandi tells all the mischievous details in hidden journaling behind the folder-matted focal photo showing the culprit grasping the jumbo cup. Brown painted rings and smudges enhance the playful coffee theme.

Sandi Minchuk, Merrillville, Indiana

Supplies: Patterned papers (Chatterbox, Daisy D's) stamps (Making Memories); rub-ons (Chatterbox); acrylic paint (Plaid); label maker (Dymo); cardstock

for the love of COFFEE

life

Madison is such a little coffee hound! She sneaks Morgan or David's coffee in the morning if no one is watching. Morgan found her feasting one day on a stash of chocolate covered coffee beans. I even caught her red handed the day of Sadie's first soccer game. Just finishing midnights, I had stopped on my drive in to get a Dunkin' Donuts french vanilla coffee to help keep myself awake. At one point, I must have set it down to cheer for Sadie. When I turned around, Miss Madie had stolen it and was trying to drink it just as fast as she could! Guess it is true what they say-Good to the last drop!

My QUEST for the Perfect CUPPA JOE

My love of coffee runs deep. It began in high school with General Foods International Coffees. My senior year I moved into the "real stuff" during evenings spent dissecting life's complexities with dad. Of course, college and law school pushed me over the edge in caffeine-powered nights of endless study. I switched to decaf in '94 after a doctor told me the caffeine was exacerbating an irregular heartbeat, but have slowely re-incorporated it over the past couple of years. Having a toddler will do that to you.

I've tried them all. Lattes, mochas, cappuccinos, frappuccinos, mochachinos, espresso… you name it, if it has coffee in it, I've tried it. But my favorite remains simple: half flavored regular (French Vanilla, at present), half flavored decaf (French Vanilla, at present) with milk, no sugar.

The "with milk" part, strangely, was an evolutionary process. For some unexplainable reason (the alignment of the planets?) I started craving half and half in my coffee during my wedding trip to Skaneateles, New York in 2000. Before that, I always drank it black. Go figure. However, during my post-partum dieting spree, I replaced the half and half with milk.

I am not a casual coffee drinker – I am a connoisseur. I have sampled them all and am fiercely loyal to my favorites. Starbucks – tastes burnt; Peets – too strong (although I can drink it if needed); Seattle's Best – too weak; Coffee Bean and Tea Leaf (an LA chain) – just right. The nectar of the Gods. Perhaps the thing I miss the most about LA. I still order Coffee Bean online but it's not the same when brewed at home – I need the paper cup.

The closest thing I've found in New Jersey is, believe it or not, Dunkin Donuts. Half French Vanilla regular, half French Vanilla decaf, milk only (or "light" as they call it on the East Coast).

And so, each day I spend 35 minutes driving to and from "Dunkins" for my morning coffee fix (and, er, sometimes for an afternoon fix as well, depending on the day…) The gas probably costs more than the coffee, which currently runs me $1.90 for a large. I could buy the beans and brew it myself, but it wouldn't be the same. I need the paper (ok, Styrofoam) cup.

4/2005 fresh

Lisa's palate is very particular when it comes to coffee. A colorful close-up of her chosen cup of joe lights up with coordinating patterned papers. Lisa created her customized title using text boxes in a word processing program. A spunky two-tone ribbon borders the page, attached to a die-cut label holder containing the date.

Lisa VanderVeen, Mendham, New Jersey

Supplies: Patterned papers (Making Memories); die-cut label holder (Deluxe Cuts); ribbon (Michaels); acrylic charm (KI Memories); pen; cardstock

---

A stop for treats is a road-trip tradition for Dee's family. She got a close-up of the goodies and set it against retro patterned papers in bright colors and white scalloped cardstock. The crisp whites, cool oranges and sweet pinks give the essence of summer, which is just when Dee loves to indulge in flavored iced coffee and donuts. Black accents break up the bright mix.

Dee Gallimore-Perry, Griswold, Connecticut

Supplies: Patterned papers, tag, chipboard flowers, ribbon, safety pin (Making Memories); decorative rub-ons (My Mind's Eye); rub-on phrase (Déjà Views, Li'l Davis Design); mesh (Magic Mesh); woven thread sentiment (Me & My Big Ideas); stamping ink; cardstock

"I had just gotten a digital camera this summer and, of course, I had it with me whenever we went on a trip. When my husband came out of Dunkin' Donuts with coffee, I realized that this was the perfect item to symbolize our trips!"

Road Trip

the beginning

the journey begins

SUMMER 2005

could not bear to be without you

What's one of the best things about taking a road trip? Stopping at Dunkin Donuts before we start on our way! In the summer, it's typically iced coffee for the 3 of us, although Daddy is sometimes known to get his typical regular coffee, too. Brendan and I always get decaf...and we started adding flavors this year...our favorite this summer? French Vanilla. Whether it's a long trip or just a trip somewhere nearby, it's always a good excuse to stop by Dunkin Donuts for coffees first! ☺

A playful memoir showcases summertime favorites on this page. Katja used focal photos of her tan-lined feet and sequined flip-flops to begin her story. A flashlight effect in image-editing software makes the two main photos glow. Supported by mini photos, the montage basks against a fresh mix of nautical patterned papers. Eclectic groupings of spunky accents add whimsy and a touch of summer fun.

Katja Kromann, Mission Viejo, California

Supplies: Patterned papers (7 Gypsies, Chatterbox, KI Memories); photo turns, flower charms (Jest Charming); metal word washers, rub-on sentiments, decorative brad, safety pin (Making Memories); word charm (Blue Moon Beads); letter stickers (American Crafts, Li'l Davis Designs); word stickers (Bo-Bunny Press); flowers (Prima); embossed word stickers (K & Company); daisy die cut (Paper House); ribbon (May Arts, Michaels, Offray); rub-on words, index tabs (Autumn Leaves); slide mount frames; letter stamps (Hero Arts); acrylic paint; fabric strips; eyelets; staples; cardstock

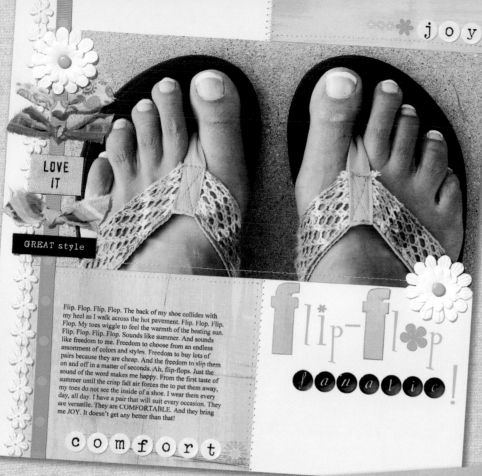

joy

LOVE IT

GREAT style

Flip. Flop. Flip. Flop. The back of my shoe collides with my heel as I walk across the hot pavement. Flip. Flop. Flip. Flop. My toes wiggle to feel the warmth of the beating sun. Flip. Flop. Flip. Flop. Sounds like summer. And sounds like freedom to me. Freedom to choose from an endless assortment of colors and styles. Freedom to buy lots of pairs because they are cheap. And the freedom to slip them on and off in a matter of seconds. Ah, flip-flops. Just the sound of the word makes me happy. From the first taste of summer until the crisp fall air forces me to put them away, my toes do not see the inside of a shoe. I wear them every day, all day. I have a pair that will suit every occasion. They are versatile. They are COMFORTABLE. And they bring me JOY. It doesn't get any better than that!

flip-flop fanatic!

comfort

The sound of flip-flop sandals flopping against her feet is music to Greta's ears. As her choice of shoe wear until the fall chill sets in, Greta playfully salutes the comfort, joy and freedom that flip-flops afford her with journaling printed on blue weathered patterned paper. Fresh aqua blues, citrus greens and crisp white accents beckon summer and match the enlarged close-up of Greta's feet sporting her favorite shoes.

Greta Hammond, Goshen, Indiana

Supplies: Patterned papers (Junkitz, KI Memories); ribbon (Junkitz, Making Memories); fabric (Imagination Project); woven label sentiments (Me & My Big Ideas, Making Memories); letter template (KI Memories); rub-on letters (Scrapworks); rub-on flowers (Autumn Leaves); epoxy letters (Li'l Davis); brads; stamping ink; thread

Shades of bright pink and glitzy glam touches help tell the story of five sassy bridesmaids. Jessie accented punchy pink patterned papers strips with large gems to play up the jeweled flip-flops in the photo. A sequined and beaded "5" in iridescent pink, pulled straight from a pair of jeans, lights up the circular blocked title. Rub-on words placed directly on the photo sum up these bridesmaids— girly girls.

Jessie Baldwin, Las Vegas, Nevada

Supplies: Patterned papers (Karen Foster Design); woven label sentiment (Me & Big Ideas); rub-on letters (Making Memories); stickers (American Crafts, KI Memories); ribbon; gems; sequined number; cardstock

funky flip flops. funky flip flops. funky flip flops. funky flip flops.

5 feet

sassy shoes

all the girls in Melinda's wedding wore matching flip-flops! 7/04

Girly Girls

dainty & delicate

A girl's passion for reading started young and is documented from ages 1 to 4½ on this page. Sue created a photo montage in image-editing software that chronologically shows her granddaughter infatuated with reading. Her journaling about the young scholar is printed on a tag tucked behind the focal photo and is accented with braided twine strung through eyelets.

Sue Hagerman, Grandview, Missouri

Supplies: Patterned papers, chipboard letters (Rusty Pickle); twine; ribbon charm (Making Memories); chipboard letters, clay tile letters (Li'l Davis Designs); letter tiles (EK Success); sentiment sticker (K & Company); rub-on letters (Creative Imaginations); cardstock

SARAH is a BORN READER.

From the minute she could pick up a book – she did! Even as a young toddler she was FASCINATED BY BOOKS, magazines, newspapers, anything printed. She would EXAMINE EVERYTHING on a page, and she always LOOKED at every page too. Talk about a LOVE OF READING! But I must admit, she takes after her mother and grandmother (me), who also loved to read.

So HERE SHE IS – at 1 YEAR OLD, 2 YEARS OLD, 3 YEARS OLD, 4 YEARS OLD, AND 4½ YEARS OLD, doing what she does best READING!! (Clockwise starting in upper left corner and big picture)   SEPTEMBER 2005

Escaping
into a good book

Though life rarely affords Lisa to get lost in a novel, reading big picture books to her toddler son is an investment in passing along her beloved hobby. The blurry photo caused by her son stepping in front of the camera was serendipitous as Lisa says it represents her life right now and his constant motion. Blocks of book cloth and leatherlike paper mimic the feel of a good book.

Lisa Hoel, San Jose, California

Supplies: Faux leather paper (source unknown); book binding cloth (source unknown); cardstock

The joy of a good book has been a life-long compulsion for me. I have loved reading every since I was big enough to get through my first Nancy Drew mystery. Going to the library and checking out a fat stack of books was a real treat. I would eagerly devour them once I got home. My parents' challenge was to keep my nose out of a book long enough to socialize with the family. I did learn more self-control over the years although I still love to lose myself in a good book. There is nothing like curling up in a comfy chair and escaping into an imaginary world. I become engrossed in the world of the characters and sometimes imagine myself entering that world and interacting with them. Oh how I hate to be interrupted! These days it's harder for me to find the time to dig into a good novel. It's one thing to let the dishes sit because I'm reading, I can't ignore my mommy duties so easily. Most of the books I read now are of the ten-page, large picture variety. However, I am excited about passing on my love of literature to my son. Already his favorite activity is bringing me a book to read to him. He will plunk his little body down next to mine on the couch and eagerly point out things in the pictures and laugh at the funny parts. I think we have a new avid reader in the making!   7.30.2005

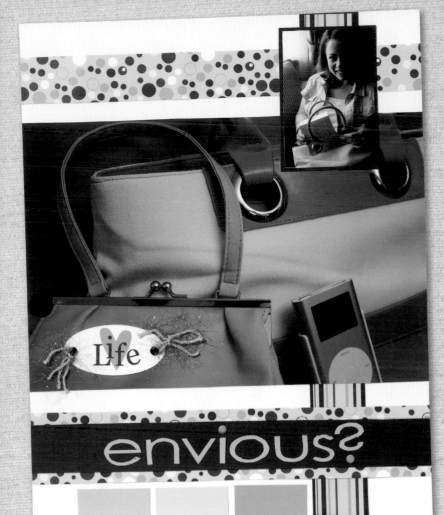

For Susan's 36th birthday there was a definite theme—green gifts. The enlarged focal photo shows a close-up of her birthday bounty while a small inset shows a self-portrait. Susan's inspired title comes from the old adage "green with envy." Green patterned paper strips in punchy stripes and polka dots festively dress the celebration page.

Susan Opel, Fort Wayne, Indiana
Photo: Elizabeth Opel, Fort Wayne, Indiana

Supplies: Patterned papers, die-cut sentiment (Heidi Grace Designs); brads; fiber; cardstock

When it comes to vintage vehicles, Julie's husband likes slammed (cool) and his dad appreciates original (classic). Her journaling represents both sides of classic vs. cool, but she decks the page in the one detail father and son agree on—paint color—shiny black. An embossed tin handcut title reflects like chrome against black-and-white patterned paper. The topics for debate in the black-and-white photo look tough against black and metal accents.

Julie Johnson, Seabrook, Texas

Supplies: Patterned paper, embossed tin, metal charms (EK Success); letter stickers (Chatterbox); cardstock

> "My husband's love affair with vintage vehicles was my inspiration. I wanted him to be proud of me so I went totally chrome."

A mouthwatering close-up tempts the taste buds, but don't worry, Amy provides her longtime favorite recipe. She's been making the staple appetizer for years and documents the ingredients along with the directions in a vertical format. Striped patterned paper in red and greens makes the dish look even tastier.

Amy Goldstein, Kent Lakes, New York

Supplies: Patterned paper (Scrapworks); monogram coaster (SEI); image (www.clipart.com); cardstock

Zesty Bruschetta with Garlic Paste

8 large plum tomatoes, chopped
1 head garlic, roasted
3 cloves garlic minced
GOOD Extra Virgin Olive Oil
fresh basil, chopped
large red onion, chopped
loaf of crusty italian bread
Kosher Salt
Lemon Juice or Red Wine Vinegar
Pepper
Parmesan Cheese
Fresh Mozzarella
Prosciuto, sliced paper thin

Begin by drizzling the head of garlic with olive oil roasting until soft in 350 - 400 degree oven. When soft remove and cool..

Slice the Italian bread diagonally and brush with olive oil. Grill each slice on BBQ or indoor grill until toasted with nice grill marks. Remove.

Squeeze garlic from outer shell into bowl. It should have the consistency of paste. Add kosher salt to taste and spread on toasted bread.

In separate bowl combine, chopped tomato, basil, garlic, salt & pepper to taste and drizzle with olive oil and a dash of lemon juice or vinegar. Toss to coat.

Spoon tomato mixture on top of toasted bread and serve with sliced fresh mozzarella and sliced prosciuto.

From atop the John Hancock Building, the hustle and bustle of big-city Chicago is silenced against this serene sunset over the cityscape and Lake Michigan's shoreline. As one of Andrea's favorite photos from her weekend escape, she reflects on the poignant memory in handwritten journaling on a bold floral graphic accented with a washer and gem center.

Andrea Steed, Rochester, Minnesota

Supplies: Patterned papers, washer (Imagination Project); letter stickers (Patchwork Paper); brad; watermark ink (Tsukineko); pen; cardstock

An altered plastic stamp holder becomes an "all-about-me" book. Laura cut patterned papers to disguise the holder and covered its handle with tied ribbons. A tab closure opens to reveal pages bound with brads and adhered to the holder's left flap. Each page touts a favorite and some include mini photos. The right flap showcases a self-portrait and journaling about Laura's many life hats.

Laura Achilles, Littleton, Colorado
Photo: David Achilles, Littleton, Colorado

Supplies: Patterned papers (KI Memories); ribbon (Doodlebug Design, May Arts, Offray); decorative tape (Heidi Swapp); letter stamps (PSX Design); rub-on letters, stickers (Carolee's Creations, Making Memories, Pebbles); binder clip (Target); stamping ink; cardstock

Dominque used a double-entendre on this page about her love affair with her new EOS Rebel XT camera. While she may be wild and crazy when it comes to taking pictures, she's certainly not a rebel without a cause. Each and every click of the button freezes precious memories for her to scrapbook. The pink and black color scheme combined with repeated circles makes the whole layout cohesive and unified.

Dominique Quintal, Longueuil, Quebec, Canada
Photo: Martine Giguére, Longueuil, Quebec, Canada

Supplies: Patterned paper (Chatterbox, KI Memories); letter stickers (Arctic Frog); brads, anchors (Junkitz); snaps (Making Memories); stamping ink; black pen; cardstock

"I thought it would be fun to do a play on words. When I got this camera as a gift from my husband, I thought the name of it was perfect to describe both my 'outside the box' approach to photography as well as the camera itself."

Life is so short. Passion to wild. My husband bought me a "totaly unexpected gadget"... An EOS digital rebel XT 8mp. Wowwwwwww, I was so excited. Now, I can take pictures and be proud of my work.... With this fantastic camera, the colours are so bright, results so wonderful. Now, I just need to create or found the good subjet and do THE clic! A good thing for a scrapmommy like me!

Wedge-cut photos and journaling blocks form a large circle to whimsically tell of Barb's passion for painting. The circle touts a paint-swatched self-portrait with handwritten journaling on patterned paper about how her love for the hobby began. Her bright and bold chipboard title is delicately embellished with hand-drawn silver scrolls and printed paint names. Colorful chipboard accents dress the page with artsy flair.

Barb Hogan, Cincinnati, Ohio

Supplies: Patterned paper (Basic Grey); cord (Stampin' Up!); chipboard accents (Imagination Project); buttons (Hobby Lobby, Making Memories, Stampin' Up!); pens; cardstock

When Torrey's artistic mother started to lose her eyesight, she switched art mediums to a more tactile one—hand-made pottery. Torrey lovingly tributes her mother's triumphant story with a series of photos showing her hands at work. To mimic her mother's pottery, Torrey created a few handmade vessels of her own from polymer clay that border the page.

Torrey Scott, Thornton, Colorado

Supplies: Patterned papers (American Crafts); textured cardstock (Bazzill); polymer clay (Sculpey); foam adhesive squares; stamping ink; sandpaper; cardstock

Ki documents a meaningful cross-stitch that she created after her first child was born with a tribute as beautiful and passionate as the stitched poem itself. She scanned the poem to capture this photograph and scanned the graph pattern from which she handcut her title. Journaling framed by a cross-stitched heart tells the story of the labor of love. Floss and a sewing needle add to the homespun feel.

Ki Kruk, Sherwood Park, Alberta, Canada

Supplies: Metallic gold paper (Golden Oak); flowers (Prima); floss (Anchor); dimensional adhesive (EK Success); pearl beads (Westrim); needle; cardstock

Laurel thrives on chaos created by juggling her many interests in the little time she has to do them. Her husband affectionately calls her "chaos creator," which she used as her title. Four doors created with folded cardstock frames, mesh and printed transparencies open to photos of Laurel's many hobbies. Mini knockers adhered to the front of the interactive panels play up the door theme while photo turns secure them closed.

Laurel Gervitz, Keller, Texas

Supplies: Patterned papers (KI Memories); vellum (Worldwin); metal mesh, cardstock frames, brads, acrylic paint (Making Memories); door knockers, clock charm (7 Gypsies); letter stickers (Creative Imaginations); die-cut letters (Li'l Davis); pen; cardstock

When Suzy was crowned with the title Memory Makers Master, she was simply shocked. She humbly journals about hopes and fears of filling her new shoes on vellum backed with distressed patterned paper. Photo turns secured with pink brads point to her enlarged self-portrait under which small photos show her range of emotions. Black rickrack and pink flowers add feminine punch to the page.

Suzy Plantamura,
Laguna Niguel, California
Photo: Jordan Piazza,
Laguna Niguel, California

Supplies: Patterned paper (Autumn Leaves, Basic Grey); vellum; letter stamps (SEI); stamping ink; flowers (Prima); brads (Making Memories); die-cut letters; rickrack; cardstock

Missy documents entering the annual Memory Makers Master artist contest with photos showing her mailing her entry. Her journaling describes the art and soul journey that led her to new heights of creativity, and despite not being crowned with the title, Missy is a winner for her creative efforts and skillful gain. Bright pink daisy and stripe patterned papers are stitched for added texture. The bold shapes and bright colors display optimism.

Missy Neal, Campbell, California
Photo: Jim Maveety, Campbell, California

Supplies: Patterned papers, fabric strips, rub-ons (Imagination Project); foam letter stamps, photo corners (Heidi Swapp); acrylic paint, letter stamps (Making Memories); cardstock

Wanda has a weakness for anything girly or cute. She couldn't resist purchasing this small iron to help her make her scrapbooking craftsmanship just perfect. The large close-up photo is the focal point on this computer-generated page while her own paper balances out the bottom. A purse, shoe and pink, purple and black color scheme make it all-girl.

Wanda Santiago-Citron,
Deerfield, Wisconsin

Supplies: Image-editing software (Digital Image Pro); stitching (www.shabbyprincess .com); purse, ribbon, shoe (source unknown)

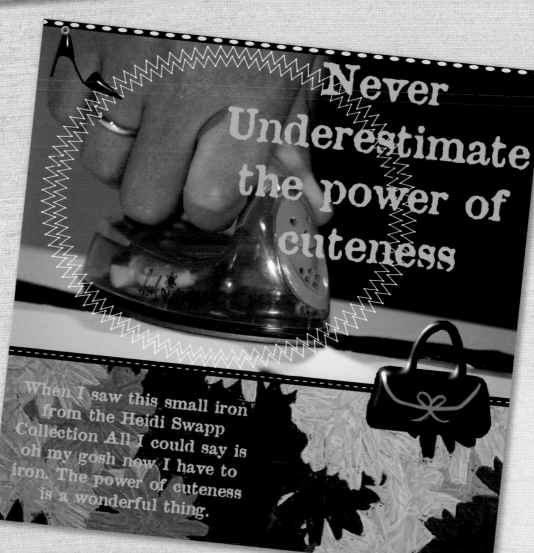

Sources

This list is representative of the many, many manufacturers who create product for scrapbooking and other crafts; many are featured on pages in this book. Please check your local retailers to find these materials, or go to a company's Web site for the latest product information. In addition, we have made every attempt to properly credit the items mentioned in this book. We apologize to any company that we have listed incorrectly, and we would appreciate hearing from you.

2DYE4
www.canscrapink.com

7 Gypsies
(877) 749-7797
www.sevengypsies.com

A2Z Essentials
(419) 663-2869
www.a2zessentials.com

A.C. Moore
www.acmoore.com

AccuCut®
(800) 288-1670
www.accucut.com

Activa® Products, Inc.
(800) 883-3899
www.activaproducts.com

Akro-Mils®
(330) 761-6340
www.akro-mils.com

All My Memories
(888) 553-1998
www.allmymemories.com

American Art Clay Co. (AMACO)
(800) 374-1600
www.amaco.com

American Crafts
(801) 226-0747
www.americancrafts.com

American Tag Company
(800) 223-3956
www.americantag.net

American Traditional Designs®
(800) 448-6656
www.americantraditional.com

Ampersand Art Supply
(800) 822-1939
www.ampersandart.com

Amscan, Inc.
(800) 444-8887
www.amscan.com

Anima Designs
(800) 570-6847
www.animadesigns.com

Anna Griffin, Inc.
(888) 817-8170
www.annagriffin.com

Armada Art, Inc.
(800) 435-0601
www.armadaart.com

Arctic Frog
(479) 636-FROG
www.arcticfrog.com

Around The Block
(801) 593-1946
www.aroundtheblockproducts.com

Art Accents, Inc.
www.artaccents.net

ARTchix Studio
(250) 370-9985
www.artchixstudio.com

Art Impressions
(800) 393-2014
www.artimpressions.com

Art Institute Glitter, Inc.
(928) 639-0805
www.artglitter.com

Artistic Expressions
(219) 764-5158
www.artisticexpressionsinc.com

Artistic Wire
(630) 530-7567
www.artisticwire.com

Artograph, Inc.
(888) 975-9555
www.artograph.com

Atkinson Designs, Inc.
(763) 441-1825
www.atkinsondesigns.com

Auto FX Software
(205) 980-0056
www.autofx.com

Autumn Leaves
(800) 588-6707
www.autumnleaves.com

A.W. Cute
(877) 560-6943
www.awcute.com

Badger Air-Brush Company
(847) 678-3104
www.badgerairbrush.com

Basic Grey™
(801) 451-6006
www.basicgrey.com

Bazzill Basics Paper
(480) 558-8557
www.bazzillbasics.com

Beacon Adhesives
(800) 865-7238
www.beaconcreates.com

Beadery®, The
(401) 539-2432
www.thebeadery.com

Beads & Plenty More
(517) 47-BEADS
www.beadsandplentymore.com

Beaux Regards
(877) 419-8488
www.beauxregards.com

Bella Press
(253) 437-1626
www.bellapress.com

Berwick Offray™, LLC
(800) 344-5533
www.offray.com

Be Unique
(909) 927-5357
www.beuniqueinc.com

Blue Cardigan Designs
(770) 904-4320
www.bluecardigan.com

Blue Moon Beads
(800) 377-6715
www.bluemoonbeads.com

Blumenthal Lansing Company
(201) 935-6220
www.buttonsplus.com

Bo-Bunny Press
(801) 771-4010
www.bobunny.com

Boutique Trims, Inc.
(248) 437-2017
www.boutiquetrims.com

Boxer Scrapbook Productions
(503) 625-0455
www.boxerscrapbooks.com

Buttons Galore
(856) 753-0165
www.buttonsgaloreandmore.com

Canson®, Inc.
(800) 628-9283
www.canson-us.com

CARL Mfg. USA, Inc.
(800) 257-4771
www.Carl-Products.com

Carolee's Creations®
(435) 563-1100
www.ccpaper.com

Carson-Dellosa Publishing Co.
(800) 321-0943
www.carsondellosa.com

Charming Place, A
(509) 325-5655
www.acharmingplace.com

ChartPak
(800) 628-1910
www.chartpak.com

Chatterbox, Inc.
(208) 939-9133
www.chatterboxinc.com

Clearsnap, Inc.
(360) 293-6634
www.clearsnap.com

Close To My Heart®
(888) 655-6552
www.closetomyheart.com

Cloud 9 Design
(763) 493-0990
www.cloud9design.biz

Club Scrap™, Inc.
(888) 634-9100
www.clubscrap.com

Cock-A-Doodle Design, Inc.
(800) 954-0559
www.cockadoodledesign.com

Collage Press
(435) 656-4611
www.collagepress.com

Collected Memories
(858) 483-9391
www.collectedmemories.com

Colorbök™, Inc.
(800) 366-4660
www.colorbok.com

Colors by Design
(800) 832-8436
www.colorsbydesign.com

Comotion Rubber Stamps
(800) 225-4894

Coronado Island Stamping
(619) 477-8900
www.cistamping.com

CottageArts.net™
www.cottagearts.net

Crafter's Workshop, The
(877) CRAFTER
www.thecraftersworkshop.com

Craf-T Products
(507) 235-3996
www.craf-tproducts.com

Crafts, Etc. Ltd.
(800) 888-0321
www.craftsetc.com

Creative Imaginations
(800) 942-6487
www.cigift.com

Creative Impressions Rubber Stamps, Inc.
(719) 596-4860
www.creativeimpressions.com

Creative Memories®
(800) 468-9335
www.creativememories.com

Creative Paperclay Company®
(805) 484-6648
www.paperclay.com

Creek Bank Creations, Inc.
(217) 427-5980
www.creekbankcreations.com

C.R. Gibson®
(800) 243-6004
www.crgibson.com

Crop In Style®
(888) 700-2202
www.cropinstyle.com

Crossed Paths™
(972) 393-3755
www.crossedpaths.net

Cross-My Heart-Cards, Inc.
(888) 689-8808
www.crossmyheart.com

C-Thru® Ruler Company, The
(800) 243-8419
www.cthruruler.com

Current®, Inc.
(800) 848-2848
www.currentinc.com

Cut-It-Up™
(530) 389-2233
www.cut-it-up.com

Daisy D's Paper Company
(888) 601-8955
www.daisydspaper.com

Daler-Rowney USA
(609) 655-5252
www.daler-rowney.com

Darby
(469) 223-4308
www.darbypaper.com

Darice, Inc.
(800- 321-1494
www.darice.com

Daylight Company, LLC
(866) DAYLIGHT
www.daylightcompany.com

Debbie Mumm®
(888) 819-2923
www.debbiemumm.com

DecoArt™ Inc.
(800) 367-3047
www.decoart.com

Déjà Views
(800) 243-8419
www.dejaviews.com

Delight
(800) 527-2548
www.jazzups.com

Delta Technical Coatings, Inc.
(800) 423-4135
www.deltacrafts.com

Deluxe Designs
(480) 497-9005
www.deluxedesigns.com

DeNami Design Rubber Stamps
(253) 437-1626
www.denamidesign.com

Design Originals
(800) 877-0067
www.d-originals.com

Destination™ Scrapbook Designs
(866) 806-7826
www.destinationstickers.com

Diane's Daughters®
(801) 621-8392
www.dianesdaughters.com

DiBona Designs
(888) 685-5538
www.dibonadesigns.com

Die Cuts With A View
(801) 224-6766
www.diecutswithaview.com

Digital Scrapbook Place, The
(866) 396-6906
www.digitalscrapbookplace.com

DMC Corp.
(973) 589-0606
www.dmc.com

DMD Industries, Inc.
(800) 805-9890
www.dmdind.com

Doodlebug Design™ Inc.
(801) 966-9952
www.doodlebug.ws

Dr. Ph. Martin's
(800) 843-8293
www.docmartins.com

Duncan Enterprises
(800) 782-6748
www.duncan-enterprises .com

Dymo
(800) 426-7827
www.dymo.com

Eco-Africa-USA, Inc.
(888) 779-7077
www.naturallypaper.com

EK Success™, Ltd.
(800) 524-1349
www.eksuccess.com

Ellison®
(800) 253-2238
www.ellison.com

Emagination Crafts, Inc.
(866) 238-9770
www.emaginationcrafts.com

Ever After Scrapbook Co.
(800) 646-0010

Everlasting Keepsakes™ by faith
(816) 896-7037
www.everlastinkeepsakes.com

Family Archives™, The
(888) 622-6556
www.heritagescrapbooks.com

Family Treasures®
(949) 290-0872
www.familytreasures.com

Fancy Pants Designs, LLC
(801) 779-3212
www.fancypantsdesigns.com

Far and Away
(509) 340-0124
www.farandawayscrapbooks.com

FiberMark
(802) 257-0365
http://scrapbook.fibermark.com

Fibers by the Yard™
(405) 364-8066
www.fibersbytheyard.com

Fiber Scraps™
(215) 230-4905
www.fiberscraps.com

Fibre-Craft® Materials Corp.
(847) 647-1140
www.fibrecraft.com

Fiskars®, Inc.
(800) 950-0203
www.fiskars.com

Flair® Designs
(888) 546-9990
www.flairdesignsinc.com

FLAX art & design
(415) 552-2355
www.flaxart.com

FontWerks
(604) 942-3105
www.fontwerks.com

FoofaLa
(402) 330-3208
www.foofala.com

Frances Meyer, Inc.®
(413) 584-5446
www.francesmeyer.com

Frost Creek Charms
(763) 684-0074
www.frostcreekcharms.com

Gauchogirl Creative
www.gauchogirl.com

Generations
(800) 905-1888
www.generationsnow.com

Glue Dots® International
(888) 688-7131
www.gluedots.com

Golden Artist Colors, Inc.
(800) 959-6543
www.goldenpaints.com

Golden Oak Papers
(509) 325-5456

Gotta Mesh™/Notions Marketing
(616) 243-8424
www.gottamesh.com

Gotta Scrap!, Inc.
(972) 772-5197
www.gottascrapgottastamp.com

Go West Studios
(214) 227-0007
www.goweststudios.com

Grafix®
(800) 447-2349
www.grafix.com

Grassroots™
(262) 695-6429
www.grassrootscreative.com

Great Balls of Fiber
(303) 697-5942
www.greatballsoffiber.com

Halcraft USA
(212) 376-1580
www.halcraft.com

Hampton Art Stamps, Inc.
(800) 229-1019
www.hamptonart.com

Heidi Grace Designs, Inc.
(608) 294-4509
www.heidigrace.com

Heidi Swapp/Advantus Corporation
(904) 482-0092
www.heidiswapp.com

Henkel Consumer Adhesives, Inc.
(800) 321-0253
www.ducktapeproducts.com

Heritage Handcrafts
(303) 683-0963
www.heritagehandcrafts.com

Hero Arts® Rubber Stamps, Inc.
(800) 822-4376
www.heroarts.com

Hillcreek Designs
(619) 562-5799
www.hillcreekdesigns.com

Hirschberg Schutz & Co., Inc.
(800) 221-8640

Hot Off The Press, Inc.
(800) 227-9595
www.paperpizazz.com

Hot Potatoes
(615) 296-8002
www.hotpotatoes.com

HyGlo®/American Pin
(480) 968-6475
www.hyglocrafts.com

Impression Obsession
(877) 259-0905
www.impression-obsession.com

Impress Rubber Stamps
(206) 901 9101
www.impressrubberstamps.com

Inkadinkado® Rubber Stamps
(800) 888-4652
www.inkadinkado.com

Inventor's Studio, The
(866) 799-3653
www.inventorsstudio.com

It Takes Two®
(800) 331-9843
www.ittakestwo.com

Janlynn® Corporation of America
(800) 445-5565
www.janlynn.com

Jaquard Products/Rupert, Gibbon & Spider,
Inc.
(800) 442-0455
www.jacquardproducts.com

Jasc Software
(800) 622-2793
www.jasc.com

Jennifer Collection, The
(518) 272-4572
www.paperdiva.net

Jesse James & Co., Inc.
(610) 435-0201
www.jessejamesbutton.com

Jest Charming
(702) 564-5101
www.jestcharming.com

JewelCraft, LLC
(201) 223-0804
www.jewelcraft.biz

JHB International
(303) 751-8100
www.buttons.com

JudiKins
(310) 515-1115
www.judikins.com

June Tailor
(800) 844-5400
www.junetailor.com

Junkitz™
(732) 792-1108
www.junkitz.com

Just For Fun® Rubber Stamps
(727) 938-9898
www.jffstamps.com

JustRite® Stampers/Millenium Marking
Company
(847) 806-1750
www.justritestampers.com

Kaleidoscope Collections, LLC
(970) 231-4076
www.kaleidoscopecollections.com

K & Company
(888) 244-2083
www.kandcompany.com

Kangaroo & Joey®, Inc.
(800) 646-8065
www.kangarooandjoey.com

Karen Foster Design
(801) 451-9779
www.karenfosterdesign.com

Keeping Memories Alive™
(800) 419-4949
www.scrapbooks.com

Ken Brown Stamps/Rubber Stamps of America
(800) 553-5031
www.stampusa.com

KI Memories
(972) 243-5595
www.kimemories.com

Kopp Design
(801) 489-6011
www.koppdesign.com

Krylon®
(216) 566-200
www.krylon.com

La Pluma, Inc.
(803) 749-4076
www.debrabeagle.com

Lara's Crafts
(214) 232-5272
www.larascrafts.com

Lasting Impressions for Paper, Inc.
(801) 298-1979
www.lastingimpressions.com

Lazar Studiowerx, Inc.
(866) 478-9379
www.lazarstudiowerx.com

LazerLetterz
(281) 627-4227
www.lazerletterz.com

Leather Factory, The
(800) 433-3201
www.leatherfactory.com

Leaving Prints™
(801) 426-0636
www.leavingprints.com

Leisure Arts/Memories in the Making
(800) 643-8030
www.leisurearts.com

Light Impressions®
(800) 828-6216
www.lightimpressionsdirect.com

Li'l Davis Designs
(949) 838-0344
www.lildavisdesigns.com

Limited Edition Rubberstamps
(650) 594-4242
www.limitededitionrs.com

Liquitex® Artist Materials
(888) 4-ACRYLIC
www.liquitex.com

Little Black Dress Designs
(360) 894-8844
www.littleblackdressdesigns.com

Lucky Squirrel
(800) 462-4912
www.luckysquirrel.com

LuminArte (formerly Angelwing Enterprises)
(866) 229-1544
www.luminarteinc.com

M & J Trimming
(800) 9-MJTRIM
www.mjtrim.com

Magenta Rubber Stamps
(800) 565-5254
www.magentastyle.com

Magic Mesh
(651) 345-6374
www.magicmesh.com

Magic Scraps™
(972) 238-1838
www.magicscraps.com

MaisyMo™ Designs
(973) 907-7262
www.maisymo.com

Making Memories
(800) 286-5263
www.makingmemories.com

Makin's Clay®/Sino Harvest Limited
www.makinsclay.com

Mara-Mi, Inc.
(800) 627-2648
www.mara-mi.com

Marvy® Uchida/ Uchida of America, Corp.
(800) 541-5877
www.uchida.com

Mary Engelbreit Studios, Inc.
(800) 443-MARY
www.maryengelbreit.com

Ma Vinci's Reliquary
http://crafts.dm.net/
mall/reliquary/

Maya Road, LLC
(214) 488-3279
www.mayaroad.com

May Arts
(800) 442-3950
www.mayarts.com

Mayco® (a division of Coloramics, LLC)
(614) 876-1171
www.maycocolors.com

MBI/MCS Industries, Inc.
(847) 749-0225
www.mcsframes.com

McCall Pattern Co., The
(212) 465-6849

McGill, Inc.
(800) 982-9884
www.mcgillinc.com

me & my BiG ideas®
(949) 883-2065
www.meandmybigideas.com

Melissa Frances/Heart & Home, Inc.
(905) 686-9031
www.melissafrances.com

Memories Complete™, LLC
(866) 966-6365
www.memoriescomplete.com

Memories in the Making/Leisure Arts
(800) 643-8030
www.leisurearts.com

Memories In Uniform
(757) 228-7395
www.memoriesinuniform.com

Meri Meri
www.merimeri.com

Michael Miller Memories
(212) 704-0774
www.michaelmillermemories.com

Micrografx®
(972) 234-1769
www.micrografx.com

Midori
(800) 659-3049
www.midoriribbon.com

Mill Hill
www.millhillbeads.com

MoBe' Stamps!
(925) 443-2101
www.mobestamps.com

MOD-my own design
(303) 641-8680
www.mod-myowndesign.com

Mohawk Paper Mills, Inc.
(800) THE-MILL
www.strathmore.com

Moments Defined, Inc.
(866) 910-4366
www.momentsdefined.com

Moonshine Design
(801) 397-3997
www.moonshinedsgn.com

Mosaic Mercantile
(877) 9-MOSAIC
www.mosaicmercantile.com

Mostly Animals Rubber Art Stamps
(800) 832-8886
www.mostlyanimals.com

Mrs. Grossman's Paper
Company
(800) 429-4549
www.mrsgrossmans.com

Mustard Moon™
(408) 299-8542
www.mustardmoon.com

My Mind's Eye™, Inc.
(800) 665-5116
www.frame-ups.com

My Sentiments Exactly
(719) 260-6001
www.sentiments.com

Nankong Enterprises, Inc.
(302) 731-2995
www.nankong.com

Nature's Pressed
(800) 850-2499
www.naturespressed.com

Neenah Paper, Inc.
(678) 566-6500
www.neenah.com

Novelcrafts
(541) 582-3208
www.novelcrafts.com

NRN Designs
(800) 421-6958
www.nrndesigns.com

nuART Handmade Papers
(630) 881-1595
www.nuartpapers.com

Nunn Design
(360) 379-3557
www.nunndesign.com

Once Upon A Charm...
(866) 6CHARMS
www.onceuponacharm.com

One Heart...One Mind®, LLC
(888) 414-3690

On The Surface
(847) 675-2520

O'Scrap/Imaginations, Inc.
(801) 225-6015
www.imaginations-inc.com

Ott-Lite Technology®
(800) 842-8848
ww.ott-lite.com

Outdoors & More Scrapbook Decor
(801) 390-6919
www.outdoorsandmore.com

Outlines™ Rubber Stamp Company, Inc.
(860) 228-3686
www.outlinesrubberstamp.com

Pageframe Designs
(877) 55frame
www.scrapbookframe.com

Paintier® Products, LLC
(586) 822-7874
www.paintier.com

Paper Adventures®
(973) 406-5000
www.paperadventures.com

Paper Company, The/ANW Crestwood
(800) 525-3196
www.anwcrestwood.com

Paper Fever, Inc.
(800) 477-0902
www.paperfever.com

PaperGami
(800) 569-2280
www.papergami.com

Paper Heart Studio
(904) 230-8108
www.paperheartstudio.com

Paper House Productions®
(800) 255-7316
www.paperhouseproductions.com

Paper Illuzionz
(406) 234-8716
www.paperilluzionz.com

Paper Inspirations™
(406) 756-9678

Paper Loft
(866) 254-1961
www.paperloft.com

Paper Love Designs
(510) 841-1088
www.paperlovedesigns.com

Paper Palette LLC, The
(801) 849-8338
www.stickybackpaper.com

Paper Parachute®
(503) 533-4513
www.paperparachute.com

Paper Patch®, The
(800) 397-2737
www.paperpatch.com

Papers by Catherine
(713) 723-3334
www.papersbycatherine.com

Paper Salon
(952) 445-6878
www.papersalon.com

Paper Source
(888) paper-11
www.paper-source.com

Paper Wizard
(909) 627-1231
www.paperwiz.net

Patchwork Paper Design, Inc.
(239) 433-4820
www.patchworkpaper.com

Pebbles Inc.
(801) 224-1857
www.pebblesinc.com

Pebéo of America
(801) 235-1520
www.pebeo.com

Pick of the Patch
(250) 479-9151
www.pickofthepatch.com

Pioneer Photo Albums, Inc.®
(800) 366-3686
www.pioneerphotoalbums.com

Plaid Enterprises, Inc.
(800) 842-4197
www.plaidonline.com

PM designs
(888) 595-2887
www.designsbypm.com

Postmodern Design
(405) 321-3176
www.stampdiva.com

Pressed Petals
(800) 748-4656
www.pressedpetals.com

Prickley Pear Rubber Stamps
www.prickleypear.com

Prima Marketing, Inc.
(909) 627-5532
www.mulberrypaperflowers.com

PrintWorks
(800) 854-6558
www.printworkscollection.com

Prism™ Papers
(866) 902-1002
www.prismpapers.com

Provo Craft®
(888) 577-3545
www.provocraft.com

Prym-Dritz Corporation
www.dritz.com

PSX Design™
(800) 782-6748
www.psxdesign.com

Pulsar Paper Products
(877) 861-0031
www.pulsarpaper.com

Punch Bunch, The
(254) 791-4209
www.thepunchbunch.com

Purple Onion Designs
www.purpleoniondesigns.com

Queen & Co.
(858) 485-5132
www.queenandcompany.com

Quest Beads & Cast, Inc.
(212) 354-0979
www.questbeads.com

Quick Quotes
(360) 520-5611
www.quickquotesinstantjournaling.com

QuicKutz, Inc.
(801) 765-1144
www.quickutz.com

Raindrops on Roses
(307) 877-6241
www.raindropsonroses.com

Ranger Industries, Inc.
(800) 244-2211
www.rangerink.com

Reminisce Papers
(319) 358-9777
www.shopreminisce.com

Robin's Nest Press, The
(435) 789-5387
robins@sbnet.com

Rocky Mountain Scrapbook Co.
(801) 785-9695
www.rmscrapbook.com

Royal Brites
(800) 669-7692
www.royalbrites.com

Royal Talens
www.talens.com

Rubba Dub Dub
(707) 748-0929
www.artsanctum.com

Rubber Stampede
(800) 423-4135
www.deltacrafts.com

Rusty Pickle
(801) 746-1045
www.rustypickle.com

S.R.M. Press, Inc.
(800) 323-9589
www.srmpress.com

Sakar Papers
(888) 400-9768
www.sakarpapers.com

Sakura Hobby Craft
(310) 212-7878
www.sakuracraft.com

Sakura of America
(800) 776-6257
www.sakuraofamerica.com

Same-Differences
(877) 610-6683
www.same-differences.com

Sandylion Sticker Designs
(800) 387-4215
www.sandylion.com

Sarah Heidt Photo Craft, LLC
(734) 424-2776
www.sarahheidtphotocraft.com

Sassafras Lass
(801) 269-1331
www.sassafraslass.com

Savvy Stamps
(866) 44-SAVVY
www.savvystamps.com

Scenic Route Paper Co.
(801) 785-0761
www.scenicroutepaper.com

Scissor Sisters
(877) PRESSTO
www.scissor-sisters.com

Scrap Artistry
(860) 521-5926
www.scrapartistry.com

ScrapArts
(503) 631-4893
www.scraparts.com

Scrapbook Wizard™, The
(435) 752-7555
www.scrapbookwizard.com

Scrap Ease®
(800) 272-3874
www.whatsnewltd.com

ScrapGoods™ (a division of The Scrap Pack)
www.scrapgoods.com

Scrapheap Re¹
www.canscrapink.com

Scrap in a Snap™
(513) 829-6610
www.scrapinasnap.com

Scrapping With Style
(704) 254-6238
www.scrappingwithstyle.com

Scrappy Cat™, LLC
(440) 234-4850
www.scrappycatcreations.com

Scrappy Doodles
(918) 280-4540
www.scrappydoodles.com

Scrap Pagerz™
(435) 645-0696
www.scrappagerz.com

Scrappin' Dreams
(417) 742-2565
www.scrappindreams.com

ScrapTherapy Designs, Inc.
(800) 333-7880
www.scraptherapy.com

Scraptivity™ Scrapbooking, Inc.
(800) 393-2151
www.scraptivity.com

Scrapworks, LLC
(801) 363-1010
www.scrapworks.com

Scrapyard 329
(775) 829-1118
www.scrapyard329.com

SEI, Inc.
(800) 333-3279
www.shopsei.com

Serendipity Designworks
(250) 743-7642
www.serendipitydesignworks.com

Sizzix®
(866) 742-4447
www.sizzix.com

Sonburn, Inc.
(800) 527-7505
www.sonburn.com

Spellbinders™ Paper Arts, LLC
(888) 547-0400
www.spellbinders.us

Staedtler®, Inc.
(800) 927-7723
www.staedtler.us

Stampabilities®
(800) 888-0321
www.stampabilities.com

Stamp Doctor, The
(866) 782-6737
www.stampdoctor.com

Stampendous!®
(800) 869-0474
www.stampendous.com

Stampers Anonymous/The Creative Block
(888) 326-0012
www.stampersanonymous.com

Stamping Sensations
(815) 589-4100
www.stampingsensations.com

Stampin' Up!®
(800) 782-6787
www.stampinup.com

Stamping Station™
(801) 444-3828
www.stampingstation.com

Stampington & Company
(877) STAMPER
www.stampington.com

Stampotique
(602) 862-0237
www.stampotique.com

Stamps by Judith
www.stampsbyjudith.com

Stamps Happen, Inc.®
(714) 879-9894
www.stampshappen.com

Sticker Studio™
(208) 322-2465
www.stickerstudio.com

Sugarloaf Products, Inc.
(770) 484-0722
www.sugarloafproducts.com

Sulyn Industries, Inc.
(800) 257-8596
www.sulyn.com

Suze Weinberg Design Studio
(732) 761-2400
www.schmoozewithsuze.com

Suzy's Zoo®
(800) 777-4846
www.suzyszoo.com

Sweetwater
(800) 359-3094
www.sweetwaterscrapbook.com

Technique Tuesday, LLC
(503) 644-4073
www.techniquetuesday.com

Ten Seconds Studio
(817) 428-0221
www.tensecondsstudio.com

Tidy Crafts
(800) 245-6752
www.tidycrafts.com

Timeless Touches™/Dove Valley Productions, LLC
(623) 362-8285
www.timelesstouches.net

Tonic® Studios USA, Inc.
(608) 836-4478
www.kushgrip.com

Top Line Creations™
(866) 954-0559
www.topline-creations.com

Traffic Works, Inc.
(323) 582-0616
www.trafficworksinc.com

Treehouse Designs
(501) 372-1109
www.treehouse-designs.com

Treehouse Memories
(801) 318-6505
www.treehousememories.com

Triangle Coatings
(510) 614-3900
www.tricoat.com

Trims and Buttons, Inc.
(213) 689-9110
www.buttons4u.com

Tsukineko®, Inc.
(800) 769-6633
www.tsukineko.com

Tumblebeasts LLC
(505) 323-5554
www.tumblebeasts.com

Uptown Design Company™, The
(800) 888-3212
www.uptowndesign.com

USArtQuest, Inc.
(517) 522-6225
www.usartquest.com

Vintage Workshop® LLC, The
(913) 341-5559
www.thevintageworkshop.com

Walnut Hollow® Farm, Inc.
(800) 950-5101
www.walnuthollow.com

We R Memory Keepers, Inc.
(801) 539-5000
www.weronthenet.com

Westrim® Crafts
(800) 727-2727
www.westrimcrafts.com

Willow Bead
(866) 488-2323
www.willowbead.com

Wimpole Street Creations
(801) 298-0504
www.wimpolestreet.com

Wintech International Corp.
(800) 263-6043
www.wintechint.com

Wishblade™, Inc.
(651) 644-5144
www.wishblade.com

Wordsworth
(719) 282-3495
www.wordsworthstamps.com

WorldWin Paper
(888) 843-6455
www.thepapermill.com

Wrights® Ribbon Accents
(877) 597-4448
www.wrights.com

Wübie Prints
(888) 256-0107
www.wubieprints.com

Zsiage, LLC
(718) 224-1976
www.zsiage.com

Index

Learn more amazing techniques
from these inspiring Memory Makers Books.

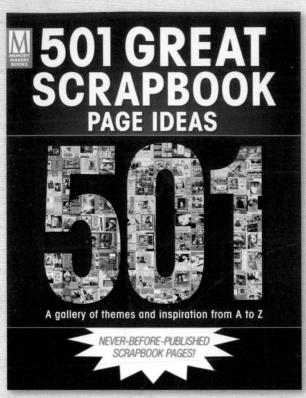

501 Great Scrapbook Pages Ideas
ISBN-13 978-1-892127-52-5
ISBN-10 1-892127-52-0
Paperback • 192 pgs. • #33358

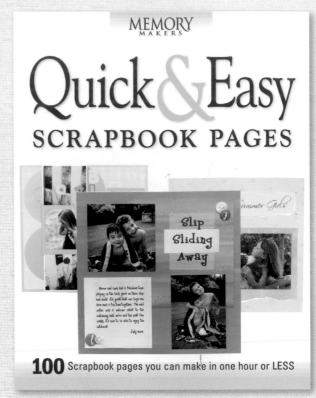

Quick & Easy Scrapbook Pages
ISBN-13 978-1-892127-20-4
ISBN-10 1-892127-20-2
Paperback • 128 pgs. • #32471

More Quick & Easy Scrapbook Pages
ISBN-13 978-1-892127-56-3
ISBN-10 1-892127-56-3
Paperback • 128 pgs. • #33360

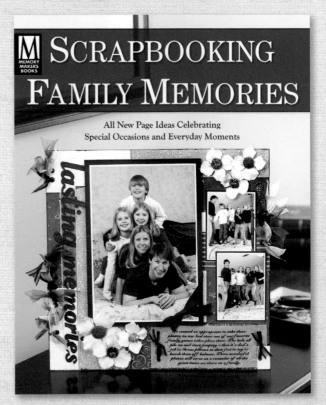

Scrapbooking Family Memories
ISBN-13 978-1-892127-59-4
ISBN-10 1-892127-59-8
Paperback • 128 pgs. • #33439